Dynamic and Stochastic Resource Economics

Essays on Biodiversity, Invasive Species, Joint Systems, and Regulation

World Scientific Series on Environmental and Energy Economics and Policy

ISSN: 2345-7503

Published

Vol. 1   Quantitative and Empirical Analysis of Energy Markets
by Apostolos Serletis

Vol. 2   The Political Economy of World Energy: An Introductory Textbook
by Ferdinand E. Banks

Vol. 3   Bridges Over Water: Understanding Transboundary Water Conflict,
Negotiation and Cooperation
by Ariel Dinar, Shlomi Dinar, Stephen McCaffrey & Daene McKinney

Vol. 4   Energy, Resources, and the Long-Term Future
by John Scales Avery

Vol. 5   Natural Gas Networks Performance after Partial Deregulation:
Five Quantitative Studies
by Paul MacAvoy, Vadim Marmer, Nickolay Moshkin & Dmitry Shapiro

Vol. 6   Energy and International War: From Babylon to Baghdad and Beyond
by Clifford E. Singer

Vol. 7   Resource and Environmental Economics: Modern Issues and
Applications
by Clement A. Tisdell

Vol. 8   Energy Conservation in East Asia: Towards Greater Energy Security
edited by Elspeth Thomson, Youngho Chang & Jae-Seung Lee

Vol. 9   Energy and Economic Theory
by Ferdinand E. Banks

Vol. 10 Quantitative and Empirical Analysis of Energy Markets
(Revised Edition)
by Apostolos Serletis

Vol. 11 Bridges Over Water: Understanding Transboundary Water Conflict,
Negotiation and Cooperation (Second Edition)
by Ariel Dinar, Shlomi Dinar, Stephen McCaffrey & Daene McKinney

Vol. 12 Dynamic and Stochastic Resource Economics: Essays on Biodiversity,
Invasive Species, Joint Systems, and Regulation
by Amitrajeet A. Batabyal

Forthcoming

Historical Energy Statistics: Global, Regional and National Trends Since
Industrialization
by T. S. Gopi Rethinaraj & Clifford E. Singer

The Implications of China's Rising Energy Use
by Peter Sheehan & Alex English

World Scientific Series on Environmental and Energy Economics and Policy – Vol. 12

Dynamic and Stochastic Resource Economics
Essays on Biodiversity, Invasive Species, Joint Systems, and Regulation

Amitrajeet A. Batabyal
Rochester Institute of Technology, USA

NEW JERSEY · LONDON · SINGAPORE · BEIJING · SHANGHAI · HONG KONG · TAIPEI · CHENNAI

Published by

World Scientific Publishing Co. Pte. Ltd.

5 Toh Tuck Link, Singapore 596224

USA office: 27 Warren Street, Suite 401-402, Hackensack, NJ 07601

UK office: 57 Shelton Street, Covent Garden, London WC2H 9HE

Library of Congress Cataloging-in-Publication Data
Batabyal, Amitrajeet A., 1965–
  Dynamic and stochastic resource economics : essays on biodiversity, invasive species, joint systems, and regulation / by Amitrajeet A. Batabyal, Rochester Institute of Technology, USA.
    pages cm. -- (World scientific series on environmental and energy economics and policy, ISSN 2345-7503 ; v. 12)
  Includes bibliographical references and index.
  ISBN 978-9814472821
  1. Environmental economics. 2. Ecology--Economic aspects. 3. Natural resources--Management. 4. Stochastic analysis. I. Title.
  HC79.E5B3725 2014
  333.701'51923--dc23

                                                                                        2013028186

British Library Cataloguing-in-Publication Data
A catalogue record for this book is available from the British Library.

Cover image: Brazilian Forest, by Martin Johnson Heade (1819–1904). Oil on Canvas. Photographic reproduction image available in the public domain at Wikimedia Commons.

In-house Editors: Philly Lim/Dipasri Sardar

Typeset by Stallion Press
Email: enquiries@stallionpress.com

Printed in Singapore

Treacherous
generals:
see my dead house,
look at broken Spain:
from every house burning metal flows
instead of flowers,
from every socket of Spain
Spain emerges
and from every dead child a rifle with eyes,
and from every crime bullets are born
which will one day find
the bull's eye of your hearts.

And you'll ask: why doesn't his poetry
speak of dreams and leaves
and the great volcanoes of his native land?

Come and see the blood in the streets.
Come and see
The blood in the streets.
Come and see the blood
In the streets!

I'm Explaining a Few Things, Pablo Neruda

CONTENTS

About the Author   xi

Acknowledgments   xiii

Part I. Introduction   1

Chapter 1   Introduction to Dynamic and Stochastic
            Resource Economics: Essays on Biodiversity,
            Invasive Species, Joint Systems, and Regulation   3

Part II. Natural Resource Management   43

Chapter 2   On Some Aspects of the Management
            of a Stochastically Developing Forest   45

Chapter 3   On the Choice Between the Stocking Rate
            and Time in Range Management   57
            with B. Biswas and E.B. Godfrey

Chapter 4   Alternate Decision Rules, the Flexibility
            Premium, and Land Development Over
            Time and Under Uncertainty   75

Chapter 5   Alternate Strategies for Managing Resistance
            to Antibiotics and Pesticides   91
            with P. Nijkamp

Part III. Biological Diversity   111

Chapter 6   An Optimal Stopping Approach
            to the Conservation of Biodiversity   113

Chapter 7   Habitat Conversion, Information Acquisition,
             and the Conservation of Biodiversity   123

Chapter 8   A Theoretical Analysis of Habitat Conversion
             and Biodiversity Conservation Over Time
             and Under Uncertainty   141

Part IV. Ecological Economics   **159**

Chapter 9   On the Optimal Management of a Class
             of Aquatic Ecological-Economic Systems   161
             with H. Beladi

Chapter 10   Necessary and Sufficient Conditions for the
             Equivalence of Economic and Ecological
             Criteria in Range Management   177

Chapter 11   Aspects of the Management of
             Ecological-Economic Systems with a Safe
             Minimum Standard   199

Part V. Invasive Species Management   **209**

Chapter 12   A Theoretical Analysis of Random Inspections
             and Fines in Invasive Species Management   211
             with S.J. Yoo

Chapter 13   Trade, the Damage from Alien Species,
             and the Effects of Protectionism Under
             Alternate Market Structures   223

Chapter 14   An Analysis of Inspections When Economic
             Cost Reduction Matters More than Biological
             Invasion Damage Control   257
             with H. Beladi

Part VI. Environmental Regulation **269**

Chapter 15 Consistency and Optimality in a Dynamic
Game of Pollution Control II: Monopoly 271

Chapter 16 A Stochastic Model of Waste Management
with On and Off Site Storage 295
with L. P. Freitas

Chapter 17 The Impact of Innovation on a Polluting
Firm's Regulation Driven Decision
to Upgrade Its Capital Stock 307
with P. Nijkamp

Index 327

ABOUT THE AUTHOR

Amitrajeet A. Batabyal is Arthur J. Gosnell Professor of Economics at the Rochester Institute of Technology (RIT). He uses microeconomic theory and a whole host of mathematical techniques to model and thereby better understand problems in natural resource, environmental, and regional economics. Dr. Batabyal has broad research interests and he has worked on problems as diverse as the design of international environmental agreements, the conduct of trade policy by developing nations when their export goods are polluting, the properties of alternate decision making rules in arranged marriages, the management of invasive species, and economic growth in innovative regions. He has published over 500 papers, books, book chapters, and book reviews in a variety of refereed scholarly outlets in ecology, economics, mathematics, operations research, and political science. He is the recipient of numerous awards including the Geoffrey J.D. Hewings Award from the North American Regional Science Council in 2003, the Moss Madden Memorial Medal from the British and Irish Section of the Regional Science Association International in 2004, the Outstanding Achievement in Research Award from the Society for Range Management in 2006, the Trustees Scholarship Award from the RIT Board of Trustees in 2007, and the Mattei Dogan Foundation Prize from the International Social Science Council in 2013.

ACKNOWLEDGMENTS

Of the 17 chapters in this book, 14 have appeared previously in different journals. Therefore, I would like to take this opportunity to express my appreciation to various publishers for granting me permission to reprint these previously published chapters. First, Chapter 2 "On Some Aspects of the Management of a Stochastically Developing Forest" originally appeared in *Ecological Modelling*, Vol. 89, pp. 67–72, 1996, Chapter 6 "An Optimal Stopping Approach to the Conservation of Biodiversity" originally appeared in *Ecological Modelling*, Vol. 105, pp. 293–298, 1998, Chapter 7 "Habitat Conversion, Information Acquisition, and the Conservation of Biodiversity" originally appeared in the *Journal of Environmental Management*, Vol. 59, pp. 195–203, 2000, Chapter 9 "On the Optimal Management of a Class of Aquatic Ecological-Economic Systems" originally appeared in the *European Journal of Operational Research*, Vol. 132, pp. 561–568, 2001, Chapter 10 "Necessary and Sufficient Conditions for the Equivalence of Economic and Ecological Criteria in Range Management" originally appeared in the *Journal of Economic Behavior and Organization*, Vol. 56, pp. 423–436, 2005, Chapter 13 "Trade, the Damage from Alien Species, and the Effects of Protectionism Under Alternate Market Structures" originally appeared in the *Journal of Economic Behavior and Organization*, Vol. 70, pp. 389–401, 2009, Chapter 16 "A Stochastic Model of Waste Management with On and Off Site Storage" originally appeared in *Ecological Economics*, Vol. 61, pp. 1–5, 2007, and I thank Elsevier for their kind permission to reprint these seven papers. Second,

Chapter 3 "On the Choice Between the Stocking Rate and Time in Range Management" originally appeared in *Environmental and Resource Economics*, Vol. 20, pp. 211–223, 2001, Chapter 4 "Alternate Decision Rules, the Flexibility Premium, and Land Development Over Time and Under Uncertainty" originally appeared in *Stochastic Environmental Research and Risk Assessment*, Vol. 18, pp. 141–146, 2004, Chapter 5 "Alternate Strategies for Managing Resistance to Antibiotics and Pesticides" originally appeared in *Environmental Economics and Policy Studies*, Vol. 7, pp. 39–51, 2005, Chapter 15 "Consistency and Optimality in a Dynamic Game of Pollution Control II: Monopoly" originally appeared in *Environmental and Resource Economics*, Vol. 8, pp. 315–330, 1996, and I thank Springer for granting me permission to reprint these four papers. Third, Chapter 8 "A Theoretical Analysis of Habitat Conversion and Biodiversity Conservation Over Time and Under Uncertainty" originally appeared in *Keio Economic Studies*, Vol. 39, pp. 33–44, 2002, and I thank the Keio Economic Society for allowing me to reprint this paper. Fourth, Chapter 17 "The Impact of Innovation on a Polluting Firm's Regulation Driven Decision to Upgrade its Capital Stock" originally appeared in *International Regional Science Review*, Vol. 31, pp. 389–403, 2008, and I thank Sage for granting me permission to reprint this paper. Finally, I note that Chapter 12 "A Theoretical Analysis of Random Inspections and Fines in Invasive Species Management" initially appeared in *Economics Bulletin*, Vol. 17, pp. 1–9, 2008.

This book would not have seen the light of day without the assistance of two groups of individuals. The first group consists of my valued coauthors Hamid Beladi, Basudeb Biswas, Luiz Freitas, E. Bruce Godfrey, Peter Nijkamp, and Seung Jick Yoo, and I thank them all for allowing me to include our jointly authored papers in this book. The second group consists of my untiring Assistant Cassandra Shellman and I thank her for all manner of assistance with this book. In addition, I acknowledge financial assistance from the Gosnell endowment at RIT.

My wife Swapna B. Batabyal and my daughter Sanjana S. Batabyal keep me company, keep me sane, and lose no opportunity to remind me that there is more to life than reading and writing about economics. I thank them both for their love and support. Finally, I dedicate this book to the memory of my brother Balarka A. Batabyal who died much too young in May 2010.

Part I
Introduction

Chapter 1

INTRODUCTION TO DYNAMIC AND STOCHASTIC RESOURCE ECONOMICS: ESSAYS ON BIODIVERSITY, INVASIVE SPECIES, JOINT SYSTEMS, AND REGULATION

We begin by pointing out that the rise in popular concern about the judicious management of natural and environmental resources has been matched by increasing scholarship by economists on several issues concerning the efficient use and management of these same resources. Second, we note that this book's primary objective is to provide a representative account of where the literature in five specific areas of natural resource and environmental economics, presently stands. These five areas are natural resource management, biological diversity, ecological economics, invasive species management, and environmental regulation. Finally, following this introductory chapter, the 16 chapters of this book show how dynamic and stochastic modeling techniques can be effectively used to construct and analyze theoretical models that shed valuable light on salient research questions in the literature.

1. Preliminaries

From the standpoint of the general public, modern interest in the judicious management of both natural and environmental resources can be said to have begun with the publication of *Silent Spring* by Rachel Carson (1962). Since then, the appearance of the alarmist *The Population Bomb* by Paul R. Ehrlich (1968) and the equally saturnine *The Limits to Growth* by Meadows *et al.* (1972) have given rise to dramatically increased concern about the depletion of our

3

exhaustible resources, the apparently poor husbandry of our renewable resources, and more generally, the excessive use of our environmental resources.[1]

This rise in popular concern about the management of our natural and environmental resources has been matched by increasing and increasingly sophisticated scholarship by economists[2] on a whole host of issues concerning the efficient use and management of our natural and environmental resources. In this regard, it is worth emphasizing that the first rigorous analysis of exhaustible resources utilizing the calculus of variations was conducted by Harold Hotelling as early as 1931. Similarly, beginning with the seminal paper by Gordon (1954) and then continuing with the work of the biologist Garrett Hardin (1968), the mathematician Colin Clark (1976), and the ecologist Marc Mangel (1985), research on renewable resources or ecological-economic systems has flourished.

This blossoming research in natural resource and environmental economics has also given rise to interest in new questions concerning the diminution in planet earth's diverse biological resources, the management of alien invasive species, and environmental regulation.[3] Collectively, this substantial and growing body of research is increasingly interdisciplinary and this interdisciplinarity has greatly expanded the scope of traditional natural resource and environmental economics.

---

1. Economists routinely distinguish between resources such as forests, fisheries, and rangelands that have a natural or biological growth rate and therefore are regenerative or renewable and resources like minerals such as coal or oil that do not have a natural growth rate — that is meaningful in the context of typical human lifetimes — and hence are non-renewable or exhaustible. This notwithstanding, as noted in Part IV of this book, with the burgeoning of research by ecological economists, it is now common to refer to renewable resources as ecological-economic systems.

2. This "tribe" of economists — to use Partha Dasgupta's (1996) terminology — is standardly referred to as natural resource and environmental economists.

3. For authoritative accounts, see Perrings et al. (1995) for biological diversity, Keller et al. (2009) for invasive species, and Baumol and Oates (1988) for environmental regulation.

Given this state of affairs, the primary objective of this book is to provide a representative account of where the literature in five specific areas of resource economics, broadly construed, presently stands. These five areas are natural resource management, biological diversity, ecological economics, invasive species management, and environmental regulation. Our secondary objective in providing this representative account is to show how dynamic and stochastic modeling techniques, familiar to researchers in operations research but typically unfamiliar to economists, can be effectively used to construct and analyze theoretical models that shed valuable light on salient research questions in the extant literature.

Specifically, following this introductory chapter, there are 16 essays (chapters) that are grouped into five parts. The four chapters comprising Part II on natural resource management address questions concerning forests, rangelands, land use, and the problem of resistance to antibiotics and pesticides. The three chapters that make up Part III on biological diversity demonstrate how the theory of optimal stopping can shed useful light on the conservation of biodiversity. Three chapters make up Part IV on ecological economics. These three chapters study aquatic ecological-economic systems, necessary and sufficient conditions under which ecological and economic management criteria are equivalent, and the use of a safe minimum standard (SMS) to manage ecological-economic systems.

Part V consists of three chapters on invasive species management. From a managerial perspective, these three chapters analyze the role of random inspections and fines, the role of trade policy (tariffs), and the tradeoff between economic cost reduction and biological invasion damage control. Finally, the three chapters comprising Part VI study particular aspects of environmental regulation. These aspects include the notions of dynamic consistency and optimality, waste management with on and off site storage, and the ways in which innovation influences the decision of a polluting firm to upgrade its capital stock. We now proceed to the contributions of the individual essays in this book.

2. The Individual Essays

2.1. *Natural resource management*

2.1.1. *A stochastically developing forest*

Economists such as Brock and Rothschild (1984) and Brock *et al.* (1988) have studied aspects of the forest management question in a stochastic setting by posing the "tree cutting" question as an optimal stopping time problem. Ecologists and foresters have used Markov and semi-Markov models to study different aspects of this forest management problem. While these analyses have certainly enhanced our comprehension of the tree cutting problem in a stochastic context, they have omitted three salient aspects of the biological *uncertainty* affecting many large and long standing forests, particularly those in developing nations. These aspects concern the probabilistic development of trees in long standing forests, the probabilistic demise of trees, and the uncertain introduction of new or previously known species into the forest. These features characterize large areas of forest land in many developing countries.

National forest managers who "inherit" such long standing forests with several different species often have a difficult time formulating forest policy. Before embarking on any policy, such managers would like to obtain information about questions that are fundamentally probabilistic in nature. What kinds of species and how many trees within a particular species can one expect to see in a mature forest? Can one say anything about the stochastic process governing the death of species? What can one say about the likelihood that a given species with a specific number of trees is the oldest — in the sense that it originated earliest — species in the forest?

These questions have not been studied previously in the extant literature in natural resource and environmental economics. Therefore, following the previous work of Bartlett (1960, pp. 17–44), Bailey (1964, pp. 117–136), and Ross (1983, pp. 156–164), Chapter 2 applies stochastic population models to the forest management problem. More specifically, a stochastically developing forest with features described in detail in the chapter is modeled with a multi-dimensional, continuous time Markov chain (CTMC). An interesting methodological connection that is made in this chapter concerns the relationship between the CTMC model and the prominent $M/G/\infty$ model[4] of queuing theory.

The first question that Chapter 2 addresses concerns the attributes of a mature or stationary forest. This involves computing the stationary probabilities of the underlying CTMC model. As the chapter points out, these stationary probabilities provide assistance to a forest manager for planning purposes in two ways. First, in the kind of forest under study, analysis shows that the limiting number of species with k trees are independent Poisson random variables. This means that interaction effects are absent between the various limiting number of species. Second, the computed stationary probabilities allow the manager to directly deduce the mean number of species with k trees. This information can be utilized by the manager to formulate logging policies that are designed to *selectively* log certain species but not others.

The second management question answered by Chapter 2 relates to the determination of the stochastic process describing the death of species. Analysis shows that the stochastic process describing the death of species depends on whether the forest under study is in a steady state at time $t = 0$ or not. If the forest is in a steady state, then the pertinent death stochastic process is a *homogeneous* Poisson process. In contrast, if the above steady state assumption does not hold then the death stochastic process is a *non-homogeneous* Poisson process.

The third and final management question answered by this chapter relates to the probabilistic determination of the age of the various species. Specifically, this chapter ascertains the likelihood that a given species with k trees is the oldest species in the forest. The

---

4. The first letter pertains to the fact that the inter-arrival time of customers in a queue has the Markovian property. The second letter arises from the fact that the server's service times have a general distribution. Finally, ∞ refers to the case in which there are (notionally) an infinite number of servers. See Wolff (1989, pp. 75–81) for a textbook account.

analysis of this last question is particularly useful because it provides a probabilistic method of dating species and this method, the chapter contends, can be the basis on which a manager makes conservation decisions. Although the stochastic analysis in Chapter 2 sheds useful light on aspects of the forest management problem, this chapter pays no attention to the economic aspects of the management of ecological-economic systems that are forests. Some of these economic aspects are addressed by Chapter 3 in the context of a different ecological-economic system, namely, rangelands.

2.1.2. *Stocking rate and time in range management*

The basic objective of Chapter 3 is to shed light on a specific controversy in the range management literature that has, unfortunately, received no theoretical attention. This controversy concerns two choice variables, namely, the stocking rate and the length of a grazing cycle that are commonly used to manage rangelands. The "stocking rate is typically expressed as animal units per section of land" (Holechek *et al.*, 1998, p. 190). In contrast, the length of a grazing cycle is defined to be the length of *time* in a calendar year during which animals graze a given rangeland.[5] The aforementioned controversy involves determining the answer to the following question. Is the stocking rate more important or is time more important in range management?

Chapter 3 answers this question by studying the decision problem faced by an optimizing private rancher who minimizes the long run expected net unit cost (LRENC) from his range operations. This rancher does so by selecting either the stocking rate or the length of time during which his animals graze his rangeland.[6] Note that

---

5. In the rest of this discussion, we shall use the terms "length of grazing cycle" and "time" interchangeably. The reader should note that both these terms refer to the length of time during which animals graze a given rangeland.

6. To keep the mathematics straightforward, in the rest of this section, we shall not focus on the profit criterion; instead, we shall focus on the LRENC criterion. However, the reader should note that maximizing profit is equivalent to minimizing net cost.

this *long run* focus means that the rancher under study cares about the expected net cost from his range operations *and* about the well being of his rangeland.

At the beginning of a grazing period, our rancher lets his animals into his fenced rangeland in accordance with a Poisson process with rate $\alpha > 0$. This rancher believes that the appropriate stocking rate for his rangeland corresponds to $A > 0$ animals. Therefore, once A animals have been allowed into the rangeland to graze, entry of additional animals is prohibited for the grazing period under consideration. As a result of his range operations, our rancher incurs costs and obtains benefits from direct and indirect sources. The direct source of net cost is modeled by supposing that the rancher incurs net cost at the rate of $\$ac$ per unit time, where a is the number of animals grazing at that time and c is the instantaneous net cost per animal. The second or indirect net cost is $\$C$ and this cost arises when the rancher closes his rangeland to additional animals. With this description of net costs, Chapter 3 uses the theory of renewal-reward processes to compute the rancher's LRENC from his range operations.

Analysis shows that the optimal stocking rate is $A^* = \sqrt{(2\alpha C)/c}$ and the optimized value of the rancher's LRENC is given by $(\text{LRENC})^*_{\text{SR}} = \sqrt{2\alpha c C} - (c/2)$. Similarly, the detailed analysis in Chapter 3 reveals that the optimal length of a grazing cycle or "time" is $T^* = \sqrt{(2C)/(\alpha c)}$ and the optimized value of the corresponding LRENC is $(\text{LRENC})^*_T = \sqrt{2\alpha c C}$. Comparing the above two optimized expressions, we see that $(\text{LRENC})^*_{\text{SR}} = \sqrt{2\alpha c C} - (c/2) < \sqrt{2\alpha c C} = (\text{LRENC})^*_T$.

The above inequality clearly tells us that the rancher's LRENC with an optimally chosen stocking rate is lower than his LRENC with an optimally chosen grazing cycle length. This is the sense in which the stocking rate is *more important* than time in range management. Put differently, if a rational rancher had to choose a single control variable from a control set consisting of the stocking rate and time, then this rancher would choose the stocking rate over time. Having focused on forests in Chapter 2 and on rangelands in Chapter 3, the objective of Chapter 4 in this book is to study management issues that arise in the context of land development and preservation over time and under uncertainty.

2.1.3. *Land development and preservation*

The work of Arrow and Fisher (1974) and Henry (1974a; 1974b) has led to the so-called Arrow–Fisher–Henry (AFH) notion of option value — sometimes called quasi-option value (QOV). This notion tells us that when land development is both indivisible and irreversible, a landowner who disregards the possibility of procuring new information about the effects of such development will invariably underestimate the benefits of preservation and hence skew the binary choice develop/preserve decision in favor of development.

Chapter 4 studies the generality of the Arrow–Fisher–Henry concept of option value by exploring the land development question in a dynamic and stochastic setting. Specifically, this chapter focuses on the expected profit of a landowner when this individual is able to choose between *time independent* and *time dependent* decision rules. The chapter first compares and contrasts the characteristics of time independent and time dependent decision rules and then discusses the magnitude of the flexibility premium emanating from the maintenance of temporal adaptability in decision making.

Units are chosen so that the numerical values of all the relevant variables and the distribution functions are drawn from the interval $(0, 1]$. The object of inquiry is a landowner who owns a plot of vacant land and who has a one-to-one and strictly monotonic profit function that is defined over offers to develop land. The landowner would like to develop his land by time $T = 1$. If the landowner fails to develop his land by time $T = 1$, then his profit is zero. This landowner receives offers to develop his land over time. These offers $O_1, O_2, O_3, \ldots$ are received in accordance with a Poisson process with a fixed rate $\lambda = 1$. The offers themselves are independent random variables that are uniformly distributed on the interval $(0, 1]$. The receipt of an offer generates a certain level of profit by means of the landowner's profit function. It is on the basis of this profit that our landowner decides whether to accept or to reject a particular offer to develop land. Because our landowner's one-to-one and strictly monotonic profit function maps offers to develop land to profit and because these offers are uniformly distributed on $(0, 1]$, the profit levels $\Pi_1, \Pi_2, \Pi_3, \ldots$ themselves are also uniformly distributed random variables on the interval $(0, 1]$.

The decision to develop land is irreversible. Accordingly there is an asymmetry associated with the binary choice accept/reject decision. If our landowner rejects a particular offer then he can always accept a later offer as long as he accepts this offer by time $T = 1$. In contrast, if our landowner accepts a particular offer (he develops his land), then the stochastic offer receipt process terminates. In other words, a decision to reject an offer preserves future options but a decision to accept an offer does not. In order to develop land by time $T = 1$, our landowner will need to use a decision rule. Chapter 4 considers two types of decision rules. The *time independent* decision rule is as follows. Our landowner decides on some threshold level of profit $\hat{\Pi}$ that is *free* of time and the landowner accepts the first offer whose profit exceeds $\hat{\Pi}$. With the *time dependent* decision rule, instead of working with a fixed $\hat{\Pi}$, our landowner works with a time dependent threshold $\hat{\Pi}(t) = (1 - t)/(3 - t)$.

The mathematical analysis in Chapter 4 yields two salient results about intertemporal land development in the presence of uncertainty. First, with the time independent decision rule, the optimal value of the profit threshold $\hat{\Pi}$ is fixed at 0.2079 and this value does *not* change with the passage of time. In contrast, with the time dependent decision rule, the profit threshold is *continually* a function of time and hence its optimal value changes over time. Second, it is formally shown that the landowner's expected profit with the time dependent decision rule which is flexible exceeds his expected profit with a time independent decision rule which is inflexible. The last chapter in Part II of this book, i.e., Chapter 5, discusses the merits of alternate strategies for managing resistance to antibiotics and pesticides.

2.1.4. *Resistance to antibiotics and pesticides*

Concern about the impacts of increasing resistance to antibiotics has been growing and current research has generated two significant findings about this problem. First, the economic cost of resistance to antibiotics and pesticides is likely to be substantial. Second, there is rising recognition of the *cost of antibiotic treatment* relative to the *cost of treatment by alternate means*. Given this state of affairs, the general purpose of Chapter 5 is to conduct a comparative *theoretical* analysis, in a probabilistic setting, of the conditions under which treatment with alternate means — involving no use of antibiotics — is more desirable than treatment with antibiotics. Specifically, this chapter addresses two queries. First, how does the presence of uncertainty influence the answer to the choice issue posed above? Second, are costs still important in distinguishing between the two strategies, or, in addition to costs, is some other aspect of the problem just as salient in helping a health care provider select between antibiotic and non-antibiotic courses of treatment?

This chapter focuses on a specific geographic area in which there exists a population of infected individuals. These individuals seek treatment for their ailment at a health care facility. It is standard practice in this facility to treat ailments with an *interventionist* strategy that involves the use of an antibiotic. The basic stock variable that an antibiotic affects is the stock of drug susceptibility. Repeated use of an antibiotic degrades the stock of drug susceptibility in a stochastic manner. The stock of drug susceptibility changes state in accordance with a Brownian motion process with drift $\beta > 0$.

With repeated use of an antibiotic, our Brownian motion process eventually gets to state r. This is the *resistant* state and once this state is reached, the default antibiotic that is currently being used is useless for subsequent treatment. When this happens, the medical facility must use a new interventionist strategy, i.e., a different antibiotic to treat the ailment in question. When this is done, our Brownian motion process returns to state 0 (the best state). The cost of using this new interventionist strategy is c^r.

The non-interventionist strategy is a no antibiotics strategy. Clearly, the health care provider may choose to treat the ailment in question with a non-interventionist strategy before the Brownian motion process hits state r. As long as the resistant state r has not been reached, the default antibiotic is successful in treating the relevant ailment with probability one. In contrast, a success score of one is not assured with the non-interventionist strategy. In particular, if the state of the Brownian motion process is k and the non-interventionist strategy is used, then this strategy will be successful (unsuccessful) in treating the ailment with probability $p(k)(1 - p(k))$. Now, if the non-interventionist strategy is successful in treating the ailment then our Brownian motion process returns to state 0. In contrast, if this strategy is unsuccessful in treating the ailment then the Brownian motion process goes to state r. The cost of attempting to cure the ailment in question in state k with the non-interventionist strategy is c^k. With this background, Chapter 5 next determines whether the interventionist strategy or the non-interventionist strategy minimizes the long run expected cost per time.

Analysis shows that the long run expected cost per unit time with a non-interventionist strategy is given by {Long Run Expected Cost}$_{NI}$ = $[\beta\{c^k + \{1 - p(k)\}c^r\}]/k$. Similarly, the long run expected cost per unit time with the interventionist strategy is {Long Run Expected Cost}$_I$ = $(\beta c^r)/r$. In addition, the analysis in Chapter 5 also shows that in a *probabilistic* setting, the answer to the above choice question depends not only on cost considerations, i.e., on c^k and c^r in the previous two mathematical expressions but *also* on the likelihood function $p(k)$.

This chapter concludes by emphasizing that in a specific geographical area, when resistance to antibiotics is an issue and decisions are made in an environment of uncertainty, the utility of interventionist versus non-interventionist treatment options depends on the costs of the two treatment options (c^k, c^r) and on the provider's *ex ante* uncertainty about the likelihood of success — the $p(k)$ function — when he uses a non-interventionist strategy. This completes the book's discussion of issues relating to natural resource management. We now proceed to discuss this book's contributions to the subject of biological diversity.

2.2. *Biological diversity*

2.2.1. *Optimal stopping and biodiversity conservation*

A consensus is now emerging among economists and ecologists that in thinking about the problem of biodiversity loss, the apposite concept to focus on is not genetic or species diversity, but the notion of ecological resilience (Perrings *et al.*, 1995; Swanson, 1995). According to this view, biodiversity matters primarily through its role in promoting resilience, "... where resilience refers to the amount of disturbance that an ecosystem can sustain before a change in the control or the structure of the ecosystem will occur" (Batabyal, 1996, p. 487). As a part of this new focus on the diversity of ecological function, Swanson (1995) has suggested that the global decline in biodiversity is best viewed as a process of natural habitat conversion. According to Swanson, if we are to ameliorate the problem of biodiversity loss, then we need to focus on this "extinction process" and the central task for a decision maker is to halt this habitat conversion process at an optimally determined point in time.

Chapter 6 pursues this way of looking at the biodiversity loss problem. Specifically, this chapter first casts the underlying conservation question within the framework of a Markov decision theoretic framework and then it uses an optimal stopping rule to provide an answer to the question about when the habitat conversion process ought to be halted. The formal analysis in this chapter is conducted using the so-called infinitesimal look ahead stopping rule (ILASR) and a theorem which provides conditions under which it is optimal to stop a stochastic process using the ILASR.

The decision problem in Chapter 6 is one faced by a national government that is interested in conserving its scarce biological resources. The government solves its problem in a dynamic and stochastic framework. Information regarding the desirability of halting the habitat conversion process is produced according to a non-homogeneous Poisson process $\{I(t): t \geq 0\}$, with a continuous, non-increasing intensity function $\gamma(t)$. Information is acquired by the government independently, and this information has a common cumulative distribution function $F(\cdot)$, with finite mean. Upon acquiring information, the government decides whether to halt the conversion of natural habitats, or to permit conversion and wait for additional information. The government's continuous, one-to-one, and strictly monotonic utility function is $\bar{u}(\cdot)$. If $i(t)$ is the information acquired by time t, then $U(t) = \bar{u}\{i(t)\}$ is the utility to the government from halting the habitat conversion process. Since $\bar{u}(\cdot)$ is a continuous, one-to-one, and strictly monotone transformation of $I(t)$, $\forall t$, the government's utility $\{U(t): t \geq 0\}$ is itself a non-homogeneous Poisson process with a continuous and non-increasing intensity function, say, $\theta(t)$. Further, successive utility realizations are independent, with cumulative distribution function $G(\cdot)$ with a finite mean.

At any point in time, should the government choose not to halt the conversion process, it incurs benefits and costs. The net benefit per unit time from not halting the habitat conversion process is B. The state at any time t is denoted by the pair $[t, U(t)]$, where $U(t)$ is the utility that will be received, should the government choose to halt the habitat conversion process at time t. If the government halts the habitat conversion process in state $[t, U(t)]$, the government's utility from t onwards will be $U(t)$. On the other hand, if the government chooses not to halt the conversion process and waits for an additional time h, then its expected utility is given by a specific mathematical expression.

From an intuitive standpoint, the government ought to halt the habitat conversion process upon acquiring information $i(t)$ at any time t if and only if the utility from halting, i.e., $U(t)$ exceeds the expected utility from postponing action and allowing habitat conversion to continue for an additional time h. Next, Chapter 6 defines the closed set S which is the set of all states for which halting the habitat conversion process now yields a higher level of utility than permitting habitat conversion to continue for an additional time h.

Because S is closed, a particular theorem can be applied to provide a mathematical condition to delineate when the habitat conversion process ought to be halted. The central implication of the analysis in Chapter 6 is that the habitat conversion process ought to be halted at time t, if, in an expected utility sense, it does not pay the government to wait for information about the consequences of halting the habitat conversion process beyond time t. Chapter 7 continues this information theoretic approach to the study of biodiversity conservation.

2.2.2. *Information and biodiversity conservation*

Despite the increased global attention to the loss of natural habitats in general and to the loss of tropical forests in particular, it does not appear as though the rate of forest conversion is slowing down. Recent studies mentioned in Chapter 7 suggest that this conversion rate is actually *increasing* in a number of countries. Given this state of affairs, the objective of Chapter 7 is to use the theory of optimal stopping to first propose and then answer the following two questions about the nexuses between natural habitat conversion and the conservation of biodiversity. First, given the link between natural habitats and biodiversity, *when* should a social planner — who is interested in conserving biodiversity — stop the habitat conversion process? Second, what is the connection between this social planner's optimal conservation policy (OCP) and the *length* of his or her planning horizon?

Chapter 7 focuses on a country such as India in which the conversion of natural habitat into developed land is taking place over time and it interprets the area of natural habitat as a measure of the stock of biodiversity. The conversion of natural habitat yields information about the consequences of development and the existing stock of biodiversity. A social planner receives this information sequentially, in packets, one packet per discrete time period. This individual has a well-defined utility function defined over information packets. Because these packets provide information about the consequences of development and the existing stock of biodiversity, the resultant utility to the social planner is also about these two things.

On receiving a particular information packet, the social planner must decide whether to act, i.e., to stop the habitat conversion process, or to do nothing and permit the conversion process to continue. Chapter 7 identifies a lower bound on the level of utility that calls for stopping the conversion process and it poses the social planner's problem as one of maximizing the probability of acting (stopping the conversion process) when the highest possible level of utility has been obtained. The information is generated in accordance with an independent and identically distributed (i.i.d) stochastic process.

The mathematical analysis in Chapter 7 produces a key result. This result tells us that when the social planner's decision making horizon is infinite, this planner should not act upon receipt of the first $(1/e)$ fraction of utility packets. He should then stop the habitat conversion process upon receipt of the first candidate[7] utility packet. In other words, the OCP calls for the social planner to wait a while, i.e., not act upon receipt of the first $(1/e)$ fraction of all utility packets. The social planner should then act and stop the habitat conversion process upon receipt of the first "candidate packet." The probability that the use of this OCP will result in the conversion process being stopped at the optimal point is shown to be $(1/e) \approx 0.37$.

The proportion of time for which it is optimal to wait before acting is *fixed*. Therefore, the analysis in Chapter 7 implies that a longer decision making horizon will result in the conservation of a relatively larger stock of biodiversity. In this way, the key result

---

7. A utility packet is a candidate if this packet is of higher utility than any previously received packet.

in the preceding paragraph demonstrates the dependence of the OCP on the *length* of the social planner's decision making horizon. More generally, this result calls for the use of long decision making horizons in the design of conservation policy. Is this result consistent with current thinking on biodiversity conservation? Chapter 7 notes that the answer to this question is yes. In this regard, Brian Kernohan — a project manager in the Minnesota Ecosystem Management Project at the Boise Cascade Corporation — and Haufler (1999, p. 238) have contended that maintaining "biological diversity involves time frames that are often far beyond traditional planning horizons." How is the analysis undertaken in Chapter 7 affected by the use of autonomous (time independent) and non-autonomous (time dependent) biodiversity conservation policies? This question is addressed in Chapter 8.

2.2.3.   *Autonomous and non-autonomous policies in biodiversity conservation*

Chapter 8 begins with the claim that the extant literature has *not* analyzed the effects that alternate policies have on the decision to conserve biodiversity and on a social planner's expected utility from conservation. As such, this chapter has three goals. First, a dynamic and stochastic model of decision making in the context of biodiversity conservation is constructed. Second, this model is used to shed light on the expected utility of a social planner when this planner is able to choose between autonomous and non-autonomous conservation policies. Finally, the chapter compares and contrasts the characteristics of autonomous and non-autonomous policies and then comments on the magnitude of the flexibility premium arising from the maintenance of temporal flexibility in decision making. The theory of optimal stopping is used to shed light on the nexus between natural habitat conversion and biodiversity conservation.

Units are chosen so that all the variables and the distribution functions are drawn from the interval (0, 1]. The chapter then focuses on a country such as Indonesia in which the conversion of natural habitat into developed land is taking place over time. It interprets the area of natural habitat as a measure of the stock of biodiversity. The conversion of natural habitat generates *information* about the consequences of development and the existing stock of biodiversity.

A social planner interested in conserving scarce biological resources receives this information sequentially over time and in packets. This planner has a utility function defined over these information packets. The social planner would like to stop the habitat conversion process by time $T = 1$. This means that if the planner fails to stop the habitat conversion process by time $T = 1$, then his utility is zero. The social planner receives information packets about the consequences of habitat conversion over time. These packets $P_1, P_2, P_3, \ldots$ are received in accordance with a Poisson process with a fixed rate $\lambda = 1$. The packets are independent random variables that are uniformly distributed on the interval $(0, 1]$. The receipt of a packet generates a certain level of utility by way of the social planner's utility function. This utility function maps information about the effects of stopping conversion to utility from stopping conversion. Upon receipt of an information packet and the corresponding utility, the social planner decides whether to stop the conversion of natural habitat or to permit conversion and wait for additional information.

In order to accomplish his objective of stopping the conversion of natural habitat by time $T = 1$, our social planner will need to use a policy. Chapter 8 considers two types of policies. When the autonomous policy is used, the social planner decides on a threshold level of utility $\hat{U}$ that is independent of time. Our social planner stops the stochastic habitat conversion process (creates a protected area) upon receipt of the first information packet whose utility exceeds $\hat{U}$. The second policy is the non-autonomous policy and in this case the threshold level of utility is a function of time t. Instead of working with a constant $\hat{U}$, the social planner now works with a time dependent threshold $\hat{U}(t) = (1 - t)/(3 - t)$.

Analysis demonstrates that when the autonomous policy is used, the optimal value of the utility threshold is fixed at $\hat{U}^* = 0.2079$

and this value leads to the social planner's maximized expected utility given by $EU_A^* = [(1 + \hat{U}^*)/2][1 - \exp\{-(1 - \hat{U}^*)\}] = 0.330425$. Similarly, when the non-autonomous policy is used, the social planner's maximized expected utility is $EU_N^* = (2/9) \int_0^1 (2 - t)dt = 0.333333$. These findings generate five specific insights.

First, the time dependence of the threshold when the non-autonomous policy is used permits the social planner to be flexible. Second, when making habitat conversion stoppage decisions (biodiversity conservation decisions) over time and under uncertainty, it pays to be flexible. Third, although the use of more complex non-autonomous policies will most likely increase the magnitude of the flexibility premium, these more complex non-autonomous policies frequently do not admit analytic solutions. Fourth, we can view the decision to create a protected area as a decision to invest in biodiversity. Finally, if we adopt this investment perspective then it is optimal to wait a while before investing and this last finding is consistent with the "value of waiting to invest" result in the investment under uncertainty literature (see Dixit and Pindyck, 1994). This concludes the present book's coverage of biodiversity. We now proceed to the three chapters in Part IV. These chapters are about problems in ecological economics.

2.3. Ecological economics

2.3.1. Aquatic ecological-economic systems

The general objective of Chapter 9 is to study aspects of the stability and the optimal management of a class of aquatic ecological-economic systems. Examples of such systems include coastal and estuarine ecological-economic systems such as the Chesapeake Bay in the USA. As Costanza *et al.* (1995) have noted, the noteworthy feature of these ecological-economic systems is that their *stability* depends on the successful functioning of a *small* number of generalist species in a broad range of ecological and economic conditions. Chapter 9 explains that the stability notion that makes most sense for this chapter is that of persistence where persistence refers to "how long a variable lasts before it is changed to another value" (Pimm, 1991, p. 21).

The specific question analyzed in this chapter is the following. How should a manager allocate his limited financial resources to optimally manage coastal and estuarine ecological-economic systems (CEE) whose persistence is determined by the successful functioning of a small number of generalist species in a wide range of ecological and economic conditions? To answer this question, the chapter focuses on a stylized CEE that consists of a finite number of species. The two generalist species in this system are species 1 and species 2 and n_1 and n_2 denote the total number of members in each of these two species.

Natural events and economic activities have an uncertain impact on the lives of the members of these two generalist species. Consequently, a member of species $i, i = 1, 2$, lives for an exponential amount of time with rate $\beta_i, i = 1, 2$. Analysis shows that the persistence of the ecological-economic system under study is $E[N]/(\beta_1 + \beta_2)$, where $E[N]$ is the expected number of species 1 and 2 members that die as a result of natural events and economic activities. The preceding expression implies that the persistence of the pertinent CEE depends on the number of members in each species (n_1, n_2) and on the rates of the two exponential lifetime distributions (β_1, β_2).

Next, Chapter 9 analyzes the management of coastal and estuarine ecological-economic systems with a limited budget given by $\$B$. The chapter poses the manager's problem as one of allocating his budget among species 1, 2, and the cost of economic activities. The benefit to society from the manager's actions designed to protect species 1 is certain and this certain dollar benefit per member of species 1 is s. In contrast, managerial actions designed to protect species 2 result in an uncertain benefit to society. Let u denote the expected dollar benefit to society per member of species 2 and let σ^2 denote the variance per unit time of benefit from species 2. Let $b \in [0, 1]$ be the fraction of the budget that the manager allocates to actions designed to protect the members of species 2. Finally,

c is the cost of economic activities. By choosing c, the manager is selecting the optimal level of economic activity. In turn, this optimal level of economic activity determines the persistence of the CEE.

As a result of managerial actions, the budget B evolves over time in accordance with a stochastic differential equation. Chapter 9 solves the manager's optimization problem and shows that, *inter alia*, the optimal $b = (n_1 s - n_2 u)/\{(w-1)\sigma^2\}$. This expression tells us three things about the management function. First, the optimal division of the manager's budget between the two generalist species of the CEE is constant and this constant is *independent* of the manager's budget. Second, the portion of the budget the manager spends on actions to protect species 2 varies directly with the number of species members n_2, the expected dollar benefit per member u, and inversely with the variance of this benefit. Finally, as s (the certain social dollar benefit per member of species 1) or n_1 (the number of species 1 members) increases, the manager ought to allocate a larger fraction of his budget to the upkeep of the generalist species 1.

From a managerial perspective, the specific focus of Chapter 9 is on the optimization of an economic criterion function and the manager's concern for the ecological stability concept of persistence is indirect. Are there circumstances involving the management of ecological-economic systems where economic and ecological criteria are equivalent? This question is addressed in Chapter 10.

2.3.2.   *Equivalence of ecological and economic criteria*

Chapter 10 studies the circumstances in which ecological and economic criteria are equivalent by focusing on rangelands. Rangelands are routinely managed with specialized grazing systems. Two salient attributes typify all specialized grazing systems. First, there are spatial and temporal control aspects to these systems. Second, the concept of rotation is a "critical feature of all specialized grazing systems" (Holechek *et al.*, 2001, p. 249). This chapter concentrates on short duration grazing which is arguably the most prominent specialized grazing system.

In this form of grazing, rangelands are managed by controlling both the length of time during which animals graze a paddock (a temporal control) and by controlling the area of this paddock (a spatial control). The basic idea in short duration grazing is threefold. First, the manager divides the rangeland under study into a number of fenced paddocks. Next, this manager allows his herd of animals to graze a particular paddock for a particular time period. Finally, the herd of animals is moved to the next paddock, and the manager continues this process in sequential fashion.

The economic criterion analyzed in this chapter is criterion [a] or the long run expected net cost of management operations. The first ecological criterion studied is criterion [b] or the long run rate at which grazing is moved from one paddock to another. The second ecological criterion studied is criterion [c] or the long run rate at which grazing has to be moved from one paddock to another because of adverse environmental factors. The theory of renewal-reward processes is used to derive expressions for these three criteria.

Now, consider an arbitrary paddock of the rangeland under study. Forage *quality* in this paddock is a *random* variable. The one-to-one and strictly monotone function $g(\cdot)$ maps the forage quality of a paddock to its "operative lifetime." Because forage quality is a random variable and because operative lifetime is a one-to-one and strictly monotonic transformation of forage quality, operative lifetime itself is a *random* variable. These operative lifetime random variables are i.i.d, and the distribution and the density functions of operative lifetime are $F(\cdot)$ and $f(\cdot)$, respectively.

The range manager will terminate grazing in the paddock and move his herd of animals to the next paddock either when T time periods have elapsed or when a stochastic and deleterious environmental event cuts down the operative lifetime of this paddock, thereby leading to a breakdown of this paddock as far as subsequent grazing is concerned. The completion of grazing in a particular paddock and the simultaneous movement of the herd of animals to the next paddock results in benefits and costs to our manager. The net cost to our manager from the completion of grazing on a paddock after T time periods (one grazing cycle) is $C(p)$. If grazing on a paddock has to be terminated because of the occurrence of a deleterious environmental event (a breakdown), then in addition to $C(p)$, our manager incurs a net cost of $C(e)$. Proposition 1 in Chapter 10 tells us that the condition $C(p) = 1 - C(e)F(T)$ is necessary and sufficient for the economic criterion (long run expected net cost) to be equivalent to the first ecological criterion (long run rate at which grazing is moved from one paddock to another). Further, the conditions $C(p) = 1$ and $C(e) = 0$ are sufficient but not necessary for the same two criteria to be equivalent. This chapter's Proposition 2 indicates that the condition $C(p) = F(T)\{1 - C(e)\}$ is necessary and sufficient for the equivalence of the economic criterion (long run expected net cost) and the second ecological criterion (long run rate at which grazing is moved from one paddock to another because of adverse environmental factors). In addition, the conditions $C(p) = 0$ and $C(e) = 1$ are sufficient but not necessary for the equivalence of these two criteria.

In sum, the analysis in Chapter 10 tells us that economic and ecological management criteria are equivalent only in exceptional circumstances. Even the weaker sufficiency conditions are unlikely to hold in practice. This means that, in general, the optimization of an economic criterion function will *not* result in the simultaneous optimization of an ecological criterion function. Therefore, if a range manager wishes to adopt an integrated ecological-economic approach to range management, then this manager will have to address economic and ecological issues *simultaneously*. Departing from the management issues studied in Chapter 10, Chapter 11 analyzes some probabilistic aspects of the management of ecological-economic systems with a so-called SMS.

2.3.3. *The safe minimum standard*

The literature reviewed in Chapter 11 shows that the optimal management of ecological-economic systems is challenging because of the presence of what Ready and Bishop (1991, p. 309) call "pure uncertainty." In addition, Margolis and Naevdal (2008) have pointed out that the management function is made even more challenging because managerial actions may result in irreversible change to some aspect of a managed ecological-economic system. This notwithstanding, Chapter 11 makes two claims. First, it contends that the existing literature has paid inadequate *theoretical* attention to the management of ecological-economic systems in the presence of both *uncertainty* and potential *irreversibility*.

Many years ago, Ciriacy-Wantrup (1952) suggested that when uncertainty and irreversibility are issues, the management function ought to pay attention to the establishment of a SMS. The idea here is to manage an ecological-economic system so that this system's ability to provide humans with a flow of vital ecosystem services — such as food production, nutrient cycling, and storm protection — does not fall below a particular standard, namely, the SMS. The second claim made by Chapter 11 is that there are also very few theoretical analyses of the management of stochastic ecological-economic systems in which the manager explicitly incorporates a SMS in his decision making. Given this state of affairs, the primary objective of Chapter 11 is to conduct such a theoretical analysis.

The object of analysis in this chapter is an arbitrary ecological-economic system such as a fishery, a forest, or a rangeland, whose evolution over time is decided by deterministic and stochastic factors. This system is modeled with a Brownian motion process denoted by $\{X(t): t \geq 0\}$. What this means is that $X(t)$ represents this ecological-economic system's ability to provide humans with a flow of vital ecosystem services at time t. Human use of this ecological-economic system begins at time $t = 0$, and hence this is also the time at which a manager is entrusted with the management of this system. At time $t = 0$, the ecological-economic system under study is devoid of any human influence and hence, moving forward in time, this system is able to provide humans with a flow of salient ecosystem services. This aspect of the problem is modeled by supposing that $X(0) = z > 0$.

If there is human use of the ecological-economic system and there is no managerial intervention of any kind then the ability of the ecological-economic system to provide humans with vital services will fall probabilistically. Therefore, the Brownian motion process $\{X(t): t \geq 0\}$ has a drift coefficient β where $\beta < 0$. To model the potential irreversibility mentioned earlier, the chapter contends that our ecological-economic system's ability to provide humans with a flow of vital ecosystem services will be irreversibly damaged when the Brownian motion process $\{X(t): t \geq 0\}$ becomes negative. As such, the use of a SMS to manage our ecological-economic system means that the manager's objective is to *never* allow $\{X(t): t \geq 0\}$ to become negative. With this background, Chapter 11 computes the steady state probability distribution function of the ecological-economic system under study given that the above described SMS is used to manage it.

Analysis shows that the steady state distribution of the ecological-economic system that is managed with a SMS is exponential with parameter β. The chapter notes that the memoryless[8] property of the exponential distribution has an interesting implication. Specifically, the manager's success in ensuring that the ecological-economic system's ability to provide humans with a flow of vital ecosystem services is *not* irreversibly damaged means that the steady state probabilistic behavior of this ecological-economic system is "history independent." This means that this system's limiting ability to provide vital ecosystem services does not reflect the previous success of managerial actions in avoiding the irreversibility mentioned previously. This concludes our discussion of this book's contributions pertaining to ecological economics. Part V of the book focuses on the management of invasive species.

---

8. See Ross (1996, pp. 35–39) or Tijms (2003, pp. 440–441) for a textbook discussion of this property.

2.4. *Invasive species management*

2.4.1. *Random inspections and fines*

Chapter 12 begins the discussion of invasive[9] species management by pointing out that, broadly speaking, there are two kinds of managerial actions that one can take to control the spread of invasive species and their harmful impacts. These are *pre-invasion* and *post-invasion* actions. The objective of pre-invasion actions is to preclude non-native species from invading a new habitat. In contrast, post-invasion actions are intended to control a non-native species, given that this species has already invaded a new habitat.

Although the extant literature has advanced our comprehension of many aspects of one kind of pre-invasive action, namely, inspections, Chapter 12 notes that there are two important issues about inspections that have received *no* attention in the literature. Therefore, the objective of this chapter is to shed light on these two issues. The first issue is to study the properties of a *random* inspection scheme. The second issue is to calculate the average total *fines* that will be collected in the long run by an inspection agency that uses this random inspection scheme to screen arriving ships for the presence of invasive species.

Consider a port of entry such as a seaport in an arbitrary country called Home. The analysis in this chapter is conducted from the standpoint of an inspection agency that has been charged with the task of inspecting arriving ships in this seaport for the presence of one or more invasive species. The term "inspection" in this chapter refers to the examination of the containers that are used by ships to move cargo or to the examination of the ballast water occasionally held by arriving ships or to the examination of both containers and ballast water.

---

9. Invasive species are also commonly known as alien, exotic, and non-native species. In the remainder of this chapter and indeed, in this book, we use these terms interchangeably.

Home engages in goods trade with a whole host of nations and hence ships from these various nations arrive in the seaport in Home to unload and/or to load cargo. Consistent with previous literature, this chapter supposes that the seaport inspection agency has distinct protocols for inspecting the arriving ships from distinct nations. In other words, ships arriving from country A are treated differently than ships arriving from country B, for any two distinct countries A and B.

This chapter uses a so-called "continuous sampling plan" to compute two key expected values. These expected values are the average fraction of all country A ships, for instance, that are and are not inspected. The acronyms AFSI and AFSNI are used to refer to these two averages. Analysis shows that in the random inspection scheme of this chapter, the average fraction of arriving ships from country A that are inspected depends on the fixed probability p that a given arriving ship will have one or more invasive species on it and on the positive integer r describing the number of ships out of which one will be inspected at random in the second stage. The chapter shows that when either $p = 1$ or $r = 1$, the random inspection scheme becomes a deterministic scheme in which all arriving ships from country A are inspected by the agency.

Next, this chapter focuses on the case in which there is an inspection protocol in place for the ships from every relevant country. Ships from all the relevant countries that fail the agency's inspection are fined and the magnitude (dollar value) of the individual ship fines are *random* variables. Upon completion of the inspection process, each ship pays a random fine to the agency and the amounts of this fine are described by the distribution law $G(y)$ where $y > 0$. Let $W(t)$ be the total amount of all the fines from the various ships that have been collected by the inspection agency by time t.

Chapter 12 computes an analytic expression for $W(t)$ and then concludes by pointing out that this expression can be utilized to assist with the general task of invasive species management in two ways. First, this expression can be used to ascertain whether it is feasible to make the conduct of inspections by our agency a revenue-neutral operation. Second, this expression can play the role of a constraint in an expected net social benefit from inspections maximization problem. Although international trade between nations lurks in the background in Chapter 12, such trade and the conditions in which it makes sense for a nation to use trade policies (tariffs) to mitigate the damage from biological invasions is investigated in Chapter 13.

2.4.2. *The utility of trade policies*

Chapter 13 extends the literature on international trade and invasive species management in three ways. First, it uses a two-country model to study the utility of tariffs as an invasive species management tool under four *different market structures.* Second, the chapter studies both *small* and *optimal* tariffs. Finally, the chapter examines the effect that tariffs have on the damage from invasive species and on *social welfare* when social welfare depends in part on the damage from alien species.

The world studied consists of two countries called Home and Foreign. Foreign exports and Home imports a particular good that could be either an agricultural good or a manufactured good. Over time, the import of this good also results in the *probabilistic* introduction of alien species from Foreign into Home. With the passage of time, scientific evidence implicating the alien species emerges, and then it becomes clear to the citizens and to the aforementioned authorities in Home that the stochastic introductions of these alien species and the resulting monetary damage are *linked* to the import of the good in question from Foreign. With this realization come calls for the use of trade policies to restrict imports and thereby reduce the introduction of the deleterious alien species.

Given this chain of events, Chapter 13 first constructs two monetary and one physical measure of the expected damage in Home from the stochastic introduction of alien species. The chapter then analyzes the impacts of small and optimal tariffs imposed by Home on the expected damage from invasive species, on prices, exports and imports, and social welfare in Home in four different market structures. The first market structure is one in which there is perfect competition and Home is a small country. In the second market structure, once again there is perfect competition but Home is now a large nation. In the third market structure, the foreign exporter is a monopolist and in the fourth market structure, the two trading nations engage in Cournot competition.

The chapter identifies several circumstances in which it makes sense to use tariffs to regulate deleterious invasive species. For instance, consider the case where perfect competition prevails and Home is a small country. Analysis shows that when social welfare depends on the mean damage from the introduction of alien species, small and optimal tariffs both *raise* welfare in Home as long as the expected total damage in Home is monetary. In contrast, when the mean total damage is physical and independent of the rate at which alien species arrive in Home, a tariff is incapable of affecting social welfare in Home, and hence, in this last case, it is optimal to not use a tariff to regulate alien species in Home.

The Chapter 13 analysis also shows that when the Home (domestic) firm engages in Cournot competition with the Foreign exporter, a number of interesting results emerge. For instance, if a small tariff increases domestic output then this tariff raises social welfare in Home irrespective of whether the expected damage from alien species introductions is monetary or physical in nature. On the other hand, if a small tariff does not raise domestic output then the imposition of a small tariff by Home will *not* necessarily raise social welfare.

Also, the analysis here shows that in addition to any profit shifting rationale, in the presence of monetary damage from alien species introductions, there is a second and arguably more important rationale for the use of import tariffs. This chapter concludes by pointing out that when tariffs are used as described, it may be possible to "kill three birds with one stone." What this means is that the Home government may be able to obtain a terms of trade benefit, shift profits away from the Foreign exporter and towards the domestic import competing firm, and reduce the monetary damage from detrimental alien species. Chapter 14 returns to the subject of inspections but with a twist. This time, inspections are analyzed in a setting in which economic cost reduction is more important to a risk loving inspector than is biological invasion damage control.

2.4.3. *Economics cost reduction versus biological invasion damage control*

DeAngelo *et al.* (2006; 2007) have studied the twin objectives of reducing the economic cost associated with inspections and reducing the likelihood of one or more biological invasions. In these two papers, greater (lesser) inspection stringency reflects an increased (decreased) concern for the possible damage from a biological invasion. Hence, an inspector who places a relatively large (small) weight on invasion damage control will, all else being equal, want to inspect ships more (less) stringently.

Chapter 14 continues the exploration of this relatively little studied issue by studying the behavior of a *risk loving* inspector in a seaport who is entrusted with the task of inspecting the container cargo on arriving ships for the presence of one or more harmful invasive species. Risk loving means that our inspector is *more* concerned about reducing the economic cost associated with inspections than he is about biological invasion damage control.

Specifically, this chapter accomplishes three tasks. First, it uses the theory of continuous time Markov chains (CTMCs) to describe a probabilistic inspection regime. Second, it mathematically explains the sense in which the inspector under study is risk loving. Finally, the chapter uses the stochastic features of the problem to compute the long run expected amount of time (LRET) an arriving ship that is inspected by the risk loving inspector spends in the seaport under study.

Ships carrying container cargo arrive at the seaport in a particular geographical region of a nation in accordance with a stationary Poisson process with rate $\lambda > 0$. Consistent with DeAngelo *et al.*

(2006; 2007), in conducting his inspections, the inspector follows one or both of the following two protocols. First, he inspects arriving ships relatively slowly and "relatively slowly" here is a proxy for more stringent inspections. More stringent inspections are conducted by our inspector if preventing one or more biological invasions is *more* important to him than reducing the economic cost from conducting inspections. Second, this same inspector can inspect arriving ships relatively quickly and "relatively quickly" in this chapter is a proxy for less stringent or more lax inspections. More lax inspections will be conducted by the inspector if he is *more* concerned about reducing the economic cost associated with inspections than he is about reducing the damage to society from one or more biological invasions. The faster (slower) inspection protocol is denoted by 1 (2).

The use of each inspection protocol results in the inspection of a single ship at any particular point in time. Given that our inspector is risk loving, Chapter 14 supposes that he would like to *minimize* the LRET a ship spends being inspected at the seaport before its cargo is cleared for transport to various inland destinations. The slower or more stringent protocol is used only when the number of ships waiting to be inspected in the seaport exceeds the critical threshold T. When the number of waiting ships in the seaport is either at or lower than the threshold T, our inspector reverts back to using the fast inspection protocol only. Given this description of the probabilistic inspection regime, Chapter 14 next computes a closed-form expression for the LRET metric.

Now, given that our inspector is risk loving, he would, in principle, like to choose suitable control variables and minimize the LRET expression. In this regard, Chapter 14 ends the discussion with two points. First, it contends that the only reasonable control variables in the model employed are the parameters β_1 and β_2 of the two exponentially distributed fast and slow inspection protocol times. Second, it notes that by selecting β_1 and β_2 optimally, the inspector will have minimized the time spent by arriving ships undergoing inspections in the seaport under study. This concludes the present book's discussion of invasive species management. We now proceed to summarize the contents of the sixth and last part of this book. This part is about environmental regulation.

2.5. *Environmental regulation*

2.5.1. *Consistency and optimality*

Chapter 15 models the interaction between a regulator and a monopolistic polluter as a deterministic Stackelberg differential game in which the regulator leads. The analysis considers dynamically inconsistent and consistent tax policies in a game in which the state, i.e., the stock of pollution, evolves in a manner known to both the players. In every case analyzed, the *production* of a certain good results in pollution. The regulator taxes the production of the polluting good and his objective is to maximize the sum of net benefits and tax revenues. The two kinds of policies available to the regulator include a unit tax an *ad valorem* tax. A key objective of the chapter is to compare the outcomes of the different games resulting from the use of these two price control instruments.

The first half of this chapter studies open loop or dynamically inconsistent taxes. This study yields three interesting results. First, it is shown that the steady state pollution effects of the two taxes are fundamentally influenced by the initial level of pollution as long as the stock dependent cost function is nonconstant. Put differently, history matters. Second, the chapter describes the conditions in which, with perfect regulatory commitment, an optimal tax policy does not involve setting zero taxes either at the beginning or at the end of the games studied. In this discussion, the chapter points out that because these optimal tax policies are inconsistent, as time progresses, the regulator will want to decrease the firm's valuation of pollution. Third, the chapter points out that when the regulator chooses to use both taxes simultaneously, it is optimal for him to levy an infinite *ad valorem* tax and to impose a unit subsidy. When he does this, he is able to force the monopolistic firm to behave competitively.

Open loop or dynamically inconsistent policies are not believable. What this means is that the forward looking firm will recognize that at time $t = 0$, the regulator will set a tax trajectory from which he will later want to deviate. Thus, such a tax trajectory will *not* be believed by the firm and hence the original policy will fail to achieve its intended objectives. This lack of credibility of open loop policies provides the rationale for the study of dynamically consistent tax policies in the second half of Chapter 15. This notwithstanding, it is important to understand that for the reasons given in the chapter, time consistent controls always result in a lower payoff to the regulator than do open loop controls except when the two kinds of controls coincide.

The analysis in Chapter 15 of dynamically consistent tax policies leads to a number of noteworthy results. We now highlight three such results. First, using specific functional forms to compare open loop unit and *ad valorem* taxes with their dynamically consistent counterparts, the chapter notes that the obtained results depend greatly on the properties of the stock dependent cost function. Depending on the magnitudes of the various parameters, there are a number of situations in which the use of time consistent taxes leads to a higher level of pollution. In addition, although time consistent taxes can lead to higher steady state levels of pollution, the use of such taxes is *more plausible* because open loop tax policies are not credible.

Second, the comparison of the steady state pollution levels with the four taxes under study generates results that are *not* general but highly dependent on the chosen functional forms for the various functions. Finally, when the regulator uses both dynamically consistent taxes to regulate pollution, it is optimal for him to impose a unit subsidy and levy an infinite *ad valorem* tax. The simultaneous use of unit and *ad valorem* taxes permits the regulator to shift and rotate the inverse demand function. Hence, he is able to confront the monopolistic firm with an infinitely elastic non-stationary function. More importantly, note that while continuous revision of the tax by the regulator alters the solution to his optimization problem, it does *not* alter his optimal course of action when he chooses to use both taxes simultaneously. The next item on the agenda in this last part of the book is waste management with on and off site storage and this topic is taken up in Chapter 16.

2.5.2.   *Waste management and storage*

Chapter 16 begins by noting that the decision faced by most waste generators is the on site *versus* off site storage decision. From the standpoint of a cost minimizing waste generator that is subject to exogenous regulatory requirements concerning the maximum amount of waste that can be stored on site, this decision involves determining the *optimal* waste production level in the time period of interest. Because off site waste storage is generally more expensive than on site storage, this optimal waste production level will have a direct bearing on a firm's long run expected cost (LREC) of waste management. The two related issues of the optimal waste production level and the on site versus off site storage decision together comprise the centerpiece of the analysis that is conducted in this chapter.

Although the extant literature has shed light on various aspects of waste management, Chapter 16 contends that this literature has paid insufficient theoretical attention to the determination of the optimal waste production level in a stochastic environment with on and off site storage. Therefore, this chapter complements the recent analysis of Batabyal and Nijkamp (2009) and studies a probabilistic model with on and off site storage that is pertinent to the management of a broad class of wastes.

The first task undertaken in this chapter is to derive a representative waste generating firm's LREC of waste management. To this end, the chapter concentrates on such a firm in a particular geographic region of a country such as the United States. This firm's goods production process yields waste that is initially stored on site. The amounts of waste that are produced in successive *months*, the time period of interest, are independent and identically distributed random variables with finite first two moments μ_1 and μ_2. Opportunities to remove the waste that is currently stored on site by our firm occur at the end of each month. The firm uses the following control rule to manage the waste it produces. If, at the end of a month, the total amount of waste on site is larger than the maximum legally permissible level or threshold W, then all waste presently stored on site is moved to a location off site. Otherwise, the on site waste is not moved. Our representative waste generating firm incurs a fixed cost F when it moves the accumulated waste stored on site to the off site location. In addition, this firm also incurs a variable cost v for each unit of waste in excess of the threshold W that it moves to the off site location. Analysis shows that the LREC for our firm is given by LREC $= \{2\mu_1^2 F + \mu_1\mu_2 v\}/\{2\mu_1 W + \mu_2\}$.

The second task undertaken in this chapter is the conduct of comparative statics exercises to show the effect that changes in the fixed cost parameter (F), the variable cost parameter (v), and the exogenous waste threshold (W) have on the LREC function. This exercise shows that, *inter alia*, the waste generating firm's long run expected cost goes up when either F or v go up.

The third and final tasks undertaken in this chapter is to demonstrate that the optimal waste production level is the solution to a particular cost minimization problem. To this end, the chapter assumes that the firm in question chooses the first moment μ_1 to minimize the LREC stated in the previous page. This exercise provides a closed form solution to the question about how much waste a firm operating in a probabilistic environment ought to produce in a month. The last chapter in this book examines the impact that innovation has on a polluting firm's regulation driven decision to upgrade its capital stock.

2.5.3. *Innovation and capital stock changes*

The general purpose of Chapter 17 is to use Tobin's (1969) *q*-theoretic investment framework to theoretically analyze the insufficiently studied *tripartite* interaction between increasing environmental regulations, the ensuing decision by a polluting firm to upgrade its capital stock, and the impact of innovation on this capital stock improvement decision. To this end, the chapter concentrates on a representative polluting firm in a regional economy which faces adjustment costs to upgrade its capital stock. A q-theoretic dynamic model of regulation driven investment by the polluting firm under study is constructed and then conditions characterizing efficient investment by this polluting firm are identified.

Next, this chapter ascertains the impact of an *unanticipated* increase in innovation on the polluting firm's steady state capital stock. Analysis with a phase diagram shows that an unanticipated increase in innovation that, *ceteris paribus*, expands the polluting firm's output Υ also increases this firm's steady state capital stock. Put differently, an increase in innovation *improves* the polluting firm's steady state capital stock and this allows the firm to better respond to the environmental regulations it confronts as a result of its production related pollution generation.

Following this discussion of the "unanticipated innovation" case, Chapter 17 addresses the impact of an *anticipated* increase in innovation on the polluting firm's steady state capital stock. Once again, analysis with a phase diagram reveals that an anticipated increase in innovation increases the polluting firm's steady state capital stock. Further, comparison with the previously studied case reveals that unanticipated and anticipated increases in innovation both lead to an increase in our polluting firm's steady state capital stock. However, the transitional dynamics or the way in which our polluting firm gets to the new steady state equilibrium from the initial equilibrium is very different.

The final question addressed in Chapter 17 is the following. What is the relationship between the polluting firm's internal shadow price of capital and the stock market value of a unit of this firm's capital? The polluting firm's internal shadow price of capital is denoted by q. V denotes the stock market value of the polluting firm. So, the stock market value of a unit of our firm's capital is V/K. The issue to be resolved is the relationship between q and V/K.

Obstfeld and Rogoff (1996, pp. 111–113) have observed that when there are no adjustment costs, we can expect the relationship $q = V/K$ to hold. In addition, Hayashi (1982) has remarked that even in the presence of adjustment costs, when a firm is a price taker, this firm's production function is linear homogenous in capital (K) and labor (L), and the adjustment cost function itself is linear homogeneous in capital (K) and investment (I), then the relationship $q = V/K$ will hold. This last equality is often referred to as the equality between "marginal" q and "average" q.

In the model utilized in Chapter 17, the adjustment cost function $\chi I^2/2$ is *not* linear homogeneous in capital (K) and investment (I). Therefore, marginal q is *unequal* to average q in this model. What this means is that the polluting firm's internal shadow price of capital is *not* equal to the stock market value of a unit of this firm's capital. In concluding this discussion, Chapter 17 points out that if the adjustment cost function of this chapter ($\chi I^2/2$) were to be replaced with the function ($\chi I^2/2K$) then marginal q would, in fact, equal average q. This is because in this last case, the adjustment cost function is linear homogeneous in both capital (K) and investment (I).

3. Conclusions

There is no gainsaying the fact that the scope of traditional resource economics has been greatly expanded by the increasingly interdisciplinary research that is now being conducted in this and related fields. Given this state of affairs, our basic objective in this book is to provide the reader with a state of the art account of where the literature in five particular areas within resource economics, broadly interpreted, now stands. Our secondary objective is to demonstrate how dynamic and stochastic approaches can be effectively used to construct and analyze theoretical models that shed valuable light on significant research questions in the existing literature.

To this end, in this introductory chapter, we have highlighted the ways in which the analyses in the 16 individual chapters collectively help accomplish this book's dual objectives. The use of dynamic and stochastic approaches to analyze interdisciplinary research questions that have a significant resource economics component to them is still in its infancy. Therefore, in the coming years, one may look forward to many interesting developments in theoretical research in this rapidly growing field of inquiry.

References

Arrow, K.J. and Fisher, A.C. (1974). Environmental Preservation, Uncertainty, and Irreversibility. *Quarterly Journal of Economics* 88:312–319.

Bailey, N.T.J. (1964). *The Elements of Stochastic Processes*. New York: Wiley.

Bartlett, M.S. (1960). *Stochastic Population Models*. New York: Wiley.

Batabyal, A.A. (1996). Review of Perrings, C., Maler, K.-G., Folke, C., Holling, C.S. and Jansson, B.-O. (eds.), *Biodiversity Loss. In Kyklos*, 49: 486–487.

Batabyal, A.A. and Nijkamp, P. (2009). Two Aspects of Waste Management from the Viewpoints of a Waste Generator and a Recipient. *Applied Economics Letters* 16:337–341.

Baumol, W.J. and Oates, W.E. (1988). *The Theory of Environmental Policy*, 2nd edn. Cambridge, UK: Cambridge University Press.

Brock, W.A. and Rothschild, M. (1984). Comparative Statics for Multidimensional Optimal Stopping Problems. *In* H. Sonnenschien (ed.), *Models of Economic Dynamics*. New York: Springer Verlag.

Brock, W.A., Rothschild, M. and Stiglitz, J.E. (1988). Stochastic Capital Theory. *In* G. Feiwel (ed.), *Joan Robinson and Modern Economic Theory*. London, UK: Macmillan.

Carson, R. (1962). *Silent Spring*. New York: Houghton Mifflin.

Ciriacy-Wantrup, S.V. (1952). *Resource Conservation*. Berkeley, California: University of California Press.

Clark, C.W. (1976). *Mathematical Bioeconomics*. New York: Wiley.

Costanza, R., Kemp, M. and Boynton, W. (1995). Scale and Biodiversity in Coastal and Estuarine Ecosystems. *In* C. Perrings, K.-G. Maler, C. Folke, C.S. Holling and B.-O. Jansson (eds.), *Biodiversity Loss*. Cambridge, UK: Cambridge University Press.

Dasgupta, P. (1996). The Economics of the Environment. *Environment and Development Economics* 1:387–428.

DeAngelo, G.J., Batabyal, A.A. and Kumar, S. (2006). On Economic Cost Minimization Versus Biological Invasion Damage Control. *In* A. Oude Lansink (ed.), *New Approaches to the Economics of Plant Health*. Heidelberg, Germany: Springer-Verlag.

DeAngelo, G.J., Batabyal, A.A. and Kumar, S. (2007). An Analysis of Economic Cost Minimization and Biological Invasion Damage Control using the AWQ Criterion. *Annals of Regional Science* 41:639–655.

Dixit, A.K. and Pindyck, R.S. (1994). *Investment Under Uncertainty*. Princeton, New Jersey: Princeton University Press.

Ehrlich, P.R. (1968). *The Population Bomb*. New York: Ballantine Books.

Gordon, H.S. (1954). The Economic Theory of a Common Property Resource: The Fishery. *Journal of Political Economy* 62:124–142.

Hardin, G. (1968). The Tragedy of the Commons. *Science* 162:1243–1247.

Haufler, J.B. (1999). Strategies for Conserving Terrestrial Biological Diversity. *In* R.K. Baydack, H. Campa III and J.B. Haufler (eds.), *Practical Approaches to the Conservation of Biological Diversity*. Washington, District of Columbia: Island Press.

Hayashi, F. (1982). Tobin's Marginal q and Average q: A Neoclassical Interpretation. *Econometrica* 50:213–224.

Henry, C. (1974a). Option Values in the Economics of Irreplaceable Assets. *Review of Economic Studies* 41:89–104.

Henry, C. (1974b). Investment Decisions under Uncertainty: The Irreversibility Effect. *American Economic Review* 64:1006–1012.

Holechek, J.L., Pieper, R.D. and Herbel, C.H. (1998). *Range Management*, 3rd edn. Upper Saddle River, New Jersey: Prentice Hall.

Holechek, J.L., Pieper, R.D. and Herbel, C.H. (2001). *Range Management*, 4th edn. Upper Saddle River, New Jersey: Prentice Hall.

Hotelling, H. (1931). The Economics of Exhaustible Resources. *Journal of Political Economy* 39:137–175.

Keller, R.P., Lodge, D.M., Lewis, M.A. and Shogren, J.F. (eds.) (2009). *Bioeconomics of Invasive Species*. New York: Oxford University Press.

Mangel, M. (1985). *Decision and Control in Uncertain Resource Systems*. Orlando, Florida: Academic Press.

Margolis, M. and Naevdal, E. (2008). Safe Minimum Standards in Dynamic Resource Problems: Conditions for Living on the Edge of Risk. *Environmental and Resource Economics* 40:401–423.

Meadows, D.H., Meadows, D.L. and Behrens, W.W. (1972). *The Limits to Growth*. New York: Universe Books.

Obstfeld, M. and Rogoff, K. (1996). *Foundations of International Macroeconomics.* Cambridge, Massachusetts: MIT Press.

Perrings, C., Maler, K.-G., Folke, C., Holling, C.S. and Jansson, B.-O. (eds.) (1995). *Biodiversity Loss.* Cambridge, UK: Cambridge University Press.

Pimm, S.L. (1991). *The Balance of Nature?* Chicago, Illinois: University of Chicago Press.

Ready, R.C. and Bishop, R.C. (1991). Endangered Species and the Safe Minimum Standard. *American Journal of Agricultural Economics* 73:309–312.

Ross, S.M. (1983). *Stochastic Processes.* New York: Wiley.

Ross, S.M. (1996). *Stochastic Processes,* 2nd edn. New York: Wiley.

Swanson, T.M. (1995). The International Regulation of Biodiversity Decline: Optimal Policy and Evolutionary Product. *In* C. Perrings, K.-G. Maler, C. Folke, C.S. Holling and B.-O. Jansson (eds.), *Biodiversity Loss.* Cambridge, UK: Cambridge University Press.

Tijms, H.C. (2003). *A First Course in Stochastic Models.* Chichester, UK: Wiley.

Tobin, J. (1969). A General Equilibrium Approach to Monetary Theory. *Journal of Money, Credit, and Banking* 1:15–29.

Wolff, R.W. (1989). *Stochastic Modeling and the Theory of Queues.* Englewood Cliffs, New Jersey: Prentice Hall.

Part II
Natural Resource Management

Chapter 2

ON SOME ASPECTS OF THE MANAGEMENT OF A STOCHASTICALLY DEVELOPING FOREST[1]

In this chapter, I focus on some important biological aspects of the forest management problem. I model a stochastically developing forest as a multi-dimensional, continuous time Markov chain. Next, I pose three questions concerning the long run characteristics of a stationary forest, the stochastic process followed by dying species, and the age of an arbitrary species in the forest. I then (a) characterize a stationary forest probabilistically, (b) describe the stochastic process governing the demise of species in this forest, and (c) provide a method for determining the age of an arbitrary species in the forest. Finally, I discuss the forest management implications of the issues raised in this chapter.

1. Introduction

Many interesting questions in stochastic capital theory concern the determination of the optimal time at which to terminate an aging process subject to biological and economic uncertainties. The optimal forest management problem is such a question. Until very recently, this management question has been analyzed in a deterministic context because the "...introduction of [uncertainty] complicates the analysis considerably" (Dasgupta, 1982, p. 182). While economists such as Brock and Rothschild (1984) and Brock et al. (1988) have analyzed aspects of the forest management

---

1. Dedicated to the memory of Sutapa Batabyal.

question in a stochastic setting, they have done so in a particular manner. Specifically, they have posed the "tree cutting" question as an optimal stopping time problem. Even the more general analysis of Clarke and Reed (1989) analyzes the management problem by positing that the price of timber follows a geometric Brownian motion process and that the logarithm of timber size follows a diffusion process whose local behavior resembles that of a Wiener process with drift.

Similarly, ecologists and foresters have also studied different aspects of this forest management problem. For instance, Hobbs and Legg (1983) and Shugart et al. (1973) have applied Markov models to study plant by plant replacement processes and the dynamics of vegetation stands, respectively. Moore (1990) has, inter alia, studied non-equilibrium age structures in Montana forests using a semi-Markov model of vegetation dynamics.

While these analyses have undeniably advanced our understanding of the tree cutting problem in a stochastic context, they have omitted three key aspects of the biological uncertainty affecting many large and long standing forests, particularly those in developing countries. These aspects pertain to the stochastic development of trees in long standing forests, the stochastic demise of trees,[2] and the uncertain introduction of new or previously known species into the forest. These features characterize large areas of forest land in many developing countries. The Amazon basin in Brazil, parts of the Chambal valley in India, and portions of the Irrawady basin in Myanmar are but three examples of forests in which the above described features play an important role in the evolution of the forest. Further, national forest managers who typically "inherit" such long standing forests with a multitude of species have a difficult time attempting to formulate forest policy. Before embarking on any policy — which from an economic standpoint would involve the formulation and solution of an appropriate optimization problem — such

---

2. Due to various reasons such as insect infestation, natural disasters, and old age.

managers would like to acquire information about questions which are inherently stochastic in nature. What kinds of species and how many trees within a particular species can one expect to see in a mature forest? Can one say anything about the stochastic process governing the demise of species? What can one say about the likelihood that a given species with a specific number of trees is the oldest — in the sense that it originated earliest — species in the forest?

To the best of my knowledge, these questions have not been addressed in the ecological literature previously. As such, in this chapter I propose to answer these three questions. In order to do so, I shall adapt and apply stochastic population models to the forest management problem (see Bartlett, 1960, pp. 17–44; Bailey, 1964, pp. 117–136; and in particular Ross, 1983, pp. 156–164). In this chapter, I shall be concerned with the biological and not the economic aspects of the management problem.[3] More specifically, I shall model the stochastically developing forest with the biological characteristics alluded to above as a multi-dimensional, continuous time Markov chain (CTMC).[4] As far as I am aware, the use of this modeling technique to study the above described questions is novel.[5] I wish to point out that this model bears considerable resemblance to the $M/G/\infty$ model[6] of queuing theory and thus I will point out some of the similarities in due course. In order to provide closed form answers to the three questions that I have posed, it will be necessary to make some distributional assumptions. Without such assumptions the problem becomes intractable and closed form answers to my questions cannot be provided.

---

3. Research on the economic aspects of the problem is ongoing and I expect to report those results separately.

4. See Bailey (1964, pp. 117–136) or Ross (1983, pp. 141–183) for more details.

5. It is important to stress that I am *not* claiming that the use of Markov models in ecology is novel. What I am claiming is that the use of the multi-dimensional CTMC to study the questions of this chapter is novel.

6. In this three-letter designation, the first letter refers to the fact that the inter-arrival times of customers in a queue has the Markovian property. The second letter refers to the fact that the server's service times have a general distribution. Finally, ∞ refers to the case in which there are an infinite number of servers. For more details see Wolff (1989, pp. 75–81).

2. The Modeling Framework

In order to answer the three outstanding questions, I shall analyze a mature, i.e., stationary forest. Suppose that new trees are "born" from existing trees in a statistically independent manner at an exponential rate γ. Due to a variety of possible reasons — some of which are listed in footnote 2 — trees are assumed to "die" independently at an exponential rate ϵ. In a queuing context, one would say that trees "depart" at an exponential rate ϵ. Finally, new individuals "enter" the forest due to reasons such as plantings, pollination by natural agents etc., according to a Poisson process with rate δ. In a queuing framework, one would say that new individuals "arrive" at rate δ. I shall assume that $\gamma < \epsilon$. This assumption will ensure ergodicity and hence the existence of stationary probabilities for my CTMC.

If I let $C_k(t)$ be the *number* of species at time t which have k trees, $k \geq 0$, and if I let $\vec{C}(t) = \{C_1(t), C_2(t), C_3(t), \ldots\}$ be the *vector* of all possible numbers of species in the forest under consideration,[7] then the vector stochastic process $\{\vec{C}(t): t \geq 0\}$ is a CTMC because along every dimension $\{C_k(t): t \geq 0\}$ for all $s \geq 0, t \geq 0$, and for non-negative integers $m, n, c(v), v \in [0, s]$, the property that

$$\Pr\{C_k(t+s) = n/C_k(s) = m, C_k(v) = c(v), 0 \leq v \leq s\}$$

$$= \Pr\{C_k(t+s) = n/C_k(s) = m\} \tag{1}$$

holds. With respect to the state vector $\vec{c} = \{c_1, c_2, c_3, \ldots\}$ $c_k > 0$, I can now define the following four states of the CTMC.[8] Let

$$A_k(t)\vec{c} = \{c_1, c_2, c_3, \ldots, c_{k-1}, c_k - 1, c_{k+1} + 1, c_{k+2}, \ldots\}, \quad k \geq 1,$$

$$\tag{2}$$

---

7. As the reader will note, I have used a countable state space to ease the mathematical exposition. If we constrain the state space to be finite, all of the subsequent analysis will carry through, albeit with greater algebraic clutter.

8. Appropriate state space definition is a crucial aspect of the modeling exercise. As van Hulst (1979) has noted in another context, if this is not done carefully, the state space can blow out to enormous size.

$$D_k(t)\vec{c} = \{c_1, c_2, c_3, \ldots, c_{k-1} + 1, c_k - 1, c_{k+1}, c_{k+2}, \ldots\}, \quad k \geq 2,$$

$$(3)$$

$$A_0(t)\vec{c} = \{c_1 + 1, c_2, c_3, \ldots\} \quad (4)$$

and let

$$D_1(t)\vec{c} = \{c_1 - 1, c_2, c_3, \ldots\}. \quad (5)$$

Equation (2) denotes the state that the CTMC is in after $\vec{c}$ when a new tree is "born" in a species with k trees, $k \geq 1$. Equation (3) denotes the state after $\vec{c}$ when a tree in a species with k trees "dies," $k \geq 2$. Equation (4) denotes the state after $\vec{c}$ when a new tree "enters" due to plantings or pollination. Finally, Equation (5) represents the state after $\vec{c}$ when a species consisting of one tree loses that tree.

Let $x\{\vec{c}, \vec{c}^{\,1}\}$ denote the CTMC's instantaneous transition rates. For my purposes, the relevant transitions are

$$x\{\vec{c}, A_0(t)\vec{c}\} = \delta, \quad (6)$$

$$x\{\vec{c}, A_k(t)\vec{c}\} = \gamma k c_k, \quad k \geq 1, \quad (7)$$

and

$$x\{\vec{c}, D_k(t)\vec{c}\} = \epsilon k c_k, \quad k \geq 1. \quad (8)$$

Before I proceed to analyze the above described forest which I have modeled as a CTMC, I note the following. In what follows, I shall assume that the forest under consideration once consisted of a bare tract of land, i.e., at time $t = 0$, $\vec{C}(0) = \vec{0}$. Further, I shall call an entering tree, a type k tree, if the species of which this tree is a member will consist of k trees at time t. Finally, I shall say that a particular species is in state k if this species consists of k trees. I am now in a position to analyze the above described forest.

3. Analysis and Results

The first question of interest to a forest manager concerns the characteristics of a mature (stationary) forest. To answer this question, I now determine the stationary probabilities for this CTMC.

By generalizing Theorem 4 of Wolff (1989, p. 74) I note that the $\{\vec{C}_k(t): t \geq 0, k \geq 1\}$ are *independent* Poisson-distributed random variables with mean $\delta \int_0^t P_k(w)dw$, where $P_k(w)$ is the probability that a species which originated at time w will consist of k trees by time t. Denote the stationary probabilities by $P(\vec{c})$. I can now state

Theorem 1. *The CTMC $\{\vec{C}(t): t \geq 0\}$ has stationary probabilities given by*

$$P(\vec{c}) = \prod_{k=1}^{\infty} \exp(-\beta_k)[\beta_k^{c_k}/c_k!], \quad \text{where } \beta_k = [1/k][\delta/\epsilon][\gamma/\epsilon]^{k-1},$$

$$k \geq 2.$$

Proof. In order to prove the theorem, I shall use (a) the *time reversibility* of $\{\vec{C}(t): t \geq 0\}$, (b) the assumption that $\vec{C}(0) = \vec{0}$, and (c) the fact that the $\{\vec{C}_k(t): t \geq 0 \ k \geq 1\}$ are independent Poisson random variables. The independence suggests that the form of the stationary probabilities should be multiplicative. As such, let the relevant stationary probabilities be given by

$$P(\vec{c}) = \prod_{k=1}^{\infty} \exp(-\beta_k)\frac{\beta_k^{c_k}}{c_k!}, \tag{9}$$

where the set $\{\beta_k\}$, $k \in [1, \infty]$ has to be determined. To determine these constants, I now show that $\{\vec{C}(t): t \geq 0\}$ is time reversible. For $P(\vec{c})$ given by Equation (9), to show time reversibility, I have to show that

$$P(\vec{c}) \cdot x\{\vec{c}, A_0(t)\vec{c}\} = P\{A_0(t)\vec{c}\} \cdot x\{A_0(t)\vec{c}, \vec{c}\}, \tag{10}$$

and

$$P(\vec{c}) \cdot x\{\vec{c}, D_k(t)\vec{c}\} = P\{D_k(t)\vec{c}\} \cdot x\{D_k(t)\vec{c}, \vec{c}\} \tag{11}$$

hold. Simple algebra tells us that Equation (10) requires that

$$\prod_{k=1}^{\infty} \exp(-\beta_k)\frac{\beta_k^{c_k}}{c_k!}\delta = \frac{\exp(-\beta_1)\beta_1^{c_1+1}}{(c_1+1)!} \prod_{k=2}^{\infty} \exp(-\beta_k)\frac{\beta_k^{c_k}}{c_k!}(c_1+1)\epsilon$$

$$\tag{12}$$

hold and Equation (11) requires that

$$\exp(-\beta_{k-1})\frac{\beta_{k-1}^{c_{k-1}-1}}{c_{k-1}!}\exp(-\beta_k)\frac{\beta_k^{c_k}}{c_k!}\epsilon k c_k$$

$$= \exp(-\beta_{k-1})\frac{\beta_{k-1}^{c_{k-1}+1}}{(c_{k-1}+1)!}\exp(-\beta_k)\frac{\beta_k^{c_k-1}}{(c_k-1)!}\gamma(c_{k-1}+1)(k-1)$$

$$(13)$$

hold. In writing Equation (13), I have canceled all the common terms. Solving Equation (13) for β_1, I get $\beta_1 = \delta/\epsilon$. Solving Equation (13) for β_k recursively by using $\beta_1 = \delta/\epsilon$, I get

$$\beta_k = \frac{1}{k}\frac{\delta}{\epsilon}\left[\frac{\gamma}{\epsilon}\right]^{k-1}, \quad k \geq 2. \tag{14}$$

I have now shown that $\{\vec{C}(t): t \geq 0\}$ is time reversible. Since the stationary probabilities given by Equation (9) do in fact solve the reversibility equations, Equation (9) does indeed give us the requisite stationary probabilities. □

Remark. The time reversibility of the above described CTMC can also be demonstrated by solving the equation $P(\vec{c}) \cdot x\{\vec{c}, A_k(t)\vec{c}\} = P\{A_k(t)\vec{c}\} \cdot x\{A_k(t)\vec{c}, \vec{c}\}$.

I have now answered the first of my three questions. That is, I have determined the characteristics of the forest under study in a steady state. Equation (9) should be of considerable help to a forest manager for planning purposes. First, while inspecting Equation (9), the manager will know that in the kind of forest under study, the limiting number of species with k trees are independent Poisson random variables. In other words, there are no interaction effects between the various limiting number of species.[9] Second, the manager will be able to infer directly, the mean number of species

---

9. Note that this is a steady state result. It does not mean that there will never be any interaction effects.

with k trees. This information is given by the individual $\beta'_k s$. This information should be of considerable use in planning logging policies, particularly those policies which are designed to *selectively* log certain species but not others.

The second management question that I have posed concerns the determination of the stochastic process which governs the demise of species. I have already argued that a key aspect of large forests is that trees die out due to a variety of reasons in an uncertain manner. Before embarking on a specific planting and/or logging policy, clearly, the forest manager would like to know the nature of the stochastic process governing species death. Access to this information will enable the forest manager to decide, *inter alia*, at what rate he/she should plant new trees and at what rate he/she should log presently standing trees. I now answer this question. Let $F(t)$ be the number of species which die out in the interval $(0, t)$. What kind of stochastic process is $\{F(t): t \geq 0\}$? The answer is contained in

Theorem 2.   *If* $\{F(t): t \geq 0\}$ *is stationary at time* $t = 0$, *then* $\{F(t): t \geq 0\}$ *is a homogeneous Poisson process with mean* δ. *If the forest is bare at* $t = 0$, *then* $\{F(t): t \geq 0\}$ *is a non-homogeneous Poisson process with intensity function* $\delta(t)$.

Proof.   To prove the theorem, I shall exploit the similarities between my CTMC model and the $M/G/\infty$ model of queuing theory. The key step lies in recognizing that my task is equivalent to determining the stochastic process followed by the *output* process of an infinite server queue with Poisson arrivals.[10] The solution to this problem is well known in queuing theory — see Ross (1985, p. 224) — and hence the claimed result follows.   □

Theorem 2 tells us that the stochastic process governing the demise of species depends fundamentally on whether the forest under study is in steady state at time $t = 0$ or not. If the forest is in steady state, then $F(t)$ is a homogeneous Poisson process.

---

10. Also see the discussion at the beginning of Section 2.

The more interesting case is when the forest is non-stationary at $t = 0$. In this case, the theorem tells us that $F(t)$ is still a Poisson process, but a non-homogeneous one. The non-homogeneity tells us that because this stochastic process does not possess stationary increments, deaths are more likely at certain times than at others. Intuitively, this is what one would expect in this latter situation.

I shall now answer the third question that I posed in Section 1. This question concerns the probabilistic determination of the age of the various species. Specifically, I am interested in determining the likelihood that a given species with k trees is the oldest species in the forest. The answer to this question is contained in the following theorem:

Theorem 3. *If in a stationary forest there exists $c_k, k > 0$, species with k trees, then the probability that a given species with k trees is the oldest — in the sense that it originated earliest — species in the forest is $k / \sum_{j=1}^{\infty} j c_j$.*

Proof. This result follows from Corollary 5.6.7 of Ross (1983, p. 164). □

Remark. The technique involved in demonstrating Theorem 3 involves first truncating the countable state space of the CTMC to a finite state space. It is important to note that this truncation involves keeping track of the various species as time progresses. In other words, keeping track of the age of the various species is an important part of the proof. For a similar application in another context, see Batabyal (1996).

The significance of Theorem 3 lies in the fact that it provides a probabilistic method of dating species. This provides the forest manager with information on the basis of which he/she can make conservation decisions.[11] The provision of such information would appear

---

11. Moore (1990) has also addressed an aspect of this conservation issue, albeit in a very different way. His approach is to maximize the mean time to local extinction for the relevant vulnerable species.

to be particularly necessary in resolving "What to preserve?"debates that are ongoing in many parts of the developing world.

4. Conclusions

In contrast with previous stochastic models of the forest management problem, in this chapter I have focused on three biological aspects of the problem which have not been addressed previously by ecologists or economists. I showed how to model a stochastically developing forest with many species of trees as a multi-dimensional CTMC. Further, I posed and answered three questions concerning (a) the long run characteristics of a stationary forest, (b) the stochastic process followed by dying species, and (c) the age of an arbitrary species in a stationary forest.

As noted by Horn (1975), Markov models have considerable predictive power. As such, the questions addressed and the answers provided in this chapter have a direct bearing on the general forest management problem. In combination with the economic aspects — on which research is ongoing — the answers provided here should offer the forest manager substantial policy guidance regarding some important but hitherto unanswered questions.

References

Bailey, N.T.J. (1964). *The Elements of Stochastic Processes.* New York: Wiley.

Bartlett, M.S. (1960). *Stochastic Population Models.* New York: Wiley.

Batabyal, A.A. (1996). The Queuing Theoretic Approach to Groundwater Management. *Ecological Modelling* 85:219–227.

Brock, W.A. and Rothschild, M. (1984). Comparative Statics for Multi-dimensional Optimal Stopping Problems. *In* H. Sonnenschien (ed.), *Models of Economic Dynamics.* New York: Springer Verlag.

Brock, W.A., Rothschild, M. and Stiglitz, J.E. (1988). Stochastic Capital Theory. *In* G. Feiwel (ed.), *Joan Robinson and Modern Economic Theory.* London, UK: Macmillan.

Clarke, H.R. and Reed, W.J. (1989). The Tree-cutting Problem in a Stochastic Environment. *Journal of Economic Dynamics and Control* 13:569–596.

Dasgupta, P. (1982). *The Control of Resources*. Oxford, UK: Basil Blackwell.

Hobbs, R.J. and Legg, C.J. (1983). Markov Models and Initial Floristic Competition in Heathland Vegetation Dynamics. *Vegetatio* 56:31–43.

Horn, H.S. (1975). Markovian Properties of Forest Succession. *In* M.L. Cody and J.M. Diamond (eds.), *Ecology and Evolution of Communities*. Cambridge, Massachusetts: Harvard University Press.

Moore, A.D. (1990). The Semi-Markov Model: A Useful Tool in the Analysis of Vegetation Dynamics for Management. *Journal of Environmental Management* 30:111–130.

Ross, S.M. (1983). *Stochastic Processes*. New York: Wiley.

Ross, S.M. (1985). *Introduction to Probability Models*, 3rd edn. Orlando, Florida: Academic Press.

Shugart, H.H., Crow, T.R. and Hett, J.M. (1973). Forest Succession Models: A Rationale and Methodology for Modeling Forest Succession over Large Regions. *Forest Science* 19:203–212.

van Hulst, R. (1979). On the Dynamics of Vegetation: Markov Chains as Models of Succession. *Vegetatio* 40:3–14.

Wolff, R.W. (1989). *Stochastic Modeling and the Theory of Queues*. Englewood Cliffs, New Jersey: Prentice-Hall.

Chapter 3

ON THE CHOICE BETWEEN THE STOCKING RATE AND TIME IN RANGE MANAGEMENT[1]

with B. Biswas and E.B. Godfrey

A long standing question in range management concerns the relative importance of the *stocking rate* versus the length of *time* during which animals graze a particular rangeland. We address this question by analyzing the problem faced by a private rancher who wishes to minimize the long run expected net unit cost (LRENC) from range operations by choosing either the stocking rate or the length of time during which his animals graze his rangeland. We construct a renewal-theoretic model and show that, in general, this rancher's LRENC with an optimally chosen stocking rate is *lower* than his LRENC with an optimally chosen grazing cycle length. From a management perspective, this means that correct stocking of the range is more important than the length of time during which animals graze the range. In addition, our research shows how to address questions concerning the desirability of temporal versus non-temporal controls in managing natural resources such as fisheries and hunting grounds.

1. Introduction

1.1. *Preliminaries*

All parts of the world that are not bare deserts, that are not cultivated, and that are not covered by bare soil, ice, or rock can be

---

1. We thank Michael Rauscher and two anonymous referees for their helpful comments on a previous version of this chapter. Batabyal acknowledges financial support from the Utah Agricultural Experiment Station, Utah State University, Logan, UT 84322-3530, by way of project UTA 024 and from the Gosnell endowment at RIT. The usual disclaimer applies.

thought of as *rangelands*. This means that rangelands include most deserts, forests, and all natural grasslands. The key feature of a rangeland is that it consists of uncultivated land that can and typically does provide habitat for browsing and grazing animals. *Browsing* refers to the consumption of leaves and twigs from woody plants such as shrubs and trees by animals. In contrast, *grazing* refers to the consumption of standing forage such as grasses by animals.

Range management is "the manipulation of rangeland components to obtain the optimum combination of goods and services for society on a sustained basis" (Holechek *et al.*, 1998, p. 5). As noted by Stoddart *et al.* (1975, pp. 2–3) and Holechek *et al.* (1998, p. 5), in contemporary times, the task of range management is based on five basic precepts. First, a rangeland is a renewable resource. Second, solar energy captured by the green plants of a rangeland can only be harvested by browsing and grazing animals. Third, the productivity of a rangeland is determined by climatic, soil, topographic, and use factors. Fourth, in comparison with cultivated lands, rangelands provide humans with food and fiber at very low energy costs. Finally, a variety of goods and services such as food, minerals, timber, and recreation are obtained from rangelands.

A range manager can manipulate the components of a rangeland in several ways. In other words, this manager can accomplish his managerial objectives[2] with a variety of choice variables. In this chapter, we are interested in shedding light on a particular controversy in the range management literature. This controversy concerns two choice variables, namely, the stocking rate and the length of a grazing cycle. The *stocking rate* concept is used in more than one way by range managers. Consequently, it is important to be clear about the precise meaning of this concept. The meaning that we shall use in this chapter tells us that the "stocking rate is typically expressed as animal units per section of land" (Holechek *et al.*,

---

2. Examples include the maximization of (i) range livestock productivity and (ii) the economic returns from the rangeland.

1998, p. 190). The *length of a grazing cycle* is more straightforward and it is defined to be the length of time in a calendar year during which animals graze a given rangeland.[3]

With these two definitions in place, we are now in a position to state the abovementioned controversy in the form of a simple question: Is the stocking rate more important or is time more important in range management? The objective of this chapter is to answer this question. We now discuss this range management controversy in greater detail and then we comment on the way in which we plan to address the underlying issues.

1.2. *The controversy*

Although there are many aspects to the task of range management, today, range scientists agree that one important aspect concerns the determination of the appropriate stocking rate. Consider the position of two standard range management texts on the subject of the stocking rate. Stoddart *et al.* (1975, p. 262) tell us that correct livestock "numbers are important for the perpetuation of the range, the well-being of the livestock, and the economic stability of the operator." Holechek *et al.* (1998, p. 221) go even further and state that proper "stocking is the most important part of successful range management."

However, not everyone agrees that the stocking rate is the most salient part of successful range management. In particular, Allan Savory (1983; 1988) and his adherents — see Goodloe (1969), Savory and Parsons (1980), and Savory and Butterfield (1999) — have forcefully argued that the stocking rate is less important than is commonly believed. Savory and Butterfield (1999, p. 41, emphasis in original) have pointed out that until "very recently no one truly explored the question of *when* animals are there as opposed to how

---

3. In the rest of this chapter, we shall use the terms "length of grazing cycle" and "time" interchangeably. The reader should note that both these terms refer to the length of time during which animals graze a given rangeland.

many there are." The central point of Allan Savory and other like minded scholars is this: Overgrazing bears "little relationship to the number of animals but rather to the *time* plants [are] exposed to the animals" (Savory and Butterfield, 1999, p. 46, emphasis in original).[4]

This polarized state of affairs raises an important question. Is the stocking rate more important or is time, i.e., the length of the grazing cycle, more important in range management? We shall answer this question by analyzing the decision problem faced by an optimizing private rancher. Keeping with standard practice in economics, we suppose that this rancher wishes to maximize the long run expected profit — or equivalently, minimize the long run expected net unit cost (hereafter LRENC) — from his range operations. This rancher does so by choosing either the stocking rate or the length of time during which his animals graze his rangeland.[5] Note that this *long run* focus means that our rancher cares about the expected net cost from his range operations *and* about the well being of his rangeland. Moreover, this focus also implies that the rancher will not stock his rangeland at a rate that the rangeland is unable to support. Our analysis shows that, in general, this rancher's LRENC with an optimally chosen stocking rate is *lower* than his LRENC with an optimally chosen grazing cycle length.

To intuitively see why this result holds, note the following two things. First, because the two choice variables under consideration here are different — the stocking rate is a *quantity* control variable and the grazing cycle length is a *temporal* control variable — the rancher's objective functions with these two choice variables are

---

4. Allan Savory's views on grazing have been variously described as time-controlled grazing, as short duration grazing, and as the Savory grazing method. For more on this and related issues, see Holechek *et al.* (1998, pp. 229–256). A related issue here concerns plant recovery times after different degrees of grazing. For more on this, see Hart *et al.* (1988), Hall *et al.* (1992), and McCreary and Tecklin (1993).

5. To keep the mathematics straightforward, in the rest of this chapter, we shall not focus on the profit criterion; instead, we shall focus on the LRENC criterion. However, the reader should note that maximizing profit is equivalent to minimizing net cost.

dissimilar. Second, in the presence of uncertainty, the two choice variables under consideration affect the rancher's objective function in different ways. The net impact of these two things is that our rancher's minimized LRENC with an optimally chosen grazing cycle length is higher than his minimized LRENC with an optimally chosen stocking rate by a specific additive factor. This additive factor is $c/2$, where c can be thought of as the instantaneous net cost of grazing an animal.

At the outset, it is important to be clear about the conclusions that can be drawn from our analysis. Our analysis tells us that when confronted with a choice *between* the stocking rate and the grazing cycle length, a rational rancher would choose the stocking rate. We are *not* saying that the grazing cycle length is irrelevant for management purposes. Further, it is our conjecture that just as part-price and part-quantity control instruments dominate pure price and pure quantity control instruments (see Roberts and Spence (1976), Weitzman (1978), and Batabyal (1995)), a hybrid control instrument that is part-stocking rate and part-time is likely to be more useful for range management than the stocking rate or the grazing·cycle length alone. Having said this, we should note that the simultaneous use of the two control variables under consideration here is not mandatory. Just as it is not always necessary to use price and quantity control instruments simultaneously to regulate pollution, similarly, in this range management context, it is not imperative that a range manager use a temporal control (grazing cycle length) and a quantity control (stocking rate) concurrently.

Given the obvious importance of this stocking rate versus time question for practical range management, one would expect this question to have been studied thoroughly. Although there are many studies that have evaluated the impact of alternate stocking rates on animal performance and on forage production,[6] and some empirical

---

6. See Holechek *et al.* (1998, pp. 248–256) and Holechek *et al.* (1999).

studies of Allan Savory's time-controlled grazing,[7] these studies have not resolved this stocking rate versus time controversy. Moreover, on the theoretical side, the matter is even less settled. To the best of our knowledge, there are *no* previous theoretical studies of this question. This state of affairs has led Holechek *et al.* (1998, p. 254) to conclude that the long "term impacts of [time-controlled] grazing ... [have yet] to be determined." As such, we now proceed to our analysis of the long run effects of the stocking rate versus time in range management.

The theoretical framework of this chapter is adapted from Batabyal (1999) and the rest of this chapter is organized as follows. Section 2 presents and analyzes a renewal-theoretic[8] model of the decision problem faced by a private rancher who wishes to minimize his LRENC from range operations by choosing the stocking rate optimally. Section 3 analyzes a similar model; however, in this section, the rancher minimizes his LRENC from range operations by choosing the length of the grazing cycle optimally. Section 4 first compares the optimized value of the rancher's LRENC from Sections 2 and 3 and thereby determines which choice variable — stocking rate or time — results in lower LRENC. Next, this section discusses the relationship between the analysis of this chapter and other related natural resource management problems. Section 5 concludes and offers suggestions for future research.

2. Range Management with an Optimally Chosen Stocking Rate

Consider a private rancher who owns livestock animals (cows) and a fenced plot of rangeland. In the model of this and the next section, our private rancher conducts his range operations with reference

---

7. See Graham *et al.* (1992), Hart *et al.* (1993), and Holechek *et al.* (1998, pp. 248–256).

8. For more on renewal theory, see Ross (1996, pp. 98–161; 1997, pp. 351–410) and Taylor and Karlin (1998, pp. 419–472).

to a particular grazing period in a calendar year. For instance, this grazing period might be from May 2 to July 15, which would correspond to the grazing period for intensive-early stocking, or it might run from May 2 to October 3, which would correspond to the grazing period for normal season-long grazing (Holechek *et al.*, 1998, pp. 231–236). At the beginning of a grazing period, our rancher lets his animals into his fenced rangeland in accordance with an arrival process. In general, this arrival process could be any renewal process. However, in both the economics and the ecology literatures, the Poisson process has been frequently used to study natural resource phenomena.[9] Consequently, we suppose that this arrival process is the Poisson process with rate α.[10] This rancher believes that the appropriate stocking rate for his rangeland corresponds to A animals. As such, once A animals have been allowed into the rangeland to graze, entry of additional animals is prohibited for the grazing period under consideration. Put differently, once A animals have been allowed in, this rancher's rangeland is closed to grazing in the current calendar year grazing period.

As a result of his range operations, our rancher incurs costs and obtains benefits from two sources. The first, or direct, source of net cost (total cost less total benefit) stems from things like the deleterious effects of grazing on the plant species of the rangeland

---

9. See Uhler and Bradley (1970), Pielou (1977), Arrow and Chang (1980), Mangel (1985), and Batabyal and Beladi (2001) for a more detailed corroboration of this claim.

10. For more on the Poisson process, see Ross (1996, pp. 59–97; 1997, pp. 249–301) and Taylor and Karlin (1998, pp. 267–332). The rate of the (Poisson) arrival process might depend on the stock of animals. One way to model this would be to work with a non-homogeneous Poisson process for which the arrival rate at time t is a function of t. That is, the arrival rate (also called the intensity function) is $\alpha(t)$, $t \geq 0$. Now if this intensity function is bounded, i.e., if $\alpha(t) \leq \beta, \forall t \geq 0$, then we can think of the non-homogeneous Poisson process as being a random sample from the homogeneous Poisson process with rate β. Specifically, we could work with this new Poisson process and the analysis would go through as indicated in the chapter. Finally, note that the range management problem being analyzed in this chapter is directly concerned with the number of animals and the length of time during which animals are *on the rancher's rangeland*. The question of how the animals leave the rangeland is not of interest. Formally, the problem being analyzed is *not* a queuing problem. As such, it is not necessary to formally model the departure process.

(a cost) and from the weight gain accruing to animals as a result of forage intake (a benefit). We capture this direct source of net cost by supposing that our rancher incurs net cost at the rate of ac per unit time, where a refers to the number of animals grazing at that time and c can be thought of as the instantaneous net cost per animal. The second, or indirect, source of net costs arises from things like the need to feed animals that have not been allowed into the rangeland (a cost) and from stocking the rangeland at the correct rate (a benefit). This benefit arises because correct stocking means that the rangeland's grazing capacity will not be exceeded. In turn, this means that this rangeland will be able to provide the rancher's animals with a flow of forage in the long run. In every calendar year grazing period, we suppose that our rancher incurs a net cost of C when he closes his rangeland to additional animals.

Now, if we say that a grazing cycle[11] for the calendar year is completed whenever the rancher closes the rangeland to additional animals, then the description of events in the previous two paragraphs constitutes a renewal-reward process.[12] This fact is useful because we can now use a key property of renewal-reward processes, namely, the renewal-reward theorem to compute our rancher's LRENC from his range operations. The reader should note that the rancher's objective function involves the minimization of an economic criterion, i.e., the long run expected net cost. The renewal-reward theorem tells us how to compute this economic criterion. Specifically, this theorem tells us that the rancher's LRENC equals the expected net cost in a grazing cycle divided by the expected length of this grazing

---

11. The use of the word "cycle" is appropriate because the events that we are studying here are cyclical in nature. First, with regard to the analysis in this section, a cycle is completed whenever the rangeland is closed to grazing by animals. Similarly, with respect to the analysis in Section 3, a cycle is completed whenever T for that calendar year expires. Second, this pattern of events is repeated every calendar year and we are examining the long run behavior of this cyclical pattern of events.

12. For more on renewal-reward processes and the renewal-reward theorem, see the references cited in Footnote 8. Also, see the motivation for the rancher's objective function in Section 1.2.

cycle. Formally, we have

$$\text{LRENC} = \frac{E[\text{net cost per grazing cycle}]}{E[\text{length of grazing cycle}]}, \qquad (1)$$

where $E[\cdot]$ is the expectation operator.

Let us now compute the two expectations on the right hand side (hereafter RHS) of Equation (1). In any given grazing cycle, let X_a denote the time between the arrival of the ath animal and the $(a+1)$th animal into the rancher's rangeland. Then the numerator on the RHS of Equation (1) is given by

$$E[\text{net cost per grazing cycle}]$$
$$= C + E[1cX_1 + 2cX_2 + 3cX_3 + \cdots + (A-1)cX_{A-1}]. \quad (2)$$

Because the rancher's cows are brought into the rangeland in accordance with a Poisson process with rate α, the mean interarrival time is $1/\alpha$. Mathematically, this means that $E[X_i] = 1/\alpha$, $i = 1, \ldots, (A-1)$. Using this result, the RHS of Equation (2) can be simplified to

$$E[\text{net cost per grazing cycle}] = C + \frac{cA(A-1)}{2\alpha}. \qquad (3)$$

In order to compute the denominator on the RHS of Equation (1), it suffices to note that the expected length of a grazing cycle is simply the expected time it takes for the animals to begin grazing on the rancher's rangeland. Because the mean interarrival time for the cows is $1/\alpha$ we get

$$E[\text{length of grazing cycle}] = \frac{A}{\alpha}. \qquad (4)$$

Now combining the results from Equations (3) and (4), we get an expression for the rancher's LRENC. That expression is

$$\text{LRENC} = \frac{\alpha C}{A} + \frac{c(A-1)}{2}. \qquad (5)$$

Having computed the expression for our rancher's LRENC we are now in a position to state this rancher's LRENC minimization problem. Specifically, this rancher chooses the stocking rate A to minimize the LRENC from his range operations. Formally, our rancher solves

$$\min_{\{A\}} \left[\frac{\alpha C}{A} + \frac{c(A-1)}{2} \right]. \tag{6}$$

Treating A as a continuous choice variable and using calculus, we see that the stocking rate that minimizes the rancher's LRENC is given by[13]

$$A^* = \sqrt{\frac{2\alpha C}{c}}. \tag{7}$$

In words, the optimal stocking rate equals the square root of the ratio of the product of twice the rate of the Poisson arrival process (α) and the indirect net cost from closing the rangeland to additional animals (C) to the instantaneous net cost per animal (c). Inspecting Equation (7) it is easy to verify two properties of the optimal stocking rate. First, as the indirect net cost per grazing cycle (C) goes up, the rancher finds it desirable to *raise* the optimal stocking rate. Second, if the instantaneous net cost per animal (c) increases, then it is in the interest of the rancher to *lower* the optimal stocking rate.

Let us now substitute the expression for the optimal stocking rate from Equation (7) into the minimand in Equation (6). This gives us an expression for the minimal LRENC that our rancher will incur by choosing the stocking rate optimally. Denote this minimal LRENC by $(\text{LRENC})^*_{\text{SR}}$. Some algebra tells us that

$$(\text{LRENC})^*_{\text{SR}} = \sqrt{2\alpha c C} - \frac{c}{2}. \tag{8}$$

---

13. The second-order condition is satisfied.

Inspecting Equation (8), we see that the minimal LRENC that our rancher will incur by choosing the stocking rate optimally equals the square root of the product of twice the rate of the Poisson arrival process (α), the instantaneous net cost per animal (c), and the indirect net cost per grazing cycle (C), less one-half the instantaneous net cost per animal.

We now study the case in which the focus of our private rancher is not on the stocking rate *per se*, but on the *length* of the grazing cycle on his rangeland. After computing the optimal length of the grazing cycle, we shall compare Equation (8) with the corresponding equation for this latter case in which the rancher's focus is on time.

3. Range Management with an Optimally Chosen Grazing Cycle Length

Instead of choosing the stocking rate optimally, our rancher now follows a different strategy. In particular, this rancher now chooses the length of the grazing cycle (T) to minimize the LRENC from his range operations. In the context of the discussion in the first paragraph of Section 2, this means that if the grazing period in a calendar year happens to be 75 days long (May 2 to July 15), then our rancher chooses T with this 75-day grazing period in mind.[14] So, in this example, the optimal T would be some real number between 0 and 75. If the optimal $T = 0$, then this means that the rancher rests his rangeland for the entire grazing period in that calendar year. At the other end, if optimal $T = 75$, then this means that the rancher's grazing cycle and the grazing period for that calendar year coincide.

_____

14. The reader should note that the length of the grazing period in a calendar year and the choice of T will depend, *inter alia*, on the geographic location of the rangeland in question. Specifically, the recovery time and the capability of a range in a wet and humid region will be very different from the recovery time and capability of a range in an arid and/or semiarid region.

In this setting, our rancher chooses the length of the grazing cycle (time) to minimize the LRENC from his range operations. Consequently, let us now compute the LRENC that is incurred by the rancher when this rancher's focus is on time rather than on the stocking rate. As in the previous section, at the beginning of the grazing period, our rancher lets his animals into his rangeland in accordance with a Poisson process with rate α. We suppose that this rancher lets his animals graze the rangeland for T units of time. In other words, when T units of time have elapsed, the rangeland is closed to grazing. This means that a grazing cycle is completed when T units of time have elapsed. As explained in the previous paragraph, the length of this grazing cycle will either be less than or equal to the length of the grazing period in a calendar year.

We shall use the renewal-reward theorem (Equation (1)) to compute our rancher's LRENC. The computation of E[net cost per grazing cycle] will be facilitated by conditioning on $N(T)$, the total number of animals that are grazing the rancher's rangeland by time T. This yields

$$E[\text{net cost per grazing cycle}/N(T)] = C + \frac{cTN(T)}{2}. \quad (9)$$

Using the properties of the expectation operator and Equation (9), we get

$$E[\text{net cost per grazing cycle}] = C + \frac{\alpha c T^2}{2}. \quad (10)$$

Now note that E[length of grazing cycle] $= T$. This result and Equation (10) together tell us that our rancher's LRENC is given by

$$\text{LRENC} = \frac{C}{T} + \frac{\alpha c T}{2}. \quad (11)$$

Having computed the expression for our rancher's LRENC, we are now in a position to state this rancher's LRENC minimization problem. This rancher chooses the length of the grazing cycle (T)

to minimize the LRENC from his range operations. Formally, our rancher solves[15]

$$\min_{\{T\}} \left[\frac{C}{T} + \frac{\alpha c T}{2} \right]. \tag{12}$$

Using calculus, we see that the grazing cycle length that minimizes the rancher's LRENC is given by[16]

$$T^* = \sqrt{\frac{2C}{\alpha c}}. \tag{13}$$

In words, the optimal length of the grazing cycle equals the square root of the ratio of the product of twice the indirect net cost from closing the rangeland (C) to the product of the rate of the Poisson arrival process (α) and the instantaneous net cost per animal (c). Inspecting Equation (13) it is easy to verify two properties of the optimal length of the grazing cycle. First, as the indirect net cost per grazing cycle (C) goes up, the rancher finds it optimal to *lengthen* the grazing cycle. Second, if the instantaneous net cost per animal (c) increases, then it is optimal for the rancher to *shorten* the grazing cycle.

Let us now substitute the expression for the optimal length of the grazing cycle from Equation (13) into the minimand in Equation (12). This gives us an expression for the minimal LRENC that our rancher will incur by choosing the grazing cycle length optimally. Denote this minimal LRENC by $(\text{LRENC})_T^*$. After some algebra, we get

$$(\text{LRENC})_T^* = \sqrt{2\alpha c C}. \tag{14}$$

Inspecting Equation (14), we see that the minimal LRENC that our rancher will incur by choosing the grazing cycle length optimally

---

15. To keep this minimization problem simple, we have not imposed a constraint requiring T to be bounded below by zero and above by the length of the grazing period in a calendar year. If the optimal T turns out to be larger than the length of the grazing period, then we simply set the optimal T equal to the length of the grazing period. For example, as discussed in the first paragraph of this section, if the length of the grazing period happens to be 75 days and the optimal T turns out to be 78 days, then we simply set this optimal T equal to 75 days.

16. The second-order condition is satisfied.

equals the square root of the product of twice the rate of the Poisson arrival process (α), the instantaneous net cost per animal (c), and the indirect net cost per grazing cycle (C).

Recall that the objective of this chapter is to answer the following question: Is the stocking rate more important or is time, i.e., the length of the grazing cycle, more important in range management? We now provide an answer to this question.

4.   Stocking Rate Versus Time in Range Management

Equation (8) gives us an expression for the LRENC incurred by our rancher when he chooses the stocking rate optimally. Similarly, Equation (14) gives us an expression for this rancher's LRENC when he chooses the length of the grazing cycle (time) optimally. Comparing these two expressions, we see that

$$(\text{LRENC})^*_{\text{SR}} = \sqrt{2\alpha cC} - \frac{c}{2} < \sqrt{2\alpha cC} = (\text{LRENC})^*_T. \qquad (15)$$

Equation (15) clearly tells us that the rancher's LRENC with an optimally chosen stocking rate is lower than his LRENC with an optimally chosen grazing cycle length. It is in this sense that the stocking rate is *more important* than time in range management. Put differently, if a rational rancher had to choose a single control variable from a control set consisting of the stocking rate and time, then this rancher would choose the stocking rate over time. We now discuss the relationship between the analysis of this chapter and other related natural resource management problems.

4.1.   *Our analysis and other resource management problems*

In addition to rangelands, a number of other natural resources are also managed with temporal and non-temporal choice variables. For instance, commercial and recreational hunters for most game, are subject to seasonal (time) restrictions. Moreover, such hunters are generally required to hunt during daylight hours. Similarly, Batabyal and Beladi (2004) have pointed out that most commercial fisheries are subject to season length (time) restrictions. Given this state of affairs, it would certainly be useful to know whether society is better off with such temporal restrictions or whether non-temporal choice variables — such as the number of animals hunted and the number of fishing boats used — result in higher welfare to society.

The theoretical framework of this chapter can be used to answer these sorts of questions. Specifically, in the context of range management decisions, our analysis leads to three conclusions. First, *ceteris paribus*, correct stocking of the range is more important than the length of time during which animals graze the range. This conclusion supports the view that proper "stocking is the most important part of successful range management" (Holechek *et al.*, 1998, p. 221). Second, there are circumstances in which the use of a non-temporal choice variable like the stocking rate leads to lower costs for the rancher. As such, it would be useful to see if one can make a general theoretical argument against the use of temporal choice variables in range management. Finally, although we have come down on the side of the stocking rate, it is clear that because of biological factors such as the differential recovery rates of plants subject to grazing, there is a difference between grazing 10 animals for 100 days and grazing 100 animals for 10 days. In other words, the length of the grazing cycle is a relevant choice variable. This suggests that from a management perspective, stochastic but relevant biological factors are likely to be better accounted for by the use of control instruments that are part-stocking rate and part-time. We now discuss this issue in greater detail.

5. Conclusions

In this chapter, we used a renewal-theoretic approach to analyze the decision problem faced by a private rancher who is interested in minimizing the LRENC from his range operations. On the basis of our analysis of two optimization problems for this rancher, we concluded that the stocking rate is more important than time in range management. To the best of our knowledge, this is the *first* theoretical answer to this stocking rate versus time question in range management.

The analysis of this chapter can be extended in a number of directions. In what follows, we suggest two possible extensions. First, the discussion in the last paragraph of Section 4.1 suggests that there might exist choice variables, intermediate between the stocking rate and time, that dominate these two control variables. With regard to this issue, consider the seminal work of Roberts and Spence (1976). Environmental economists now know that it is possible to construct an "intermediate" control instrument that is part-price (fee or tax) and part-quantity (emissions permit scheme). Roberts and Spence (1976) showed that this intermediate control instrument can always be converted into a pure price or pure quantity control instrument. Consequently, in comparison with either a pure price or pure quantity control instrument, a regulator will do at least as well — and often much better — with this intermediate control instrument. A useful extension of this chapter would be to determine whether this logic carries over to the subject of range management. In other words, the open question is to check whether it is possible to construct, in a dynamic and stochastic setting, a control instrument that is intermediate in the sense that it is part-stocking rate and part-time. If it is possible to do so, then it should be fairly straightforward to demonstrate that this intermediate control instrument dominates a pure stocking rate and a pure time control instrument.

Second, in Section 2, we studied the decision problem faced by a private rancher who owns a single species of livestock animals (cows). As such, it would be useful to ascertain whether the results of this chapter hold when this rancher's decision problem with the stocking rate as a choice variable is modified to account for situations in which the rancher owns more than one animal species. Studies of range management that incorporate these aspects of the problem into the analysis will provide additional insight into the roles that the stocking rate and time play in successful range management.

References

Arrow, K.J. and Chang, S.S.L. (1980). Optimal Pricing, Use, and Exploration of Uncertain Natural Resource Stocks. *In* P.T. Liu (ed.), *Dynamic Optimization and Mathematical Economics.* New York: Plenum Press.

Batabyal, A.A. (1995). Leading Issues in Domestic Environmental Regulation: A Review Essay. *Ecological Economics* 12:23–39.

Batabyal, A.A. (1999). Aspects of the Optimal Management of Cyclical Ecological-economic Systems. *Ecological Economics* 30:285–292.

Batabyal, A.A. and Beladi, H. (2001). Aspects of the Theory of Financial Risk Management for Natural Disasters. *Applied Mathematics Letters* 14:875–880.

Batabyal, A.A. and Beladi, H. (2004). Time Restrictions in Natural Resource Management: A Dynamic and Stochastic Analysis. *European Journal of Operational Research* 157:775–783.

Goodloe, S. (1969). Short Duration Grazing in Rhodesia. *Journal of Range Management* 22:369–373.

Graham, K.T., Torell, L.A. and Allison, C.D. (1992). Costs and Benefits of Implementing Holistic Resource Management on New Mexico Ranches. New Mexico Agricultural Experiment Station Bulletin 672.

Hall, L.M., George, M.R., McCreary, D.D. and Adams, T.E. (1992). Effects of Cattle Grazing on Blue Oak Seedling Damage and Survival. *Journal of Range Management* 45:503–506.

Hart, R.H., Samuel, M.J., Test, P.S. and Smith, M.A. (1988). Cattle Vegetation and Economic Responses to Grazing Systems and Grazing Pressure. *Journal of Range Management* 41:282–286.

Hart, R.H., Clapp, S. and Test, P.S. (1993). Grazing Strategies, Stocking Rates and Frequency Intensity of Grazing on Western Wheatgrass and Blue Grama. *Journal of Range Management* 46:122–127.

Holechek, J.L., Pieper, R.D. and Herbel, C.H. (1998). *Range Management*, 3rd edn. Upper Saddle River, New Jersey: Prentice Hall.

Holechek, J.L., Thomas, M., Molinar, F. and Galt, D. (1999). Stocking Desert Rangelands: What We've Learned. *Rangelands* 21:8–12.

Mangel, M. (1985). *Decision and Control in Uncertain Resource Systems.* Orlando, Florida: Academic Press.

McCreary, D.D. and Tecklin, J. (1993). Tree Shells Accelerate Valley Oak Restoration on Grazed Rangelands (California). *Restoration and Management Notes* 11:152.

Pielou, E.C. (1977). *Mathematical Ecology*. New York: Wiley.

Roberts, M. and Spence, M. (1976). Effluent Charges and Licenses under Uncertainty. *Journal of Public Economics* 5:193–208.

Ross, S.M. (1996). *Stochastic Processes*, 2nd edn. New York: Wiley.

Ross, S.M. (1997). *Introduction to Probability Models*, 6th edn. San Diego, California: Academic Press.

Savory, A. (1983). The Savory Grazing Method or Holistic Resource Management. *Rangelands* 5:155–159.

Savory, A. (1988). *Holistic Resource Management*. Washington, District of Columbia: Island Press.

Savory, A. and Parsons, S.D. (1980). The Savory Grazing Method. *Rangelands* 2:234–237.

Savory, A. and Butterfield, J. (1999). *Holistic Management*, 2nd edn. Washington, District of Columbia: Island Press.

Stoddart, L.A., Smith, A.D. and Box, T.W. (1975). *Range Management*, 3rd edn. New York: McGraw Hill.

Taylor, H.M. and Karlin, S. (1998). *An Introduction to Stochastic Modeling*, 3rd edn. San Diego, California: Academic Press.

Uhler, R.S. and Bradley, P.G. (1970). A Stochastic Model for Determining the Economic Prospects of Petroleum Exploration over Large Regions. *Journal of the American Statistical Association* 65:623–630.

Weitzman, M.L. (1978). Optimal Rewards for Economic Regulation. *American Economic Review* 68:683–691.

Chapter 4

ALTERNATE DECISION RULES, THE FLEXIBILITY PREMIUM, AND LAND DEVELOPMENT OVER TIME AND UNDER UNCERTAINTY[1]

The Arrow–Fisher–Henry (AFH) analysis of land development under uncertainty has been conducted in a two-period model. Recently, Capozza and Helsley (1990), Batabyal (1996; 1997; 2000), and others have analyzed the question of land development under uncertainty in a multi-period setting. We extend this literature by examining the role that time independent and time dependent decision rules play in the decision to develop land over time and under uncertainty. We first construct a dynamic and stochastic model of decision making in the context of land development. Next, we use this model to analyze the expected profit of a landowner when this landowner uses, respectively, time independent and time dependent decision rules. Finally, we compare and contrast the properties of time independent and time dependent decision rules and we discuss the magnitude of the premium stemming from the maintenance of temporal flexibility in decision making.

1. Introduction

Natural resource and environmental economists have been interested in the question of (possibly irreversible) land development

1. We thank two anonymous referees and George Christakos for their helpful comments on a previous version of this chapter. As well, we thank the Gosnell endowment at RIT for financial support. The usual disclaimer applies.

under uncertainty at least since Weisbrod (1964). Since then, Arrow and Fisher (1974) and Henry (1974a; 1974b) have shed considerable light on this development question. Specifically, these researchers have identified a notion known as option value. The so-called Arrow–Fisher–Henry (AFH) notion of option value — sometimes called quasi-option value (QOV) — tells us that when development is both indivisible and irreversible, a landowner who disregards the possibility of procuring new information about the effects of such development will invariably underestimate the benefits of preservation and hence skew the binary choice develop/ preserve decision in favor of development.

Does this AFH result hold when the development decision is *divisible*?[2] Epstein (1980), Hanemann (1989), and Batabyal (1999) have analyzed various facets of this question and these researchers have shown that when the development decision is divisible, the AFH result will not hold in general. One can also inquire about the nature of the development decision when this decision is made in a *multi-period* setting. Because the AFH analysis is conducted in a two-period model, the apposite development question is "Do I develop today or tomorrow?" In contrast, in a multi-period setting, the apposite question is "When do I develop?" This follows from the fact that a landowner's decision problem now is not over two periods but over $n > 2$ periods.

Markusen and Scheffman (1978), Arnott and Lewis (1979), and Capozza and Helsley (1989) have all studied this question in a deterministic setting. However, when the apposite development decision is irreversible, the use of a certainty framework will bias results about when land ought to be developed. In fact, as we have learned from the investment under uncertainty literature,[3] uncertainty will

---

2. By divisible we mean that it is possible to develop some fraction of a landowner's land and not necessarily the entire landholding. Put differently, the development decision is not an "all or nothing" type of decision.

3. For additional details on this literature, see McDonald and Siegel (1986), Pindyck (1991), Dixit and Pindyck (1994), and Hubbard (1994).

generally impart an option value to undeveloped land and delay the development of land from, say, agricultural to urban use. Therefore, if we are to comprehend when land ought to be developed in the presence of irreversibilities, then it is important to explicitly account for the presence of uncertainty.

Recently, Titman (1985), Capozza and Helsley (1990), and Batabyal (1996; 1997; 2000) have studied the question of land development under uncertainty. Assume that the value of vacant land in the first period exceeds the wealth of a landowner who wishes to construct a building. In this setting, Titman (1985) has shown that a wealth maximizing landowner is better off leaving his land vacant. However, the bulk of Titman's (1985) analysis is carried out in a two-period model. Consequently, this paper does not really address the multi-period nature of the land development problem. In the context of a "first hitting time" problem,[4] Capozza and Helsley (1990) show that land ought to be converted from rural to urban use at the first instance in which the land rent surpasses the reservation rent. In contrast with this "first hitting time" approach, Batabyal (1996; 1997) has used the theory of Markov decision processes to provide, respectively, a discrete time and a continuous time analysis of the "When do I develop land" question. In both these papers, a specific stopping rule is employed to ascertain when a stochastic "revenue from development" process ought to be terminated. Batabyal (2000) has analyzed a model in which the possibility that a landowner may never develop his land is accounted for. In this setting, Batabyal (2000) characterizes an optimal decision rule for the landowner and points out that the use of this decision rule involves a probabilistic comparison of the revenue obtainable from accepting a particular offer, i.e., developing now, with the revenue to be obtained by preserving now and developing later. It turns out that when this decision rule is used, the landowner's optimal course

---

4. For additional details on this, see Dixit and Pindyck (1994, pp. 83–84) and Ross (1996, pp. 363–366).

of action involves waiting a while and then developing land upon receipt of the first so-called "candidate" offer.

While these papers have certainly advanced our understanding of some aspects of the land development question over time and under uncertainty, it is still true that the extant literature has *not* analyzed the effects that alternate decision rules have on the decision to develop land and on a landowner's expected profit from development. Consequently, our chapter has three objectives. First, we construct a dynamic and stochastic model of decision making in the context of land development. Next, we use our model to shed light on a question that, to the best of our knowledge, has not been analyzed previously in the literature. This question concerns the expected profit of a landowner when this individual is able to choose between *time independent* and *time dependent* decision rules. Finally, we compare and contrast the attributes of time independent and time dependent decision rules and then we discuss the magnitude of the flexibility premium stemming from the maintenance of temporal adaptability in decision making.

To see why the distinction between time independent and time dependent decision rules is salient, note that time independent decision rules are inflexible. In contrast, time dependent decision rules are flexible. As such, intuitively one expects to observe a flexibility premium associated with the use of a time dependent decision rule. Specifically, as far as the sign of this flexibility premium is concerned, we expect it to be positive. This reflects the fact that there is an advantage to our landowner from the use of a time dependent decision rule. Further, as far as the magnitude of this flexibility premium is concerned, we expect the use of a "more complicated" time dependent decision rule to lead to a larger (and positive) flexibility premium. For instance, *ceteris paribus*, the size of the flexibility premium can be expected to be larger with a non-linear time dependent decision rule than with a linear time dependent decision rule. Indeed, one of our objectives is to explore the sign and the magnitude of this flexibility premium. This is done in Section 4 of the chapter.

The rest of this chapter is organized as follows. Section 2 presents the theoretical framework. Section 3 uses this framework and provides a detailed analysis of the effects of time independent and time dependent decision rules on the expected profit of a landowner contemplating land development. Section 4 talks about the attributes of time independent and time dependent decision rules and then comments on the sign and the magnitude of the premium arising from the maintenance of temporal flexibility in decision making. Section 5 concludes and offers suggestions for future research.

2. The Theoretical Framework

In order to keep things from getting unduly convoluted, in the rest of this chapter we shall choose units so that the numerical values of all the relevant variables and the distribution functions are drawn from the interval $(0, 1]$. Now, consider a landowner who owns a plot of vacant land and who has a one-to-one and strictly monotonic profit function that is defined over offers to develop land. For concreteness, we suppose that our landowner would like to develop his land by time $T = 1$.[5] Therefore, if the landowner fails to develop his land by time $T = 1$, then his profit is zero.

Our landowner receives offers to develop his land over time. These offers $O_1, O_2, O_3, \ldots$ are received in accordance with a Poisson process[6] with a fixed rate $\lambda = 1$. The offers themselves are independent random variables that are uniformly distributed on the interval $(0, 1]$. The receipt of an offer generates a certain level

---

5. Given our earlier assumption about the choice of units and the interval $(0, 1]$, the specific value $T = 1$ makes our subsequent computations tractable. However, the reader should note that by an appropriate choice of units and interval, an analysis of the sort conducted in this chapter can be carried out for any finite value of T. Also, note that by employing this constraint, we are ensuring that our landowner will develop his land. The relevant question is: "When?" Finally, this constraint excludes the possibility that our landowner may never wish to develop his land. However, this last possibility has already been analyzed in Batabyal (2000).

6. For comprehensible discussions of the Poisson process, see Ross (1996, pp. 59–97) and Taylor and Karlin (1998, pp. 267–331).

of profit by means of the landowner's profit function. It is on the basis of this profit that our landowner decides whether to accept or to reject a particular offer to develop land. Now, because our landowner's one-to-one and strictly monotonic profit function maps offers to develop land to profit and because these offers are uniformly distributed on $(0, 1]$, the profit levels $\Pi_1, \Pi_2, \Pi_3, \ldots$ themselves are also uniformly distributed random variables on the interval $(0, 1]$.

Following AFH, we suppose that the decision to develop land is irreversible. Consequently, there is an asymmetry associated with the binary choice accept/reject decision. If our landowner rejects a particular offer then he can always accept a later offer as long as he accepts this offer by time $T = 1$. In contrast, if our landowner accepts a particular offer (he develops his land), then the stochastic offer receipt process terminates. Put differently, a decision to reject an offer preserves future options but a decision to accept an offer does not.[7] The reader should note that this asymmetry and the desire to develop land by time $T = 1$ constraint together will play a fundamental role in our subsequent analysis.

In order to accomplish his objective of developing his land by time $T = 1$, our landowner will need to use a decision rule. In this chapter we shall consider two types of decision rules. The first decision rule is the time independent one and this rule is of the following type. Our landowner decides on some threshold level of profit $\hat{\Pi}$ that is *free* of time. With this decision rule, our landowner will accept the first offer whose profit exceeds $\hat{\Pi}$. For example, using this time independent decision rule, if our landowner accepts the fourth offer, then it must be true that $\Pi_1 \leq \hat{\Pi}, \Pi_2 \leq \hat{\Pi}, \Pi_3 \leq \hat{\Pi}$, and

---

7. A question that arises now relates to the fate of rejected offers. Specifically, should it be possible to recall a previously rejected offer? Batabyal (1996) has already analyzed the effects of recall on the decision to accept or to reject an offer to develop land. He has shown that theoretical circumstances exist in which the ability to recall a previously rejected offer has no impact on the landowner's ultimate decision. Given this finding, in the rest of this chapter, we disallow the possibility of recalling a previously rejected offer.

$\Pi_4 > \hat{\Pi}$. The second decision rule is the time dependent decision rule and in this case the threshold level of profit is a function of time t. In other words, instead of working with a fixed $\hat{\Pi}$, our landowner will now work with a *time dependent* threshold $\hat{\Pi}(t)$, where $\hat{\Pi}(t) = (1 - t)/(3 - t)$.

Before closing this section we should point out that time dependent decision rules can be of various levels of intricacy. Most of the more intricate decision rules do not permit the researcher to obtain closed-form solutions. As such, in this chapter we have chosen to work with a relatively simple (but non-linear) decision rule because it allows us to obtain closed-form solutions and because, consistent with our objectives, the use of this rule enables us to compare the effects of time independent and time dependent decision rules in a straightforward manner. We now proceed to our analysis of the time independent decision rule.

3. Alternate Decision Rules and their Effects

3.1. *The time independent decision rule*

Our objective in this section is to compute the expected profit of our landowner when he uses a time independent decision rule with profit threshold $\hat{\Pi}$. To this end, let us first calculate the probability of developing land by time $T = 1$ when this decision rule is used. Because the profit stochastic process deriving from the stochastic offer receipt process is a Poisson process with rate $\lambda = 1$, we can tell that the probability we seek is

$$\text{Prob}\{\text{land developed by } T = 1\} = 1 - \exp\{-(1 - \hat{\Pi})\}. \quad (1)$$

Our next task is to ascertain the expected profit of the offer that results in our landowner agreeing to develop his land by time $T = 1$. Now recall that these profit levels are uniformly distributed on the interval $(0, 1]$. Hence, given that our landowner develops his land by time $T = 1$, the expected profit of the offer that results in land development is $(1 + \hat{\Pi})/2$. We can now determine our landowner's expected profit $E\Pi_{TI}$ from the development of land with a time independent decision rule. This is given by multiplying $(1 + \hat{\Pi})/2$ by the probability on the right hand side (RHS) of Equation (1). We get

$$E\Pi_{TI} = \left[\frac{1 + \hat{\Pi}}{2}\right][1 - \exp\{-(1 - \hat{\Pi})\}]. \qquad (2)$$

Equation (2) tells us that when a time independent decision rule is used, the expected profit from land development is the product of two terms in square brackets. Both these terms in the square brackets contain the profit threshold $\hat{\Pi}$. Note that Equation (2) is also our landowner's objective function. Consequently, with this information in mind, we can now ask the following question: What value of the profit threshold $\hat{\Pi}$ should our landowner pick in order to maximize his expected profit from the development of land? This question can be answered by letting our landowner solve

$$\max_{\hat{\Pi}} \left[\left[\frac{1 + \hat{\Pi}}{2}\right][1 - \exp\{-(1 - \hat{\Pi})\}]\right]. \qquad (3)$$

This is a straightforward but laborious maximization problem. With some simplification, this maximization problem can be restated as $\max_{\hat{\Pi}}[1/2 - (1/2)\exp\{-(1 - \hat{\Pi})\} + \hat{\Pi}/2 - (\hat{\Pi}/2)\exp\{-(1 - \hat{\Pi})\}]$. The first-order necessary condition to this expected profit maximization problem is $\exp\{-(1 - \hat{\Pi})\} + (\hat{\Pi}/2)\exp\{-(1 - \hat{\Pi})\} - 1/2 = 0$. It is possible to rewrite this first-order necessary condition. This gives us $\log_e(2 + \hat{\Pi}) - (1 - \hat{\Pi}) = 0$. Finally, this last equation can be expressed as

$$\hat{\Pi} + \log_e(2 + \hat{\Pi}) = 1. \qquad (4)$$

Because $\hat{\Pi} \in (0, 1]$, it is easy to verify that the solution to Equation (4) is given by $\hat{\Pi}^* = 0.2079$. This means that if our landowner sets the value of the profit threshold $\hat{\Pi}^* = 0.2079$, then he will have maximized his expected profit from the development of his plot of land.

What is the maximized value of our landowner's expected profit? This question can be answered by substituting $\hat{\Pi}^* = 0.2079$ into Equation (2). This tells us that our landowner's maximized expected profit from land development is

$$E\Pi^*_{TI} = \left[\frac{1 + \hat{\Pi}^*}{2}\right][1 - \exp\{-(1 - \hat{\Pi}^*)\}] = 0.330425. \quad (5)$$

Equation (5) tells us that the expected profit to our landowner when he uses the optimal time independent decision rule is 0.330425. In other words, this is the highest level of expected profit that our landowner can hope to attain with a time independent decision rule. This state of affairs naturally leads to the following query. Can our landowner do better by using a time dependent decision rule? We now proceed to answer this question.

3.2. *The time dependent decision rule*

Our goal now is to compute the landowner's expected profit from land development when he uses a time dependent decision rule of the form $\hat{\Pi}(t) = (1-t)/(3-t)$. Continuing in the same manner as in the previous section, let us first determine the likelihood of developing the plot of land by time $T = 1$ when the above time dependent decision rule is used. Because the decision rule now is time dependent, the likelihood that we are interested in can be determined by calculating the probability of developing land in a small time interval $[t, t + dt]$. Using the properties of the Poisson process (see Ross (1996, pp. 59–97) and Taylor and Karlin (1998, pp. 267–331)), we get

$$\text{Prob\{developing land within } [t, t + dt]\}$$

$$= \exp\left\{-\int_0^t (1 - \hat{\Pi}(s))\,ds\right\}\{1 - \hat{\Pi}(t)\}dt. \quad (6)$$

Comparing Equations (1) and (6), we see that the time dependence of the decision rule complicates the computation of the likelihood of land development. We now need to calculate the expected profit of the offer that results in our landowner developing his land by time $T = 1$. Once again continuing as in the previous section, we obtain a similar expression for this expected profit. Consequently, we can now ascertain our landowner's expected profit $E\Pi_{TD}$ from the development of land with a time dependent decision rule. This is given by multiplying $(1 + \hat{\Pi}(t))/2$ by the probability on the RHS of Equation (6) and then integrating the resulting expression between 0 and 1. Mathematically, we have

$$E\Pi_{TD} = \int_0^1 \left[\frac{1 + \hat{\Pi}(t)}{2} \right]$$

$$\times \exp\left\{ -\int_0^t (1 - \hat{\Pi}(s))ds \right\} \{1 - \hat{\Pi}(t)\}dt. \qquad (7)$$

Equation (7) tells us that when a time dependent decision rule is used, the expected profit from land development is the product of two terms. As in the previous section, both these terms contain the profit threshold $\hat{\Pi}(\cdot)$. Also, observe that Equation (7) is our landowner's objective function. However, because of the time dependent nature of our landowner's decision rule, we cannot now calculate an optimal $\hat{\Pi}^*$ as we did in the previous section.

Even so, we can still ask: What is the maximized value of our landowner's expected profit when he uses a time dependent decision rule? To answer this question, we will need to complete the integrations in Equation (7). Let us first complete the integration in the expression for the probability of developing land in the interval $[t, t + dt]$, i.e., in the second term on the RHS of Equation (7). Integrating, we get

$$\exp\left\{ -\int_0^t (1 - \hat{\Pi}(s))ds \right\} \{1 - \hat{\Pi}(t)\}dt$$

$$= \frac{1}{9} \left(\frac{2}{3 - t} \right) \exp\{2\log_e(3 - t)\}dt. \qquad (8)$$

Using Equation (8), we can substantially simplify the objective function delineated by Equation (7). This simplification yields

$$E\Pi_{TD} = \frac{2}{9} \int_0^1 (2 - t)dt. \tag{9}$$

Now completing the integration in Equation (9), we get

$$E\Pi^*_{TD} = \frac{2}{9} \int_0^1 (2 - t)dt = 0.333333. \tag{10}$$

Equation (10) tells us that the expected profit of our landowner when he uses a time dependent decision rule is 0.333333. Put differently, this is the highest level of expected profit that our landowner can hope to attain with the time dependent decision rule $\hat{\Pi}(t) = (1 - t)/(3 - t)$. We now compare and contrast the attributes of time independent and time dependent decision rules and then we discuss the magnitude of the premium arising from the maintenance of temporal flexibility in decision making.

4. Time Independent Versus Time Dependent Decision Rules

In principle, for reasons given in Section 1, we expect time independent and time dependent decision rules to yield very different payoffs to our landowner. Our analysis thus far allows us to shed light on this and related issues. Specifically, we can use Table 1 to

Table 1. A comparison of time independent and time dependent decision rules.

Criterion of interest	Time independent decision rule	Time dependent decision rule
Optimal value of profit threshold	$\hat{\Pi}^* = 0.2079$	$\hat{\Pi}(t) = \frac{1-t}{3-t}$
Maximal expected profit from land development	$E\Pi^*_{TI} = 0.330425$	$E\Pi^*_{TD} = 0.333333$
Magnitude of the flexibility premium	$E\Pi^*_{TD} - E\Pi^*_{TI} = 0.002908 > 0$	

compare and contrast the attributes of these two distinct decision rules. Reading horizontally, the second row of Table 1 reveals the basic difference in the two rules. In the time independent case, the optimal value of the profit threshold $\hat{\Pi}$ is fixed at 0.2079 and this value does *not* change with the passage of time. In contrast, when our landowner's decision rule is time dependent, the profit threshold is *continually* a function of time and hence its optimal value will generally change with the passage of time.

The third row of Table 1 gives us exact values of the expected profit from land development when these two decision rules are used by our landowner. Relative to a time independent decision rule, a time dependent decision rule allows a landowner to be flexible in the face of changing circumstances. As indicated in the second last paragraph of Section 1, new information about the consequences of land development or preservation cannot be incorporated into the time independent decision rule. In contrast, time dependent decision rules permit our landowner to alter the value of the profit threshold with the passage of time.

The second aspect of flexibility pertains to the constraint describing our landowner's desire to develop his land by a certain time. To see this clearly, consider the following example: We have chosen units so that the time by which our landowner would like to develop his land is $T = 1$. For the purpose of this example, let us measure time in years and let us suppose that the age constraint is $T = 65$ years. Then, it is reasonable to say that the optimal value of $\hat{\Pi}$ for our landowner when he is 30 years old will most likely be different from the optimal value of $\hat{\Pi}$ when this landowner is 63 years old. Now, in contrast with a time independent decision rule, the use of a time dependent decision rule allows our landowner to alter the value of $\hat{\Pi}$ over time and hence, in general, this decision rule is more flexible and therefore more desirable. The third row of Table 1 shows that this reasoning is correct because $E\Pi^*_{TD} = 0.333333 > 0.330425 = E\Pi^*_{TI}$.

How much more desirable is the time dependent decision rule? The simple answer is: Not much more. As shown in the fourth row of Table 1, the premium associated with the maintenance of temporal flexibility in decision making is positive but only 0.002908. Consequently, relative to a time dependent decision rule, our landowner does almost as well by using a time independent decision rule. This finding is most likely due to the fact that we have worked with a relatively straightforward time dependent decision rule in this chapter. As we change the form of the time dependent decision rule, the magnitude of the associated flexibility premium will typically change. Further, the use of more intricate time dependent decision rules will, most likely, increase the magnitude of this flexibility premium. Having said this, the reader should note that as indicated in the last paragraph of Section 2, these more intricate time dependent decision rules frequently do not admit closed-form solutions.

5. Conclusions

In this chapter, we provided a theoretical analysis of alternate forms of decision making in the context of land development over time and under uncertainty. To the best of our knowledge, ours is the *first* chapter to provide a comparative analysis of the attributes of time independent and time dependent decision rules in a land development setting. After pointing out the basic difference between time independent and time dependent decision rules, our analysis showed that time dependent decision rules are generally more desirable than time independent decision rules because the expected profit from the development of land when a time dependent decision rule is used exceeds the expected profit from land development with a time independent decision rule. In other words, there is a positive flexibility premium associated with the use of a time dependent decision rule.

The analysis of this chapter can be extended in a number of directions. In what follows, we suggest two possible extensions. First, in a setting similar to that of this chapter, one could analyze the land development decision when this decision is divisible. Miller and Lad

(1984) and Batabyal (1999) have made a start in this direction but there are many facets of this divisibility issue — such as the impact of learning on the "What fraction of my land do I develop" question — that remain inadequately addressed in the literature.

Second, the time dependent decision rule that we have studied in this chapter involves altering the *value* of the profit threshold. However, the *form* of the decision rule itself does not change. Consequently, it would be useful to compare and contrast the attributes of the time dependent decision rule of this chapter with a different decision rule that involves the temporal modification of the form of the decision rule. An examination of these aspects of the problem will allow richer analyses of the connections between alternate rules and the decision to develop land over time and under uncertainty.

References

Arnott, R.J. and Lewis, F.D. (1979). The Transition of Land to Urban Use. *Journal of Political Economy* 87:161–169.

Arrow, K.J. and Fisher, A.C. (1974). Environmental Preservation, Uncertainty, and Irreversibility. *Quarterly Journal of Economics* 88:312–319.

Batabyal, A.A. (1996). The Timing of Land Development: An Invariance Result. *American Journal of Agricultural Economics* 78:1092–1097.

Batabyal, A.A. (1997). The Impact of Information on Land Development: A Dynamic and Stochastic Analysis. *Journal of Environmental Management* 50:187–192.

Batabyal, A.A. (1999). On Some Aspects of Land Development when the Decision to Develop is Divisible. *Resources Policy* 25:173–177.

Batabyal, A.A. (2000). An Optimal Stopping Approach to Land Development under Uncertainty. *Annals of Regional Science* 34:147–156.

Capozza, D.R. and Helsley, R.W. (1989). The Fundamentals of Land Prices and Urban Growth. *Journal of Urban Economics* 26:295–306.

Capozza, D.R. and Helsley, R.W. (1990). The Stochastic City. *Journal of Urban Economics* 28:187–203.

Dixit, A.K. and Pindyck, R.S. (1994). *Investment Under Uncertainty*. Princeton, New Jersey: Princeton University Press.

Epstein, L.G. (1980). Decision Making and the Temporal Resolution of Uncertainty. *International Economic Review* 21:269–283.

Hanemann, W.M. (1989). Information and the Concept of Option Value. *Journal of Environmental Economics and Management* 16:23–37.

Henry, C. (1974a). Option Values in the Economics of Irreplaceable Assets. *Review of Economic Studies* 41:89–104.

Henry, C. (1974b). Investment Decisions under Uncertainty: The Irreversibility Effect. *American Economic Review* 64:1006–1012.

Hubbard, R.G. (1994). Investment under Uncertainty: Keeping One's Options Open. *Journal of Economic Literature* 32:1816–1831.

Markusen, J.R. and Scheffman, D.T. (1978). The Timing of Residential Land Development: A General Equilibrium Approach. *Journal of Urban Economics* 5:411–424.

McDonald, R. and Siegel, D. (1986). The Value of Waiting to Invest. *Quarterly Journal of Economics* 101:707–727.

Miller, J.R. and Lad, F. (1984). Flexibility, Learning, and Irreversibility in Environmental Decisions: A Bayesian Approach. *Journal of Environmental Economics and Management* 11:161–172.

Pindyck, R.S. (1991). Irreversibility, Uncertainty, and Investment. *Journal of Economic Literature* 29:1110–1152.

Ross, S.M. (1996). *Stochastic Processes*, 2nd edn. New York: Wiley.

Taylor, H.M. and Karlin, S. (1998). *An Introduction to Stochastic Modeling*, 3rd edn. San Diego, California: Academic Press.

Titman, S. (1985). Urban Land Prices under Uncertainty. *American Economic Review* 75:505–514.

Weisbrod, B.A. (1964). Collective-Consumption Services of Individualized Consumption Goods. *Quarterly Journal of Economics* 78:471–477.

Chapter 5

ALTERNATE STRATEGIES FOR MANAGING RESISTANCE TO ANTIBIOTICS AND PESTICIDES[1]

with P. Nijkamp

How should one manage the problem of resistance to antibiotics and pesticides? The formal modeling of this question is very much in its infancy. Therefore, we construct a dynamic and stochastic model of antibiotic or pesticide use to investigate the relative merits of two kinds of treatment options for overseeing the problem of resistance. In particular, we identify a likelihood function and then, *inter alia*, we show that this function has an important bearing on how we might best address the problem of resistance.

1. Introduction

Our era is sometimes called the "life sciences era." As the medical and the biological sciences have advanced, so has the ability of humans to successfully control a variety of deleterious organisms. Indeed, with the passage of time, humans have used a variety of antibiotics and pesticides to cure humans, animals, and plants of a whole host of previously lethal diseases. A good example of an antibiotic that has been widely used to cure all manner of infections including staphylococci causing infections is penicillin. Similarly, the

1. We thank Eiji Hosoda, two anonymous reviewers, and session participants at the 2004 North American Regional Science Council (NARSC) conference in Seattle and the 2005 Eastern Economic Association (EEA) conference in New York City for their helpful comments on a previous version of this chapter. In addition, Batabyal thanks the Gosnell endowment at RIT for financial support. The usual disclaimer applies.

so-called *Bt* plant pesticides are prominent examples of pesticides that have been engineered to express the *Bacillus thuringiensis (Bt)* δ endotoxins that effectively attack and kill a prominent pest, namely, the European corn borer (Secchi and Babcock, 2003).

Although humans have enjoyed remarkable success in mitigating the detrimental effects of bacteria and agricultural pests, it is now becoming increasingly clear that this success has not come without a cost. Consider the case of antibiotics. As noted by Garrett (1994), Elbasha (2003), and Howard (2004), the fundamental problem is this: When antibiotics eliminate drug susceptible bacterial strains, they create a fertile setting for drug resistant strains to prosper. As a result, the effectiveness of antibiotics is reduced by repeated use and the rate of this reduction is often rapid. This is the problem of *resistance* to the use of antibiotics and a similar problem arises with the repeated use of pesticides.

In a fairly comprehensive study, the Institute of Medicine (1992) noted that multiple drug resistance induced by the use of antibiotics can lead to treatment costs of $150,000 per patient. The reader should note that this figure is an order of magnitude *higher* than the costs of traditional treatment. Similarly, in the German context, Fleischer and Waibel (2003) have documented a case in which the cost of maize herbicide use *increased* from less than DM 40 million in 1987 to about DM 111.7 million in 1993. Only a few years after the introduction of the first antibiotic, penicillin, in the late 1940s, penicillin resistant infections caused by the bacterium *Staphylococcus aureus* (*S. aureus*) began to emerge. As Bren (2002) has noted, these so-called "staph" infections are varied and they can range from urinary tract infections to bacterial pneumonia. Methicillin, one of the most potent antibiotics available to treat "staph" infections is now no longer effective against some strains of *S. aureus*. In fact, very recently, it has been reported that some strains of *S. aureus* are now resistant to the antibiotic Vancomycin. This means that even Vancomycin — one of the most lethal antibiotics around — may be in danger of losing its effectiveness against some kinds of "staph" infections.

Because of this unfortunate state of affairs, for well over a decade now, concern about the effects of increasing resistance to antibiotics has been growing. The fact that there are now so many concrete instances of resistance to antibiotics has led several writers — see Amabile-Cuevas (1997), Buhner (1999), and McKenna (2003) — to focus explicitly on *alternate* treatment options to antibiotics. The discussion in this and the previous paragraph leads to two noteworthy findings. First, the economic cost of resistance to antibiotics and pesticides is non-negligible and is in fact likely to be substantial. Second, for quite some time now, there has been increasing concern in the world about the *cost of antibiotic treatment* relative to the *cost of treatment by alternate means*. A theoretical discussion of this second finding will form the centerpiece of our subsequent analysis in this chapter.

Given the salience of antibiotic and pesticide resistance, one can ask what researchers have contributed to increasing our understanding of this problem. In this regard, two observations are pertinent. First, although there does exist a medical and biological sciences literature on this subject, as Rowthorn and Brown (2003, p. 43) have noted, "epidemiologists and biologists in the research community have not responded by building optimization models." Second, despite the fact that there is a clear economic dimension to the problem of antibiotic and pesticide resistance, optimal "human drug use has been addressed within an economic context by only a handful of economists" (Wilen and Msangi, 2003, p. 19).

Some of the most noteworthy contributions by economists on the subject of resistance are contained in the recent edited book by Laxminarayan (2003).[2] Many of the chapters in this book

---

2. Hueth and Regev (1974), Brown and Layton (1996), and Laxminarayan and Brown (2001) are three important papers on the subject of resistance that appeared before Laxminarayan (2003). These three papers and the relevant medical and biological sciences literature on resistance are discussed by the authors of the individual chapters in Laxminarayan (2003). Therefore, readers interested in a more detailed review of the literature than we provide in this chapter should consult these references.

construct and analyze theoretical models of antibiotic and pesticide use and management. Using dynamic analysis, Rowthorn and Brown (2003) point out that a social planner ought to begin antibiotic use by exclusively using the antibiotic that is effective against the bacterial strain that is the most prevalent. However, if this antibiotic is also the more expensive one, then the above strategy may or may not continue to be an optimal strategy. Laxminarayan and Weitzman (2003) use a static framework and show that although treatment homogeneity is valued in the medical profession, when the possibility of resistance is acknowledged, there are circumstances in which it makes more sense to treat an infectious disease with a combination of antibiotics. Morel *et al.* (2003) study the regulation of *Bt* corn in the presence of pesticide resistance. Their probabilistic analysis tells us that a transgenic crop ought to be released into the environment only if the irreversible costs are lower than the sum of the irreversible benefits and the present value of an infinite stream of instantaneous additional net benefits.

Given the documented concern about the costs of treatment with antibiotics relative to the costs of treatment with alternate options, the general purpose of this chapter is to conduct a comparative *theoretical* analysis, in a stochastic setting, of the conditions under which treatment with alternate means — involving no use of antibiotics — is more desirable than treatment with antibiotics. Specifically, because there are virtually *no* stochastic analyses of this question, we wish to show how stochastic modeling can shed valuable light on this antibiotic use versus no antibiotic use question. We stress that our objective in this chapter is *not* to conduct either an empirical or a simulation analysis of the above question. Further, in our subsequent discussion, we shall identify and discuss salient cost terms, a parameter, and a likelihood function that *are* location specific. Even so, the reader should understand that the purpose of such identification is to point to those aspects of the problem that, while being location specific as far as *magnitudes* are concerned, are germane in general. Concretely, what this means is that our analysis will *not* be concerned with empirical details about things such as the social infrastructure or the geographic environment of a particular locality. In addition, our use of the phrase "as far as magnitudes are concerned" above, is intended to point out that the actual sizes of the cost terms and the pertinent parameter will typically vary from location to location.

Now it turns out that very recently, Wilen and Msangi (2003) have addressed aspects of this antibiotics versus no antibiotics use question, albeit in a non-stochastic or *deterministic* setting. These researchers use an optimal control framework to compare and contrast the properties of what they call "interventionist" and "ecological" strategies. The interventionist strategy always uses an antibiotic to treat an ailment and the ecological strategy is a no treatment strategy.[3] Which strategy ought a health care provider to use to cure an ailment? Wilen and Msangi (2003) show that the answer to this question depends on the magnitude of the treatment *cost* parameter. When this magnitude is low, the interventionist strategy leads to lower total treatment and damage costs. In contrast, when this magnitude is high, the ecological strategy results in lower aggregate treatment and damage costs.

In the "real world," a health care provider typically makes decisions about the antibiotic versus no antibiotic use question in an environment of *uncertainty*. Particularly, when a non-antibiotic course of treatment is used, this provider will typically not know — or know only imperfectly — what the likelihood of success is.[4]

---

3. As Wilen and Msangi (2003, p. 19) explain, the ecological policy is non-interventionist in the sense that when this strategy is used, a disease is allowed "to progress in a manner dictated by the natural interaction among bacteria exhibiting interspecific and intraspecific competition."

4. In the rest of this chapter, to illustrate our theoretical points, we shall frequently refer to one specific but very common ailment, namely, acute otitis media or AOM. AOM is a middle ear infection that may cause a change in the normal eardrum, which is located at the inner end of the ear canal. Now, to see the points that we have been making in the text of the chapter, note that because of the problem of resistance, it is sometimes suggested that instead of treating AOM with an antibiotic such as amoxicillin, a non-antibiotic option such as homeopathic treatment ought to be considered. However, as Jacobs *et al.* (2001) have clearly pointed out, one of the problems that has prevented the widespread use of homeopathy to treat AOM is the *uncertainty* concerning the likelihood of success when this non-antibiotic option is used.

Therefore, in this chapter, we extend the Wilen and Msangi (2003) analysis by introducing *uncertainty* into the analysis. Specifically, we ask two questions. First, how does the presence of uncertainty affect the answer to the choice question that we posed in the previous paragraph? Second, in a stochastic framework, are costs still salient in distinguishing between the two strategies, or, in addition to costs, is some other aspect of the problem just as important in helping a health care provider choose between antibiotic and non-antibiotic courses of treatment? By answering these two questions, we show how theoretical analysis, and in particular stochastic modeling, can help shed light on the practical issue of choosing between antibiotic and no antibiotic treatment options.

The rest of this chapter is organized as follows: Section 2 describes a dynamic and stochastic model of antibiotic or pesticide use. Section 3 first analyzes interventionist and non-interventionist strategies (to be explained in the next section) for overseeing the problem of resistance. Next, this section identifies a particular likelihood function and it shows that in addition to cost considerations, whether the problem of resistance is best addressed with an interventionist strategy or a non-interventionist strategy depends fundamentally on this likelihood function. Finally, Section 4 concludes and discusses ways in which the research of this chapter might be extended.

2.   The Theoretical Framework

We now begin our analysis by adopting a stochastic modeling approach. The model of this chapter is based on previous research by Antelman and Savage (1965), Ross (1983, Chapter 6), and Batabyal and Yoo (1994). At the outset, the reader should note that from a modeling perspective, the questions of the development of resistance to either an antibiotic or to a pesticide are formally equivalent. Therefore, even though in what follows we shall describe our model in terms of antibiotic use, the model is equally pertinent to the case in which a pesticide is being used.

Consider a specific geographic area in which there exists a population of infected individuals. These individuals seek treatment for their ailment at a health care facility such as a physician's office or a hospital. We assume that it is standard practice in this health care facility to treat relevant ailments with an *interventionist* strategy that involves the use of an antibiotic. This assumption is consistent with standard medical practice in the United States and in large parts of western Europe.[5] To see this clearly, suppose the malady under consideration is AOM. In this case it is common to attempt to cure this ailment by prescribing the antibiotic amoxicillin. In fact, as Laxminarayan and Weitzman (2003) have pointed out, in 1997, nearly 60% of all cases of AOM in the United States were treated with amoxicillin. This example is indicative of our general point that the default treatment of choice in the majority of ailments in the United States and western Europe is an antibiotic and, hence, in what follows, we call this default selection the *interventionist* strategy.

The fundamental stock variable that an antibiotic affects is what we shall call the stock of drug susceptibility. Conceptually, this stock is very much like an exhaustible natural resource stock. Just as repeated extraction draws down the stock of an exhaustible resource such as coal, similarly, repeated use of an antibiotic degrades the stock of drug susceptibility. This phenomenon essentially describes an economic case of declining marginal benefits. It is important to understand that this degradation process is typically stochastic and *not* deterministic. We shall account for this feature by thinking of the stock of drug susceptibility as a stochastic process that can exist in one of many possible states. To this end, let state 0 be the best possible state. In other words, this state corresponds to the highest possible level of the stock of drug susceptibility. Further, to model the probabilistic degradation process, we suppose that the stock

---

5. For a more detailed corroboration of this claim in the case of AOM, see Jacobs *et al.* (2001) and Bosker (2004).

of drug susceptibility changes state in accordance with a Brownian motion process with drift $\beta > 0$.[6]

With repeated use of an antibiotic, our Brownian motion process changes state and eventually it gets to state r. This is the *resistant* state and the idea here is that once this state is reached, the default antibiotic that is currently being used is useless for subsequent treatment. When this happens, our medical facility must use a new interventionist strategy, i.e., a different antibiotic to treat the ailment in question. When this is done, our Brownian motion process is assumed to return to state 0. In other words, the stock of drug susceptibility is, once again, as high as it could possibly be.[7] We shall denote the cost of using this new interventionist strategy by c^r.

Let us now delineate the *non-interventionist* strategy for treatment. The reader should note that we are using the label "non-interventionist" in a general way. Therefore, following Wilen and Msangi (2003), one non-interventionist strategy would be a no treatment strategy. However, in the context of this chapter, homeopathic, herbal, or other natural treatments, in addition to doing nothing, are all non-interventionist strategies. In other words, a non-interventionist strategy is a no antibiotics strategy. Put somewhat differently, a non-interventionist strategy is essentially the "passive" counterpart of an active treatment strategy. It comprises

---

6. Note that unlike the present study, most of the extant literature — see Wilen and Msangi (2003) and Rowthorn and Brown (2003) for examples — has modeled this degradation process as a deterministic process. For more on the Brownian motion process, see Ross (1983, Chapter 6) and Ross (2003, Chapter 10).

7. In the "real world," it is possible that when bacteria are resistant to drug "A" then they will also be partially resistant to drug "B." If this is in fact the case in a specific instance and an interventionist course of action is taken, then, with the passage of time, a substitute for drug "B" will have to be found. Although what we have just mentioned is a possibility, the reader should note that this is certainly not inevitable. To see this, consider, once again, the case of AOM. As Bosker (2004) has pointed out, when treating AOM with an interventionist strategy, the default antibiotic is typically amoxicillin. When resistance to amoxicillin is an issue, the "different antibiotic" that we have just talked about is often chosen from the trinity of azithromycin, cefuroxime, and ceftriaxone.

a rather heterogeneous class of medical options ranging from no antibiotics provision to homeopathic treatments. We shall treat this class as a single class, but without loss of generality, a set of specific non-interventionist strategies may be identified and analytically treated in our subsequent modeling efforts. Clearly, our health care provider may choose to treat the ailment in question with a non-interventionist strategy before the Brownian motion process hits state r. In other words, this provider may choose to eschew use of the antibiotic and treat the ailment in question with a non-interventionist strategy before the resistant state for the default antibiotic that is currently being used is reached.

As long as the resistant state r has not been reached, we suppose that the default antibiotic is successful in treating the relevant ailment with probability one.[8] However, to keep the problem interesting and to be consistent with actual practice where there typically tends to be greater uncertainty about the success of less used non-antibiotic treatment options, we suppose that a success score of one is not the case with the non-interventionist strategy. In particular, if the state of the Brownian motion process is k and the non-interventionist strategy is used, then this strategy will be successful in treating the ailment with probability $p(k)$ and it will be unsuccessful with probability $1 - p(k)$. This likelihood function is explicitly a function of the *state* in which the non-interventionist strategy is used. However, because these alternate states indirectly proxy the biological and the social aspects of the treatment choice question, the likelihood function $p(\cdot)$ itself also indirectly accounts for these biological and social aspects. Note that this likelihood function $p(\cdot)$ will typically vary depending on the ailment being analyzed. Now, if the non-interventionist strategy is successful in treating the ailment then our Brownian motion process returns to state 0. In

---

8. This "success with probability one" supposition may be a little too rigid. One way to account for this issue would be to specify and work with an appropriate probability function — in addition to the one we employ — in the analysis.

contrast, if this strategy is unsuccessful in treating the ailment then the Brownian motion process is assumed to go to state r.[9] The cost of attempting to cure the ailment in question in state k with the non-interventionist strategy is c^k.

In the second paragraph of this section, we noted that our analysis concerns a "specific geographic area." What this means is that the cost terms (c^r, c^k), the drift parameter β, and the likelihood function $p(k)$ are *specific* to this geographic area. Put differently, the cost terms, the drift parameter, and the likelihood function are *local* in nature and we are *not* saying that local conditions do not matter. Further, when the geographic area under consideration is changed, the magnitudes of (c^r, c^k, β) may well change and so may the nature of the likelihood function. The reader should note that our analysis in this chapter is fully compatible with such local variation in the magnitudes of (c^r, c^k, β) and in the likelihood function. Our task now is to determine whether the interventionist strategy or the non-interventionist strategy minimizes the long run expected cost per time.

3. Interventionist Versus Non-interventionist Strategies

3.1. *The long run expected cost per time*

The issue of the cost of medical treatment has been the subject of intensive economic research. In this regard, various alternative methodologies may be distinguished. In this chapter, to compute the pertinent cost function, we shall use renewal theory.[10] Further,

---

9. We realize that the failure of the non-interventionist strategy does not necessarily mean that our Brownian motion process must go to state r. We make this assumption mainly to keep the subsequent mathematics from getting unduly complicated. Indeed, in principle, it is possible to focus on the case in which our Brownian motion process goes to some intermediate state m, where m is worse than k but better than state r.

10. Excellent textbook accounts of renewal theory can be found in Taylor and Karlin (1998, Chapter 7) and in Ross (2003, Chapter 7).

we shall restrict attention to non-interventionist strategies that attempt to treat the ailment when our Brownian motion process is in state k, where $0 < k < r$. Given this restriction, the reader will note that returns by our Brownian motion process to state 0 constitute renewals. Therefore, we can use the well known renewal-reward theorem[11] to compute the long run expected cost that we seek.

Now, if we think of a cycle being completed every time a renewal occurs, then the renewal-reward theorem tells us that the long run expected reward is given by the expected return earned in a cycle divided by the length of this cycle. The reader should note that this last sentence about the long run expected reward is *not* a hypothesis of ours. Instead, it is one way of stating what the renewal-reward theorem tells us. In this chapter, the object of interest is a cost, i.e., a negative reward. This notwithstanding, we stress that the renewal-reward theorem continues to apply.

Adapting the renewal-reward theorem to the problem we are analyzing, we get

$$\text{Long Run Expected Cost} = \frac{E[\text{Cost per Cycle}]}{E[\text{Length of Cycle}]}, \qquad (1)$$

where $E[\cdot]$ is the expectation operator. It is straightforward to compute the numerator on the right hand side (RHS) of Equation (1). Some reflection tells us that the expected cost per cycle equals $c^k + \{1 - p(k)\}c^r$. Therefore, in symbols we have

$$E[\text{Cost per Cycle}] = c^k + \{1 - p(k)\}c^r. \qquad (2)$$

The computation of the expected length of a renewal cycle is more complicated. We proceed as in Batabyal and Yoo (1994). Let

---

11. For more on the renewal-reward theorem, see Ross (1983, p. 78) or Ross (2003, p. 417). This theorem has been used previously in the literature to model all manner of natural resource and environmental phenomena. See Batabyal and Yoo (1994), Batabyal (1999), and Batabyal and Beladi (2002) for more details.

us denote the expected time it takes for our Brownian motion process to reach state k with the function $g(k)$. Now, because a Brownian motion process has independent and stationary increments,[12] for any two states k and l, we can write

$$g(k + l) = g(k) + g(l). \tag{3}$$

Equation (3) and the aforementioned properties of Brownian motion processes together tell us that the function $g(k)$ is linear and specifically that $g(k) = a \cdot k$, where a is a constant. Now, following the procedure described in Batabyal and Yoo (1994), we can tell that the constant $a = 1/\beta$ and hence $g(k) = k/\beta$. This last finding allows us to conclude that

$$E[\text{Length of Cycle}] = \frac{k}{\beta}. \tag{4}$$

Now, using Equations (2) and (4) together, we have

$$\{\text{Long Run Expected Cost}\}_{\text{NI}} = \frac{E[\text{Cost per Cycle}]}{E[\text{Length of Cycle}]}$$

$$= \frac{\beta[c^k + \{1 - p(k)\}c^r]}{k}. \tag{5}$$

According to Equation (5), the long run average cost of treating the ailment under consideration with the *non-interventionist* strategy is given by the ratio of the weighted sum of the two cost terms c^k and c^r to the state k, $0 < k < r$, in which this strategy is utilized.

Our next task is to determine the long run expected cost for the interventionist strategy. For this strategy, it should be clear to the reader that $E[\text{Cost of Cycle}] = c^r$. Similarly, following the logic of the derivation that led to Equation (4), we infer that $E[\text{Length of Cycle}] = r/\beta$. Therefore, putting these two pieces of

---

12. For more on these concepts, the reader should consult Ross (1983, Chapter 6) and Ross (2003, Chapter 10).

information together, we deduce that

$$\{\text{Long Run Expected Cost}\}_\text{I} = \frac{E[\text{Cost per Cycle}]}{E[\text{Length of Cycle}]} = \frac{\beta c^r}{r}. \quad (6)$$

In words, Equation (6) tells us that the long run average cost of treating the ailment under study with the *interventionist* strategy is given by the ratio of the product of the drift parameter of our Brownian motion process β and the cost of using a new interventionist strategy c^r to the resistant state r.

Inspecting Equation (5) it is clear that for a *given* likelihood function $p(k)$, we can always use calculus to minimize this long run expected cost function. This notwithstanding, we now provide two examples to highlight an important point and that point is this. The *choice* between the interventionist strategy and the non-interventionist strategy (see Equations (5) and (6)) depends in large part on the likelihood function $p(k)$.

3.2. The likelihood function and its salience

In our first example the likelihood function is $p(k) = 1 - k/r$. In this case $1 - p(k) = k/r$. Substituting this last expression in Equation (5) and then simplifying, we get

$$\{\text{Long Run Expected Cost}\}_\text{NI}$$

$$= \frac{\beta c^k}{k} + \frac{\beta c^r}{r} > \frac{\beta c^r}{r} = \{\text{Long Run Expected Cost}\}_\text{I}. \quad (7)$$

Equation (7) clearly tells us that when the likelihood function is $p(k) = 1 - k/r$, the optimal course of action for our health care provider is to *always* use the interventionist strategy, i.e., always use an antibiotic. In this case, it makes no sense to use the non-interventionist strategy because this strategy results in higher long run expected costs. If this example were about pesticide use then, in this setting, we would say that a pesticide regulator ought *never* to use organic fertilizer (a non-interventionist strategy). Instead, (s)he ought to continue to use the currently used pesticide.

As a second example, consider the probability function

$$p(k) = \begin{cases} \dfrac{e^{-\theta k} - e^{-\theta r}}{1 - e^{-\theta r}} & \text{if } 0 < k < r \\ 0 & \text{if } k \geq r. \end{cases} \tag{8}$$

In this case, let us first substitute the value of $p(k)$ from Equation (8) into Equation (5). This gives us

$$\{\text{Long Run Expected Cost}\}_{\text{NI}} = \frac{\beta \left[c^k + \dfrac{c^r(1 - e^{-\theta k})}{1 - e^{-\theta r}} \right]}{k}. \tag{9}$$

Now, as in the first example, the health care provider ought to pursue the interventionist strategy if the RHS of Equation (9) is greater than $\beta c^r / r$, the long run expected cost with the interventionist strategy.

Suppose, for the moment, that the non-interventionist strategy is optimal. Then, the optimal course of action for our health care provider can be determined by differentiating the RHS of Equation (9) with respect to k and then simplifying. This tells us that our health care provider ought to use the non-interventionist strategy in state k^* where k^* satisfies

$$\theta k^* e^{-\theta k^*} + e^{-\theta k^*} = \frac{c^r + c^{k^*}(1 - e^{-\theta r})}{c^r}. \tag{10}$$

Wilen and Msangi (2003) showed that in a *deterministic* setting, the choice between the interventionist strategy and the non-interventionist strategy depends on the magnitude of the treatment cost parameter. Our analysis shows that in a *probabilistic* setting, the answer to this choice question depends not only on cost considerations, i.e., on c^k and c^r in Equations (5) and (6), but *also* on the nature of the likelihood function $p(k)$. We now have answers to the two questions we posed in the second last paragraph of Section 1.

Our primary theoretical finding in this chapter is that in a *specific* geographical area or *locality*, when (i) resistance to antibiotics is an issue and (ii) decisions are made in an environment of uncertainty, the question as to whether it makes more sense to use an interventionist or a non-interventionist treatment option depends fundamentally on the costs of the two treatment options and on the provider's *ex ante* uncertainty about the likelihood of success when (s)he uses a non-interventionist strategy. The reader should note that this finding is *not* just of theoretical importance but also of great practical significance. We have already documented (with citations) the practical salience of *costs* in Section 1 and hence we shall not repeat this point here.

We now use the ailment of AOM to stress the practical relevance of the uncertainty aspect of our investigation. Because of resistance to amoxicillin and to some other antibiotics, health care providers have pondered the usefulness of non-interventionist strategies such as homeopathy to cure AOM. Now, our theoretical analysis tells us that a key determinant of the usefulness of homeopathy ought to be the probability function $p(\cdot)$ describing the likelihood of success when this homeopathic option is used to cure AOM. Is there any real evidence to support this contention? The answer is yes. For instance, in a private pediatric practice in Seattle, in an attempt to determine the above-mentioned likelihood of success or the $p(\cdot)$ function, Jacobs *et al.* (2001) studied 75 children between the ages of 18 months and 6 years who had been diagnosed with AOM and then treated with homeopathic medicine. Friese *et al.* (1996) and Barnett *et al.* (2000) have made similar attempts to determine, respectively, the likelihood of success or the $p(\cdot)$ function for homeopathic treatment options in specific parts of Germany and the United States.

4. Conclusions

In this study, we introduced uncertainty into the analysis and thereby generalized the Wilen and Msangi (2003) study of the choice between the interventionist strategy and the non-interventionist strategy in dealing with the problem of resistance caused by the repeated use of antibiotics and pesticides. Specifically, we asked and answered two questions. First, we showed exactly how the presence of uncertainty affects the answer to the aforementioned choice issue. Second, we pointed out that in a stochastic framework, the answer to the above choice question depends not only on cost considerations but also on the likelihood of success or the $p(\cdot)$ function when the non-interventionist strategy is used. Finally, we provided citations and "real world" evidence to substantiate our claim about the salience of cost considerations *and* the likelihood of success function.

The analysis contained in this chapter can be extended in a number of directions. In what follows, we suggest five possible extensions. First, the reader will note that we modeled the probabilistic movement toward the resistant state with a Brownian motion process. As such, it would be useful to investigate the extent to which the results of this chapter hold when alternate stochastic processes are used to model the random movement toward the resistant state. Second, it would be useful to compare the approach of this chapter — in which, outside the resistant state, the default antibiotic is successful in curing the ailment under study with certainty — with an alternate approach in which the default antibiotic's success is probabilistic and not deterministic. Third, an important and promising research direction would be to position this chapter's analysis, with its focus on costs, onto an alternate analysis in which the explicit focus is on human health because lifetime additions have clear personal benefits over a long time period. Fourth, subsequent research might also highlight related issues such as the motives for accepting interventionist or non-interventionist strategies (see Travisi *et al.* (2006)). Finally, given the salience of the likelihood function $p(\cdot)$, more experimental research is needed to obtain an appropriate and solid statistical basis for its specification. Indeed, there is much scope for innovative behavioral and statistical research in the new field of resistance economics.

References

Amabile-Cuevas, C.F. (1997). *Antibiotic Resistance*. Georgetown, Texas: Landes Bioscience.

Antelman, G. and Savage, I.R. (1965). Surveillance Problems: Wiener Processes. *Naval Research Logistics Quarterly* 12:35–55.

Barnett, E.D., Levatin, J.L., Chapman, E.H., Floyd, L.A., Eisenberg, D., Kaptchuk, T.J. and Klein, J.O. (2000). Challenges of Evaluating Homeopathic Treatment of Acute Otitis Media. *Pediatric Infectious Disease Journal* 19:273–275.

Batabyal, A.A. and Yoo, S.J. (1994). Renewal Theory and Natural Resource Regulatory Policy under Uncertainty. *Economics Letters* 46:237–241.

Batabyal, A.A. (1999). Aspects of the Optimal Management of Cyclical Ecological-Economic Systems. *Ecological Economics* 30:285–292.

Batabyal, A.A. and Beladi, H. (2002). On the Choice of the Optimal Temporal Control in Renewable Resource Management. *Stochastic Environmental Research and Risk Assessment* 16:325–332.

Bosker, G. (2004). Antibiotic Selection for Acute Otitis Media. Available at http://hypertension-consult.com/Secure/textbookarticles/PrimaryCare_Book/30.htm, [accessed on 14 March 2005].

Bren, L. (2002). Battle of the Bugs: Fighting Antibiotic Resistance. *FDA Consumer Magazine*, July–August. Available at http://www.fda.gov/fdac/features/2002/402_bugs.html [accessed on 5 January 2012].

Buhner, S.H. (1999). *Herbal Antibiotics*. North Adams, Massachusetts: Storey Publishing.

Brown, G.M. and Layton, D.F. (1996). Resistance Economics: Social Cost and the Evolution of Antibiotic Resistance. *Environment and Development Economics* 1:349–355.

Elbasha, E.H. (2003). Deadweight Loss of Bacterial Resistance due to Overtreatment. *Health Economics* 12:125–138.

Fleischer, G. and Waibel, H. (2003). Elements of Economic Resistance Management Strategies — Empirical Evidence from Case Studies in Germany. *In* R. Laxminarayan (ed.), *Battling Resistance to Antibiotics and Pesticides*. Washington, District of Columbia: Resources for the Future Press.

Friese, K.H., Kruse, S. and Moeller, H. (1996). Acute Otitis Media in Children: Comparison Between Conventional and Homeopathic Therapy. *HNO* 44:462–466.

Garrett, L. (1994). *The Coming Plague*. New York: Penguin Books.

Howard, D.H. (2004). Resistance-Induced Antibiotic Substitution. *Health Economics* 13:585–595.

Hueth, D. and Regev, U. (1974). Optimal Agricultural Pest Management with Increasing Pest Resistance. *American Journal of Agricultural Economics* 56:543–553.

Institute of Medicine (1992). *Emerging Infections.* Washington, District of Columbia: National Academy Press.

Jacobs, J., Springer, D.A. and Crothers, D. (2001). Homeopathic Treatment of Acute Otitis Media in Children: A Preliminary Randomized Placebo-controlled Trial. *Pediatric Infectious Disease Journal* 20:177–183.

Laxminarayan, R. (ed.) (2003). *Battling Resistance to Antibiotics and Pesticides.* Washington, District of Columbia: Resources for the Future Press.

Laxminarayan, R. and Brown, G.M. (2001). Economics of Antibiotic Resistance: A Theory of Optimal Use. *Journal of Environmental Economics and Management* 42:183–206.

Laxminarayan, R. and Weitzman, M.L. (2003). Value of Treatment Heterogeneity for Infectious Diseases. *In* R. Laxminarayan (ed.), *Battling Resistance to Antibiotics and Pesticides.* Washington, District of Columbia: Resources for the Future Press.

McKenna, J. (2003). *Natural Alternatives to Antibiotics.* Villa Park, Illinois: Newleaf Books.

Morel, B., Farrow, R.S., Wu, F. and Casman, E.A. (2003). Pesticide Resistance, the Precautionary Principle, and the Regulation of *Bt* Corn: Real Option and Rational Option Approaches to Decision making. *In* R. Laxminarayan (ed.), *Battling Resistance to Antibiotics and Pesticides.* Washington, District of Columbia: Resources for the Future Press.

Ross, S.M. (1983). *Stochastic Processes.* New York: Wiley.

Ross, S.M. (2003). *Introduction to Probability Models,* 8th edn. San Diego, California: Academic Press.

Rowthorn, R. and Brown, G.M. (2003). Using Antibiotics when Resistance is Renewable. *In* R. Laxminarayan (ed.), *Battling Resistance to Antibiotics and Pesticides.* Washington, District of Columbia: Resources for the Future Press.

Secchi, S. and Babcock, B.A. (2003). Pest Mobility, Market Share, and the Efficacy of Refuge Requirements for Resistance Management. *In* R. Laxminarayan (ed.), *Battling Resistance to Antibiotics and Pesticides.* Washington, District of Columbia: Resources for the Future Press.

Taylor, H.M. and Karlin, S. (1998). *Introduction to Stochastic Modeling,* 3rd edn. San Diego, California: Academic Press.

Travisi, C.M., Nijkamp, P., Vighi, M. and Giacomelli, P. (2006). Managing Pesticide Risk for Non-target Ecosystems with Pesticide Risk Indicators: A Multicriteria Approach. *International Journal of Environmental Technology and Management* 6:141–162.

Wilen, J.E. and Msangi, S. (2003). Dynamics of Antibiotic Use: Ecological Versus Interventionist Strategies to Manage Resistance to Antibiotics. *In* R. Laxminarayan (ed.), *Battling Resistance to Antibiotics and Pesticides*. Washington, District of Columbia: Resources for the Future Press.

Part III

Biological Diversity

Chapter 6

AN OPTIMAL STOPPING APPROACH TO THE CONSERVATION OF BIODIVERSITY[1]

In the past two decades, a considerable amount of concern has been expressed in academic and in non-academic circles about the decline in the world's diverse biological resources. Recently, Swanson (in: *Biodiversity Loss: Economic and Ecological Issues.* Cambridge University Press, Cambridge, 1995) has suggested that the problem of biodiversity loss is really a problem of regulating the natural habitat conversion process in which naturally existing species have systematically been replaced by human chosen ones. In this way of looking at the problem, a decision maker's central task is to determine the optimal point at which this conversion process should be halted. In this chapter, I show how the theory of optimal stopping can be applied to model the biodiversity loss problem as described above. Specifically, I pose the underlying conservation question within the framework of a Markov decision process. I then show how to determine the optimal point at which this conversion process should be halted.

1. Introduction

In the last two decades, a considerable amount of concern has been expressed in academic and in non-academic circles about the loss

1. I acknowledge financial support from the Faculty Research Grant program at Utah State University, and the Utah Agricultural Experiment Station, Utah State University, Logan, UT 84322-3530, by way of project UTA 024. This work was approved as journal paper no. 4936. I thank an anonymous referee for his output. I alone am responsible for the output.

of diversity in the world's biological resources. As Perrings *et al.* (1995a) have noted, there are many levels at which one can discuss the problem of biodiversity loss. Most popular characterizations have portrayed the problem as essentially one of genetic and species diversity loss. This notwithstanding, a consensus is emerging among economists and ecologists that in thinking about biodiversity loss, the appropriate concept to focus on is not genetic or species diversity, but the notion of ecological resilience (Perrings *et al.*, 1995b; Swanson, 1995b). According to this view, biodiversity matters primarily through its role in promoting resilience, "... where resilience refers to the amount of disturbance that an ecosystem can sustain before a change in the control or the structure of the ecosystem will occur" (Batabyal, 1996a, p. 487).

As a part of this new focus on the diversity of ecological function, Swanson (1995a) has suggested that the global decline in biodiversity is best viewed as a process of natural habitat conversion in which naturally occurring species have been systematically replaced by human selected ones. According to Swanson, if we are to ameliorate the problem of biodiversity loss, we need to focus on this "extinction process." In this view of the underlying problem, the central task for a decision maker is to halt this habitat conversion process at an optimally determined point in time.

In this chapter, I shall pursue this way of looking at the biodiversity loss problem. Specifically, I shall cast the underlying conservation question within the framework of a Markov decision theoretic framework (Derman, 1970). I shall then use an optimal stopping rule to provide an answer to the question of when the habitat conversion process should be halted.

The rest of this chapter is organized as follows. Section 2 formulates and discusses the theoretical framework in detail. Section 3 offers concluding comments and discusses directions for future research.

2. The Theoretical Framework

My model is based on Ross (1970, pp. 188–190) and on Batabyal (1997), and the spirit of the analysis is related to that contained in Batabyal's unpublished 1997 manuscript; "An information theoretic perspective on the conservation of biodiversity." I shall first describe the infinitesimal look ahead stopping rule (ILASR) and a theorem which provides conditions under which it is optimal to stop using the ILASR. As Ross (1970, p. 188) has noted, the ILASR can be thought of as a policy which stops a stochastic process precisely in those states for which stopping immediately yields a higher payoff than waiting an additional time h. Let S be the set of states for which stopping immediately yields a higher payoff than waiting an additional time h. Then it can be shown that Theorem 1 in (Ross, 1970, p. 188) applies and this says: If S is closed, i.e., once a stochastic process enters S, the process cannot exit S, then under certain regularity conditions, the ILASR is optimal.

The biodiversity conservation problem can now be cast in a Markov decision theoretic framework. This will then enable me to use Theorem 1 to determine when the habitat conversion process should be halted. I shall model the underlying decision problem as one that is faced by a national government which is interested in conserving its scarce biological resources.[2] The government solves its problem in a dynamic and stochastic framework. The framework is dynamic because the underlying conservation question involves halting a phenomenon — the conversion of natural habitats — that is taking place over time. The framework is stochastic because the habitat conversion process is stochastic and because the

---

2. I have posed the decision making problem at the level of a country. However, a change of scale — to a region within a country or to a region encompassing more than one country — does not affect the analysis qualitatively.

decision to halt this conversion process depends fundamentally on the uncertain availability of information regarding the desirability of such an action.

I assume that this information is produced according to a non-homogeneous Poisson process $\{I(t) : t \geq 0\}$, with a continuous, non-increasing intensity function $\gamma(t)$. Information is acquired by the government independently, and this information has a common cumulative distribution function $F(\cdot)$, with finite mean. By letting the information acquisition process follow a non-homogeneous Poisson process I am leaving open the possibility that it is more likely that information will be received at certain times than at other times. Since it is unlikely that the conversion of natural habitats is taking place uniformly over time, allowing for the above possibility would appear to be necessary. I assume that any information that is not used immediately by the government in deciding whether or not to halt the habitat conversion process, can be used subsequently. The specific source of information production is not critical to my analysis. It could be the result of research and development undertaken by the government, or it could be the result of activities undertaken by private agencies. In any event, from the perspective of the government, information is costly to acquire. As such, I shall incorporate this cost in the overall decision problem faced by the government.

Upon acquiring information, the government decides whether to halt the conversion of natural habitats, or to permit conversion and wait for additional information. Let $\bar{u}(\cdot)$ be the government's utility function. I assume that $\bar{u}(\cdot)$ is a continuous, one-to-one, and strictly monotone function. This utility function maps information about halting conversion to utility from halting conversion. In other words, if $i(t)$ is the information acquired by time t, then $U(t) = \bar{u}\{i(t)\}$ denotes the utility to the government from halting the habitat conversion process. Further, since $\bar{u}(\cdot)$ is a continuous, one-to-one, and strictly monotone transformation of $I(t), \forall t$, it follows that the government's utility $\{U(t) : t \geq 0\}$ is itself a non-homogeneous Poisson process with a continuous and non-increasing intensity function, say, $\theta(t)$.[3] Further, successive utility realizations are independent, with cumulative distribution function $G(\cdot)$. This distribution function also has a finite mean.

At any point in time, should the government choose not to halt the conversion process, it incurs benefits and costs. The benefits stem from retaining flexibility. The government leaves open the possibility that more and better information will be received in the future which may call into question the wisdom of a current decision to halt the habitat conversion process. The costs arise from two sources. First, the government has to pay to obtain information about the conversion process. Second, it loses the current utility from halting this conversion process. I shall denote the net benefit per unit of time from not halting the habitat conversion process by B.

The state (see Fig. 1) at any time t is denoted by the pair $[t, U(t)]$, where $U(t)$ is the utility that will be received, should the government choose to halt the habitat conversion process at time t. The reader should note that with this specification of the state, I have a two action — halt or do not halt — Markov decision process. If the government halts the habitat conversion process in state $[t, U(t)]$, the government's utility from t onwards will be $U(t)$. On the other hand, if the government chooses not to halt the conversion process and waits for an additional time h, then its expected utility will be

$$\left\{ 1 - \int_t^{t+h} \theta(r)\,dr \right\} \cdot U + \int_t^{t+h} \theta(r)\,dr \cdot E[\max(\Upsilon, U)]$$

$$+ Bh + o(h). \tag{1}$$

In Equation (1), Υ is a random variable representing the utility to the government from information received in $[t, t + h]$ and $E[\cdot]$ is the expectation operator. The $o(h)$ term is a technical requirement which stems from the definition of a non-homogeneous Poisson

---

3. See Wolff (1989, p. 26) for further details.

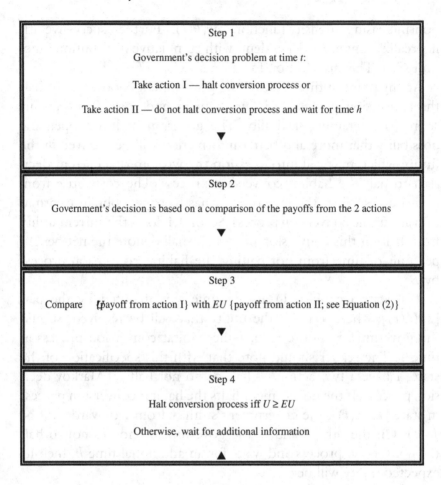

Fig. 1. Conceptual diagram of the optimal stopping approach.

process. Specifically, because $\{U(t) : t \geq 0\}$ is a non-homogeneous Poisson process, $\text{prob}\{U(t + h) - U(t) = 1\} = \theta(t)h + o(h)$. See Ross (1996, Chapter 2) for further details. Equation (1) can be simplified to

$$U + \int_t^{t+h} \theta(r)\,dr \int_U^\infty (y - U)\,dG(y) + Bh + o(h). \qquad (2)$$

Intuitively speaking, the government should halt the habitat conversion process upon acquiring information $i(t)$ at any time t if and only if the utility from halting, i.e., $U(t)$ exceeds the expected utility — given in Equation (2) — from postponing action and allowing habitat conversion to continue for an additional time h. Alternately put, the habitat conversion process should be halted now if and only if

$$U \geq U + \int_t^{t+h} \theta(r)dr \int_U^\infty (y - U)dG(y) + Bh + o(h). \quad (3)$$

Now canceling the common terms on both sides of Equation (3), dividing both sides of Equation (3) by h and then letting $h \to 0$ yields

$$0 \geq \theta(t) \int_U^\infty (y - U)dG(y) + B. \quad (4)$$

Equation (4) gives us the condition for determining whether the habitat conversion process should be halted now. From Equation (4), I can define the set S, i.e., the set of all states for which halting the habitat conversion process now yields a higher level of utility than permitting habitat conversion to continue for an additional time h. This set is

$$S = \left\{ (t, U) : \theta(t) \int_U^\infty (y - U)dG(y) \leq -B \right\}. \quad (5)$$

The reader should note that S is a closed set. This follows from the fact that as t increases, $\theta(t)$ does not increase and the integral in Equation (5) does not increase as well. I can now apply Theorem 1 — which I stated at the beginning of this section — and conclude that the government should halt the habitat conversion process at time t if and only if the utility from halting the habitat conversion process is $U(t)$, where $U(t)$ solves

$$\theta(t) \int_U^\infty (y - U)dG(y) = -B. \quad (6)$$

Equations (5) and (6) together tell us that the habitat conversion process should be halted at time t, if, in an expected utility sense, it does not pay the government to wait for information about the consequences of halting the habitat conversion process beyond time t.

2.1. *An example*

This example is adapted from Batabyal (1996b); the government utilities (in dollar terms) have been chosen so as to be consistent with the range mentioned by Simpson *et al.* (1996, p. 164). Our government is considering whether or not to halt the habitat conversion process that is at work in its country. As indicated in the previous discussion, this government receives information about the consequences of halting this habitat conversion process at any particular time. Suppose that there are only three states — states 0, 1, and 2 — in which the utilities to the government (in dollar terms) from halting the habitat conversion process are $38 000, $40 000, and $42 000, respectively. Let the probabilities of obtaining these utilities be $P_0 = 1/2$, $P_1 = 3/8$, and $P_2 = 1/8$, respectively. Further, let $B = -\$50$ be the net benefit per unit of time from not halting the habitat conversion process. Finally, suppose that the government uses a discount factor of $\beta = 0.99$ in making its decision.

To provide an answer to the "when to halt the habitat conversion process" question, suppose that once a decision to halt the process has been made, the corresponding Markov decision process goes to state infinity, and that it stays there indefinitely, accruing a net benefit of $B = \$0$. Now standard computations tell us that in this example, the government's optimal policy calls for not halting the habitat conversion process when the utility is $38 000 and halting the conversion process when the utility is either $40 000 or $42 000. Further, the government should halt the conversion process in state 1; this decision results in the receipt of utility in the amount of $40 000.

3. Conclusions

In this chapter I modeled the question of biodiversity conservation as an optimal stopping time problem within the context of a

Markov decision process. In this context, I provided an answer to the question as to when the habitat conversion process should be halted optimally. This answer involves a comparison of the utility obtainable from halting the habitat conversion process at time t, i.e., $U(t)$, with the expected utility to be obtained by not halting and waiting for new information beyond time t.

The analysis of this chapter can be generalized in a number of directions. In what follows, I suggest three possible extensions. First, one can make the net benefit from waiting — the B term — explicitly stochastic. When this is done, the government's decision will depend on the interaction between this stochastic process and the utility stochastic process.

Second, alternate specifications for the information production function can be analyzed. In this chapter, I have provided a rather simple specification in which information is produced in accordance with a non-homogeneous Poisson process. More general specifications will permit more elaborate analyses of the connections between information production and the optimal time at which the habitat conversion process should be halted.

Finally, one can consider the impact on the optimal time to halt the conversion process when the government uses randomized or non-stationary stopping rules. An analysis of this aspect of the problem will enable us to compare the implications of using alternate stopping rules for the conservation of biodiversity.

References

Batabyal, A.A. (1996a). Review of Perrings, C., Maler, K.-G., Folke, C., Holling, C.S. and Jansson, B.-O. (eds.), *Biodiversity Loss. In Kyklos*, 49: 486–487.

Batabyal, A.A. (1996b). The Timing of Land Development: An Invariance Result. *American Journal of Agricultural Economics* 78:1092–1097.

Batabyal, A.A. (1997). The Impact of Information on Land Development: A Dynamic and Stochastic Analysis. *Journal of Environmental Management* 50:187–192.

Derman, C. (1970). *Finite State Markovian Decision Processes.* New York: Academic Press.

Perrings, C., Maler, K.-G., Folke, C., Holling, C.S. and Jansson, B.-O. (1995a). Introduction: Framing the Problem if Biodiversity Loss. *In* C. Perrings, K.-G. Maler, C. Folke, C.S. Holling and B.-O. Jansson (eds.), *Biodiversity Loss.* Cambridge, UK: Cambridge University Press.

Perrings, C., Maler, K.-G., Folke, C., Holling, C.S. and Jansson, B.-O. (eds.) (1995b). *Biodiversity Loss.* Cambridge, UK: Cambridge University Press.

Ross, S.M. (1970). *Applied Probability Models with Optimization Applications.* San Francisco, California: Holden-Day.

Ross, S.M. (1996). *Stochastic Processes,* 2nd edn. New York: Wiley.

Simpson, R.D., Sedjo, R.A. and Reid, J.W. (1996). Valuing Biodiversity for Use in Pharmaceutical Research. *Journal of Political Economy* 104:163–185.

Swanson, T.M. (1995a). The International Regulation of Biodiversity Decline: Optimal Policy and Evolutionary Product. *In* C. Perrings, K.-G. Maler, C. Folke, C.S. Holling and B.-O. Jansson (eds.), *Biodiversity Loss.* Cambridge, UK: Cambridge University Press.

Swanson, T.M. (ed.) (1995b). *The Economics and Ecology of Biodiversity Decline.* Cambridge, UK: Cambridge University Press.

Wolff, R.W. (1989). *Stochastic Modeling and the Theory of Queues.* Englewood Cliffs, New Jersey: Prentice-Hall.

Chapter 7

HABITAT CONVERSION, INFORMATION ACQUISITION, AND THE CONSERVATION OF BIODIVERSITY[1]

We analyze two questions concerning the conservation of biodiversity in a dynamic and stochastic framework. First, given the link between natural habitats and biodiversity, when should a social planner stop the habitat conversion process? Second, what is the nexus between a social planner's optimal conservation policy and the length of this individual's planning horizon? We obtain the following two results. First, the optimal conservation policy calls for the social planner to wait a while, i.e., not act upon the receipt of the first $(1/e)$ fraction of all utility packets. The social planner should then stop the habitat conversion process upon receipt of the first candidate packet. The probability that the use of this optimal conservation policy will result in the conversion process being halted at the optimal point is $(1/e) \approx 0.37$. Second, because the proportion of time for which it is optimal to wait before acting is fixed, longer planning horizons result in the conservation of relatively larger stocks of biodiversity.

1. Introduction

In recent times, a great deal of concern has been expressed about the decline in the world's diverse biological resources. Ecologists and economists now agree that not only are we losing biological diversity

1. We thank four anonymous referees and particularly Roy Haines-Young for their helpful comments on two previous versions of this chapter. We acknowledge financial support from the Faculty Research Grant program at Utah State University, and from the Utah Agricultural Experiment Station, Utah State University, Logan, UT 84322-4810, by way of grant UTA 024. Approved as journal paper # 4993. The usual disclaimer applies.

(hereafter biodiversity), we are losing it at an unprecedented rate (Swanson, 1995a, p. xi). Although popular explanations for the problem of biodiversity loss abound, it is only very recently that ecologists and economists have begun to pool their resources to systematically study issues pertaining to the loss and the conservation of biodiversity (Perrings *et al.*, 1995a; Swanson, 1995a). An important conclusion emanating from this joint "ecological-economic" approach to the subject is that when viewing the problem of biodiversity loss, it is generally inappropriate to concentrate on the loss of genetic information. Instead, what researchers should be focusing on are the connections between biodiversity loss and the associated loss of ecosystem resilience (Perrings *et al.*, 1995b, pp. 16–17).

Beyond this general finding, ecologists and economists have analyzed three specific issues related to biodiversity. These issues concern the valuation of biodiversity, a determination of the causes for the decline in biodiversity, and the measurement of biodiversity. The valuation of biodiversity has become an important issue not only because of the demonstrated link between biodiversity loss and the loss of ecosystem resilience, but more narrowly, because of its close link to "biodiversity prospecting," and hence to the potential discovery of new pharmaceutical products. Polasky and Solow (1995), Simpson *et al.* (1996) and others have investigated this valuation issue. These researchers have shown that by deriving a demand curve for native genetic resources, one can determine the marginal willingness to pay for the marginal species and the marginal hectare of threatened habitat.

Inquiries into the causes for the decline in biodiversity have been conducted by Barbier and Rauscher (1995), Gadgil (1995), and Southgate (1995) (also see Swanson (1995a) and Perrings *et al.* (1995a) and the references therein). By demonstrating a causal link between myopic policy making and a diminution in biodiversity, these authors have highlighted the need for designing conservation policies which take into account the economics and the ecology of the biodiversity loss problem. In particular, Gadgil (1995, p. 107) notes that such policies must acknowledge that the problem of biodiversity loss is closely connected to "the ever-growing resource demands of [citizens of the First World and the Third World elite]...and their willingness to permit resource degradation in tracts outside their domain of concern."

Finally, the measurement issue has been studied by Weitzman (1992; 1993; 1995), Solow *et al.* (1993), and Solow and Polasky (1994). These researchers have shown that the genetic distance between related species can be used to come up with an effective measure of biodiversity. This measure recognizes that the "optimal conservation policy may be defined as the feasible action that yields the highest discounted expected value of diversity (plus whatever other net benefits are attributed to various components)" (Weitzman, 1995, p. 22). It is important to understand that this measurement issue has been guided by the realization that conservation resources are scarce. As a consequence, in order to determine how these scarce resources should be allocated across competing needs, it is necessary to measure biodiversity.

While this body of research has undoubtedly shed light on many aspects of the biodiversity conservation question, a number of outstanding questions remain. The purpose of this chapter is to pose and answer two such questions. It is important to first note the relationship between natural habitats and biodiversity. The conversion of natural habitats inevitably leads to a loss of biodiversity. For instance, Smith *et al.* (1995, p. 134) have noted that overexploitation, the introduction of exotic species, and habitat conversion are "the three primary causes of...extinctions and endangerments..."[2]

The problems associated with habitat conversion are very serious. Consider the case of tropical forests, generally recognized to be a salient source of biodiversity. As noted by Myers (1992,

---

2. For more on the relationship between habitat conversion and biodiversity loss, see Myers (1992), Wilson (1992), Ehrlich (1994), Hartwick (1995), and Krautkraemer (1995). In particular, Myers (1992, pp. 379–383) provides a country by country review of conversion rates in tropical forests.

pp. 175–176), commercial logging, fuelwood gathering, cattle raising, and forest farming operations collectively result in the conversion of approximately 200,000 Km^2 of primary forest every year. This massive conversion of tropical forests has given rise to a number of startling statistics. Here are two such statistics. First, the tropical forests of West Africa, the Greater Antilles, India, Madagascar, the Philippines, and Atlantic Brazil have already been reduced to *less than* 10% of their original areas (Terborgh and van Schaik, 1997). Second, as pointed in Terborgh (1992), outside of protected areas, tropical forests are expected to endure for *only about* 35 to 40 more years. It is unfortunate that despite the increased global attention to the loss of tropical forests, it does not appear as though the rate of forest conversion is slowing down. Recent studies (Whitmore and Sayer, 1992; Aldhous, 1993) suggest that this conversion rate is actually *increasing* in a number of countries.

With these sobering statistics in mind, the two questions that comprise the subject matter of this chapter are: (1) given the link between natural habitats and biodiversity, *when* should a social planner — who is interested in conserving biodiversity — stop the process of habitat conversion? (2) what is the nexus between this social planner's optimal conservation policy (OCP) and the *length* of his/her planning horizon? The theory of optimal stopping can be used to shed light on these two questions. For more on the theory of optimal stopping, see Ross (1983), Harris (1987), Dixit and Pindyck (1994), and Batabyal (1998). The reader should note that although the *significance* of these optimal stopping questions has been recognized by researchers, the questions themselves have not been analyzed previously (see Polasky and Solow (1995, p. 303), and Swanson (1995b, pp. 226–227) for a more detailed corroboration of this claim).

In the remainder of this chapter, we provide an optimal stopping perspective on these two questions. This chapter's model is adapted from Gilbert and Mosteller (1966). The work that is most closely related to that presented here is Batabyal (1998). Batabyal (1998) also analyzes the conservation of biodiversity over time and under uncertainty. However, his analysis is conducted within the framework of a Markov decision process. This chapter's analysis is more general because we do not make any distributional assumption about the stochastic process that we work with. Moreover, as indicated above, an important objective of this chapter is to study the link between a social planner's OCP and the *length* of his/her planning horizon; this issue has not been analyzed by Batabyal (1998).

To characterize the social planner's OCP, we exploit the connections between the preservation of natural habitats and the conservation of biodiversity. We also show that the social planner's optimal policy is closely related to the length of his/her planning horizon.

2. The Theoretical Framework

Consider a country such as India in which the conversion of natural habitat into developed land is taking place over time.[3] As Wilson (1992) and Krautkraemer (1995) have noted, estimates of the rate of species loss are generally based on the rate of habitat loss. As a consequence, we have interpreted the area of natural habitat as a measure of the stock of biodiversity.[4] The conversion of natural habitat yields information about the consequences of development and the existing stock of biodiversity. This link between habitat conversion and information acquisition has been previously documented; for instance, Swanson (1995b, p. 247) has observed that sequential "decision making regarding...conversions implies the

---

3. We have posed the decision making problem at the level of a country. However, a change of scale — to a region within a country or to a region encompassing more than one country — does not affect the analysis qualitatively.

4. This kind of interpretation has been used previously in the literature. For more details, see Barrett (1995, p. 285). However, note that for some "hot spot" habitats (see Myers, 1992, pp. xxi–xxii), the use of the area of natural habitat as a measure of the stock of biodiversity will need to be augmented to account for the fact that these "hot spot" habitats contain species that are at risk and are found nowhere else. This augmentation can be accomplished by letting the social planner's utility function depend on both the information packets and on a second variable — such as the number of endemic species per unit area — that is an indicator of biodiversity quality.

passage of time, and one component of time is the accumulation of information."

A social planner — who is interested in conserving the scarce biological resources in his/her country — receives this information sequentially, in packets, one packet per discrete time period. To proceed further, we have to specify an objective function for this social planner. To this end, we suppose that this social planner has a well defined utility function.[5] In microeconomic theory, the utility function is generally defined over goods. Here, the relevant goods are the information packets. The social planner's utility is defined over such packets. Note that because these packets provide information about the consequences of development and the existing stock of biodiversity, the resultant utility to the social planner is also about these two things. In particular, although the levels of utility associated with distinct information packets will vary, it is certainly not the case that the only way in which the social planner can generate utility is by halting the habitat conversion process.

On receiving a particular information packet, the social planner must decide whether to act, i.e., to stop the habitat conversion process,[6] or to do nothing and permit the conversion process to continue. We identify a lower bound on the level of utility that calls for stopping the conversion process, i.e., we pose the social planner's problem as one of maximizing the probability of acting (stopping the conversion process) when the highest possible level of utility has been obtained. The social planner solves his/her problem in a dynamic and stochastic framework. The framework is dynamic because the actual decision making in the setup of this

---

5. This means that the utility function possesses certain standard properties such as continuity. For more on this, see Varian (1992, pp. 94–97).

6. The reader should think of this action, i.e., stopping the habitat conversion process as one that results in the creation of a protected area. Examples of such protected areas are Corbett National Park in India, Pico da Neblina National Park in Brazil, and Sierra Nevada National park in Colombia.

chapter involves stopping a process — the conversion of natural habitat — that is taking place over time.[7] The framework is stochastic because the conversion process itself is stochastic and because the decision to stop this process depends fundamentally on the uncertain availability of information regarding the desirability of such an action.

We assume that this information is generated in accordance with an independent and identically distributed (i.i.d) stochastic process. This means that a particular information packet is received at time t with a certain probability, independent of any previous or subsequent information packets. The specific source of these packets is not critical to the analysis. It could be the result of analysis conducted by governmental research and development departments or it could be the result of government sponsored activities undertaken by private and/or non-profit agencies.

Let $\bar{u}(\cdot)$ be the social planner's continuous, one-to-one, and strictly monotone utility function. This function maps information about the effects of stopping conversion to utility from stopping conversion. Because $\bar{u}(\cdot)$ is a continuous, one-to-one, and strictly monotone transformation of the stochastic process that generates information, it follows that the social planner's utility, U retains the properties of the randomly generated information packets (see Wolff (1989, p. 26) for further details). In other words, we can think of utility as being generated sequentially, in packets, and in accordance with an i.i.d stochastic process. Upon receipt of an information packet and the corresponding utility, the social planner decides whether to stop the conversion of natural habitat, i.e., whether to create a protected area, or to permit conversion and wait for additional information. The reader should bear in mind that essentially

---

7. The reader should note the manner in which the problem is dynamic. Although we have not modeled the dynamics of habitat change explicitly, the maintained assumption is that the effects of habitat change are revealed to the social planner by means of the stochastically generated information packets.

it is information that is the driving force behind the social planner's decision as to when to stop the habitat conversion process.

Let us first focus on the more relevant case of a known, finite number (n) of utility packets.[8] As indicated above, upon receipt of a packet, the social planner must decide whether to stop the conversion process or to do nothing and wait for additional utility packets. The nature of utility is such that if the social planner does not act upon receipt of a particular packet, then the corresponding level of utility associated with that packet becomes useless for future decision making. The social planner has no access to any prior knowledge about the probabilistic nature of the utility packets. We model this by positing that the only knowledge the social planner is privy to is the relative *rank* of a utility packet, as compared to previous packets.[9] The social planner's objective is to maximize the probability of receiving the utility packet of highest rank when all $n!$ orderings of the various packets are equally likely. It is understood that the social planner will stop the habitat conversion process (create a protected area) when he believes that he has received the packet with the highest relative rank. By pursuing this objective, the social planner will in effect be maximizing his/her utility from the creation of a protected area in his/her country.[10]

From the standpoint of the social planner, the situation described above involves sequential decision making. In this connection, let us call a utility packet a *candidate* if this packet is of higher utility than any previously received packet. We are in state a, if the ath packet, $1 \leq a \leq n$, has just been received and this packet is a candidate. Let $\Upsilon(a)$ denote the best action that the social planner can take

---

8. Recall that because the number of packets and the number of time periods coincide, n is also the social planner's decision making horizon.

9. Here, rank is a proxy for level, i.e., if the level of utility associated with packet 1 is higher than the level associated with packet 2, then packet 1 will have a higher relative rank.

10. Note that positive discounting of future packets by the social planner will not alter the analysis in any significant manner. The only change is that instead of focusing on the actual utility of the various packets, the social planner will now focus on the discounted utility. Accordingly, the assignment of ranks will reflect discounted utilities rather than actual utilities.

in this setting. Then $\Upsilon(a)$ can be expressed mathematically by the following equation:

$$\Upsilon(a) = \max[P(a)\,R(a)], \quad a = 1, \ldots, n. \tag{1}$$

In Equation (1), $P(a)$ is the probability that the packet with the highest level of utility will materialize if the ath packet is acted upon and $R(a)$ is the best action that the social planner can take if the ath packet is not acted upon. Now conditioning[11] on the event that the ath packet is a candidate, we get:

$$P(a) = P[\text{packet is of highest utility of } n/\text{packet is of highest utility of } a]$$

$$= a/n. \tag{2}$$

It is now possible to give a concrete interpretation to $R(a)$. $R(a)$ is the *maximal* probability of acting upon the packet of highest utility when the previous a packets have not been acted upon. The reader should note that (i) $P(a)$ is increasing in a and (ii) from the social planner's perspective, the case in which the first a packets have not been acted upon is at least as good as the case in which the first $a+1$ packets have not been acted upon. These two observations tell us that $R(a)$ is decreasing in a. Now because $P(a)$ is increasing in a (see Equation (2)) and $R(a)$ is decreasing in a, we know that there must exist a packet b such that

$$a/n = P(a) \le R(a), \quad a \le b \tag{3}$$

and

$$a/n = P(a) > R(a), \quad a > b \tag{4}$$

hold. From Equations (3) and (4), the structure of the social planner's OCP can be determined intuitively. This OCP says the following: For some utility packet $b \le n - 1$, do not act, i.e., do not stop the habitat conversion process; then act (stop the conversion process and create a protected area) upon receipt of the first candidate packet.

---

11. When calculating a particular probability or an expectation, it is often useful to "condition" on an appropriate random variable. This explains why conditioning is a popular procedure in probability theory. For more on this, see Ross (1993, pp. 100–106).

Recall that the social planner will act when he believes that he has received the packet with the highest level of utility. As a consequence, our next task is to determine the probability — $[P_{OCP}(\text{highest})]$ — of receiving the highest utility packet when this OCP is followed. From Ross (1993, p. 100), it follows that this probability is given by

$$P_{OCP}(\text{highest}) = \sum_{a=1}^{a=n-b} P_{OCP}[\text{highest of } n/a + b \text{ packet recd}]$$

$$\cdot P_{OCP}[a + b \text{ packet recd}]. \qquad (5)$$

Now following the line of reasoning that led to Equation (2), the conditional probability on the right hand side (RHS) of Equation (5) can be simplified. This yields

$$P_{OCP}[\text{highest of } n/a + b \text{ packet recd}] = (a + b)/n. \qquad (6)$$

The second probability on the RHS of Equation (5) can also be simplified by writing this probability as a joint probability. This simplification yields

$$P_{OCP}[a + b \text{ packet recd}] = [b/(a + b - 1)] \times [1/(a + b)]. \qquad (7)$$

With Equations (6) and (7), the expression for $P_{OCP}(\text{highest})$ in Equation (5) can be rewritten. This gives

$$P_{OCP}(\text{highest}) = (b/n) \sum_{c=b}^{c=n-1} (1/c), \qquad (8)$$

where $c = a + b - 1$. The probability in Equation (8) is what the social planner wishes to maximize. Inspection of Equation (8) tells us that the function on the RHS of this equation is *not* differentiable. This means that in the finite number of utility packets — and the finite decision making horizon — case, calculus cannot be used to solve this maximization problem. Below, we focus attention on the asymptotic case in which $n \to \infty$. The reader should think of this asymptotic case as an *approximation* to the more relevant finite decision making horizon case.

For large n, the RHS of Equation (8) can be approximated well by the natural logarithm function. Using this approximation, we get[12]

$$P_{OCP}(\text{highest}) = (b/n) \log_e[(n-1)/b]. \tag{9}$$

Let $f(v) \equiv (v/n) \log_e[(n-1)/v] = P_{OCP}(\text{highest})$. We can now state the social planner's optimization problem. This planner solves

$$\max_v[(v/n) \log_e[(n-1)/v]]. \tag{10}$$

The first-order necessary condition to this problem is

$$v^* = (n-1)/e. \tag{11}$$

Substituting v^* from Equation (11) into $f(\cdot)$ gives

$$f(v^*) = P_{OCP}(\text{highest}) = 1/e \tag{12}$$

because $[(n-1)/n] \to 1$ as $n \to \infty$. Equation (12) contains the correct expression for the social planner's OCP. In turn, this equation leads to

Theorem 1. *For the infinite decision making horizon case, the social planner should not act upon receipt of the first $(1/e)$ fraction of utility packets; he should then stop the habitat conversion process upon receipt of the first candidate packet.*

2.1. *Discussion*

Theorem 1 provides us with an answer to the "When to halt the habitat conversion process" question. This theorem tells us that the OCP calls for the social planner to wait a while, i.e., not act upon receipt of the first $(1/e)$ fraction of all utility packets. The social planner should then act and stop the habitat conversion process

---

12. Note that although Equation (9) bears some resemblance to the information theoretic Shannon–Wiener function (see Krebs, 1994, pp. 704–705), the probability described in Equation (9) and the Shannon–Wiener function are dissimilar concepts. The Shannon–Wiener function seeks to construct an index of species diversity by determining the informational content of a sample. In contrast, the purpose of Equation (9) is to provide a differentiable approximation to the probability of receiving the highest utility packet when the OCP of this chapter is followed.

upon receipt of the first candidate packet. The probability that the use of this OCP will result in the conversion process being stopped at the optimal point can be easily computed. This probability is $(1/e) \approx 0.37$.

To see the connection between the theoretical result stated in Theorem 1 and actual conservation policy, consider the case of protected areas such as Corbett National Park in India, Pico da Neblina National Park in Brazil, and Sierra Nevada National Park in Colombia. As indicated in Footnote 6, the reader should interpret the act of stopping the habitat conversion process as one that results in the creation of a protected area. Why is it optimal to wait a while before creating a protected area? This is because waiting a while permits the social planner to "ascertain areas of high biodiversity and conservation priority and to plan effective protected area networks" (MacKinnon, 1997, p. 40). A specific case in point is the Conservation Needs Assessment (CNA) project in Papua New Guinea. By waiting a while, the CNA project was able to "compile and synthesize large quantities of geographical and distributional data relevant to biodiversity conservation" (MacKinnon, 1997, p. 40).

Theorem 1 also demonstrates the dependence of the OCP on the *length* of the social planner's decision making horizon. To see the relevance of this result for actual conservation policy, consider the more relevant finite decision making horizon case.[13] If we think of a time period as being 1 year long and the decision making horizon is 10 years, then Theorem 1 says that habitat conversion should be stopped after 3.7 years. In a similar way, if the decision making horizon is 20 years, then Theorem 1 says that habitat conversion should be stopped after 7.4 years. That is, in the 10 years decision making horizon case, natural habitat is preserved for 6.3 years and in the 20 years decision making horizon case, natural habitat is

---

13. Strictly speaking, Theorem 1 holds only for the asymptotic ($n \to \infty$) case. Further, as indicated previously, the asymptotic case is an approximation to the finite decision making horizon case. In particular, as n gets small, the quality of the approximation decreases. In reading the rest of this paragraph, the reader should keep these details in mind.

preserved for 12.6 years. Because the proportion of time for which it is optimal to wait before acting is *fixed*, we see that a longer decision making horizon will result in the conservation of a relatively larger stock of biodiversity.

The reader will note that a particular contribution of Theorem 1 is that it specifies the *exact nature* of the functional relationship between the length of a social planner's decision making horizon and the number of time periods for which biodiversity is conserved. Generally speaking, Theorem 1 calls for the use of long decision making horizons in the design of conservation policy. Is this result consistent with current thinking on the subject of biodiversity conservation? The answer to this question is yes. In this regard, Haufler (1999, p. 28) — a wildlife manager at the Boise Cascade Corporation in Boise, Idaho — has noted that "time frames need to be long enough to consider the disturbance regimes and successional processes affecting the ecological communities." Along the same lines, Brian Kernohan — a project manager in the Minnesota Ecosystem Management Project at the Boise Cascade Corporation in International Falls, Minnesota and Haufler (1999, p. 238) have pointed out that maintaining "biological diversity involves time frames that are often far beyond traditional planning horizons."

Theorem 1 has three additional implications. First, when pondering the OCP described in this theorem, it is important to take the following into account. The decision maker in this chapter is a social planner who takes all of society's welfare into account. Social welfare depends not only on biodiversity conservation but also on things like housing, industries, and roads, all of which typically involve the conversion of natural habitats. As a consequence, in deciding how long to wait before halting the conversion of natural habitats, the social planner optimally trades off these competing benefits and costs. This suggests that intertemporal studies of biodiversity conservation ought to *endogenize* the length of the decision making horizon. Second, it is never optimal to wait for the entire length of the decision making horizon before acting to halt the conversion of natural habitat. Third, the shorter the decision making horizon, the shorter is the length of the waiting period. In particular, when the decision making horizon is one period long, the social planner should stop the conversion of natural habitat immediately. To the best of our knowledge, these linkages between the length of the decision making horizon and optimal biodiversity conservation policy have not been studied previously.

The theoretical analysis of this chapter provides some insights into the temporal dimension of the biodiversity conservation question. The obtained results of this chapter, as in all theoretical papers, depend on the assumptions made. In particular, we assumed that information is generated in accordance with an i.i.d stochastic process. Although this is a salient assumption, it is important to remember that this assumption is routinely made in other areas of economics — such as econometrics — that study stochastic processes. This chapter's OCP is not independent of either the stock of biodiversity or the benefits of habitat conversion. This is because the OCP *depends* on the sequentially received information packets and the information that these packets contain is about the existing stock of biodiversity and the consequences of development (habitat conversion). Finally, note that no scaling of any kind is needed to obtain the result stated in Theorem 1.

The act of stopping the habitat conversion process (creating a protected area) can be interpreted as one that "invests" in biodiversity. With this interpretation of the problem, Theorem 1 tells us that it is optimal to wait a while before making this investment. In this way, Theorem 1 nicely complements the "value of waiting to invest" result that is to be found in the investment under uncertainty literature.[14]

---

14. For more on this literature, see Pindyck (1991), Dixit and Pindyck (1994), and Batabyal (1996; 1997). The present chapter differs from Batabyal (1996) in three ways. First, Batabyal (1996) conducts his analysis in a Markov decision theoretic framework; we do not make any similar distributional assumption. Second, the stopping rules used in these two studies are different. Third, Batabyal (1996) does not analyze the link between the optimal stopping rule and the length of the decision making horizon; this chapter does.

3. Conclusions

In this chapter, we have analyzed two questions about biodiversity conservation by studying the optimal stopping time of the related habitat conversion process. In this setting, in response to the "When to stop the habitat conversion process" question, we provided an OCP for the social planner. With this policy, a social planner makes a probabilistic comparison of the utility from stopping the conversion process upon receipt of a specific information packet with the utility from not stopping and waiting for new information. Because the proportion of time for which it is optimal to wait before acting is fixed, a salient policy implication of this analysis is that, *ceteris paribus*, longer decision making horizons will result in the conservation of a relatively *larger* stock of biodiversity.

The analysis of this chapter can be extended in a number of directions. First, note that the social planner's OCP is of an "all or nothing" type. This means that the social planner either stops all conversion or permits all conversion to continue. An examination of the social planner's optimization problem when partial stopping is a possibility, will permit a more elaborate analysis of the connections between information production and the optimal point at which the habitat conversion process should be stopped. Second, if the social planner learns about the statistical properties of the information generation process over time, then it is likely that he will eventually know the distribution from which the utility packets are generated. One could then analyze the impact of this knowledge on the "When to halt the habitat conversion process" question. An analysis of this aspect of the problem will enable one to study the ways in which learning affects the nature of optimal biodiversity conservation policies.

References

Aldhous, P. (1993). Tropical Deforestation: Not Just a Problem in Amazonia. *Science* 259:1390.

Barbier, E.B. and Rauscher, M. (1995). Policies to Control Deforestation: Trade Intervention versus Transfers. *In* C. Perrings, K.-G. Maler, C. Folke, C.S. Holling and B.-O. Jansson (eds.), *Biodiversity Loss*. Cambridge, UK: Cambridge University Press.

Barrett, S. (1995). On Biodiversity Conservation. *In* C. Perrings, K.-G. Maler, C. Folke, C.S. Holling and B.-O. Jansson (eds.), *Biodiversity Loss*. Cambridge, UK: Cambridge University Press.

Batabyal, A.A. (1996). The Timing of Land Development: An Invariance Result. *American Journal of Agricultural Economics* 78:1092–1097.

Batabyal, A.A. (1997). The Impact of Information on Land Development: A Dynamic and Stochastic Analysis. *Journal of Environmental Management* 50:187–192.

Batabyal, A.A. (1998). An Optimal Stopping Approach to the Conservation of Biodiversity. *Ecological Modelling* 105:293–298.

Dixit, A.K. and Pindyck, R.S. (1994). *Investment Under Uncertainty*. Princeton, New Jersey: Princeton University Press.

Ehrlich, P.R. (1994). Energy Use and Biodiversity Loss. *Philosophical Transactions of the Royal Society*, Series B 344:99–104.

Gadgil, M. (1995). Prudence and Profligacy: A Human Ecological Perspective. *In* T.M. Swanson (ed.), *The Economics and Ecology of Biodiversity Decline*. Cambridge, UK: Cambridge University Press.

Gilbert, J.P. and Mosteller, F. (1966). Recognizing the Maximum of a Sequence. *Journal of the American Statistical Association* 61:35–73.

Harris, M. (1987). *Dynamic Economic Analysis*. New York: Oxford University Press.

Hartwick, J.M. (1995). Decline in Biodiversity and Risk-adjusted Net National Product. *In* T.M. Swanson (ed.), *The Economics and Ecology of Biodiversity Decline*. Cambridge, UK: Cambridge University Press.

Haufler, J.B. (1999). Strategies for Conserving Terrestrial Biological Diversity. *In* R.K. Baydack, H. Campa III and J.B. Haufler (eds.), *Practical Approaches to the Conservation of Biological Diversity*. Washington, District of Columbia: Island Press.

Kernohan, B.J. and Haufler, J.B. (1999). Implementation of an Effective Process for the Conservation of Biological Diversity. *In* R.K. Baydack, H. Campa III and J.B. Haufler (eds.), *Practical Approaches to the Conservation of Biological Diversity*. Washington, District of Columbia: Island Press.

Krautkraemer, J.A. (1995). Incentives, Development, and Population: A Growth-theoretic Perspective. *In* T.M. Swanson (ed.), *The Economics and*

Ecology of Biodiversity Decline. Cambridge, UK: Cambridge University Press.

Krebs, C.J. (1994). *Ecology*, 4th edn. Menlo Park, California: Addison-Wesley.

MacKinnon, K. (1997). The Ecological Foundations of Biodiversity Protection. *In* R. Kramer, C. van Schaik and J. Johnson (eds.), *Last Stand*. New York: Oxford University Press.

Myers, N. (1992). *The Primary Source*. New York: W.W. Norton.

Perrings, C., Maler, K.-G., Folke, C., Holling, C.S. and Jansson, B.-O. (eds.) (1995a). *Biodiversity Loss*. Cambridge, UK: Cambridge University Press.

Perrings, C., Maler, K.-G., Folke, C., Holling, C.S. and Jansson, B.-O. (1995b). Introduction: Framing the Problem if Biodiversity Loss. *In* C. Perrings, K.-G. Maler, C. Folke, C.S. Holling and B.-O. Jansson (eds.), *Biodiversity Loss*. Cambridge, UK: Cambridge University Press.

Pindyck, R.S. (1991). Irreversibility, Uncertainty, and Investment. *Journal of Economic Literature* 29:1110–1152.

Polasky, S. and Solow, A.R. (1995). On the Value of a Collection of Species. *Journal of Environmental Economics and Management* 29:298–303.

Ross, S.M. (1983). *Introduction to Stochastic Dynamic Programming*. San Diego, California: Academic Press.

Ross, S.M. (1993). *Introduction to Probability Models*, 5th edn. San Diego, California: Academic Press.

Simpson, R.D., Sedjo, R.A. and Reid, J.W. (1996). Valuing Biodiversity for use in Pharmaceutical Research. *Journal of Political Economy* 104:163–185.

Smith, F.D.M., Daily, G.C. and Ehrlich, P.R. (1995). Human Population Dynamics and Biodiversity Loss. *In* T.M. Swanson (ed.), *The Economics and Ecology of Biodiversity Decline*. Cambridge, UK: Cambridge University Press.

Solow, A.R. and Polasky, S. (1994). Measuring Biological Diversity, *Environmental and Ecological Statistics* 1:95–103.

Solow, A.R., Polasky, S. and Broadus, J. (1993). On the Measurement of Biological Diversity. *Journal of Environmental Economics and Management* 24:60–68.

Southgate, D. (1995). Economic Progress and Habitat Conservation in Latin America. *In* T.M. Swanson (ed.), *The Economics and Ecology of Biodiversity Decline*. Cambridge, UK: Cambridge University Press.

Swanson, T.M. (ed.) (1995a). *The Economics and Ecology of Biodiversity Decline*. Cambridge, UK: Cambridge University Press.

Swanson, T.M. (1995b). The International Regulation of Biodiversity Decline: Optimal Policy and Evolutionary Product. *In* C. Perrings,

K.-G. Maler, C. Folke, C.S. Holling and B.-O. Jansson (eds.), *Biodiversity Loss*. Cambridge, UK: Cambridge University Press.

Terborgh, J. (1992). *Tropical Deforestation*. Burlington, North Carolina: Carolina Biological Supply.

Terborgh, J. and van Schaik, C. (1997). Minimizing Species Loss: The Imperative of Protection. *In* R. Kramer, C. van Schaik and J. Johnson (eds.), *Last Stand*. New York: Oxford University Press.

Varian, H.R. (1992). *Microeconomic Analysis*, 3rd edn. New York: W.W. Norton.

Weitzman, M.L. (1992). On Diversity. *Quarterly Journal of Economics* 107:363–406.

Weitzman, M.L. (1993). What to Preserve: An Application of Diversity Theory to Crane Conservation, *Quarterly Journal of Economics* 108:157–184.

Weitzman, M.L. (1995). Diversity Functions. *In* C. Perrings, K.-G. Maler, C. Folke, C.S. Holling and B.-O. Jansson (eds.), *Biodiversity Loss*. Cambridge, UK: Cambridge University Press.

Whitmore, T.C. and Sayer, J.A. (1992). *Tropical Deforestation and Species Extinction*. London, UK: Chapman and Hall.

Wilson, E.O. (1992). *The Diversity of Life*. Cambridge, Massachusetts: Harvard University Press.

Wolff, R.W. (1989). *Stochastic Modeling and the Theory of Queues*. Englewood Cliffs, New Jersey: Prentice-Hall.

Chapter 8

A THEORETICAL ANALYSIS OF HABITAT CONVERSION AND BIODIVERSITY CONSERVATION OVER TIME AND UNDER UNCERTAINTY[1]

We exploit the known links between natural habitats and biodiversity to pose and study the biodiversity conservation question as an optimal stopping problem. We extend the extant literature on this question by studying the role that autonomous and non-autonomous policies play in the decision to conserve biodiversity over time and under uncertainty. We first construct a dynamic and stochastic model of decision making in the context of biodiversity conservation. Next, we use this model to analyze the expected utility of a social planner when this planner uses, respectively, autonomous and non-autonomous policies. Finally, we compare and contrast the properties of autonomous and non-autonomous conservation policies and we discuss the magnitude of the flexibility premium stemming from the maintenance of temporal flexibility in decision making.

1. Introduction

A considerable amount of concern has been expressed in recent times about the decline in the world's diverse biological resources.

1. We thank an anonymous referee and Makoto Yano for their helpful comments on a previous version of this chapter. As well, we thank the Gosnell endowment at RIT for financial support. This chapter is dedicated to the memory of A.N. Batabyal (1937–2002). The usual disclaimer applies.

Economists and ecologists now acknowledge that not only are we losing biological diversity (hereafter biodiversity), we are losing it at an unparalleled rate (Swanson, 1995a, p. xi). Casual explications for the problem of biodiversity loss abound. However, it is only very recently that economists and ecologists have begun to combine their resources to systematically analyze issues relating to the loss and the conservation of biodiversity.[2] A salient conclusion emanating from this joint "ecological-economic" approach to the subject is that when considering the problem of biodiversity loss, it is generally inappropriate to focus on the loss of genetic information. Instead, what researchers should be concentrating on are the nexuses between biodiversity loss and the parallel loss of ecosystem resilience (Perrings *et al.*, 1995b, pp. 16–17).

Beyond this general finding, economists and ecologists have analyzed three additional issues related to biodiversity. These issues concern the measurement of biodiversity, a determination of the causes for the decline in biodiversity, and the valuation of biodiversity. The measurement issue has been studied by Weitzman (1992; 1993; 1995), Solow *et al.* (1993), and Solow and Polasky (1994). These scholars have shown that the genetic distance between related species can be used to devise an effective measure of biodiversity. This measure recognizes that the "optimal conservation policy may be defined as the feasible action that yields the highest discounted expected value of diversity (plus whatever other net benefits are attributed to various components)" (Weitzman, 1995, p. 22). It is salient to comprehend that this measurement issue has been guided by the realization that conservation resources are scarce. Consequently, in order to ascertain how these scarce resources ought to be allocated across competing needs, it is necessary to measure biodiversity.

---

2. For more on this joint research, see the papers in Perrings *et al.* (1995a) and Swanson (1995a).

Studies of the causes for the decline in biodiversity have been conducted by Barbier and Rauscher (1995), Gadgil (1995), and Southgate (1995).[3] By revealing a causal connection between myopic policy making and a diminution in biodiversity, these researchers have pointed to the need for devising conservation policies that take into account the economics and the ecology of the biodiversity loss problem. Specifically, Gadgil (1995, p. 107) has pointed out that such policies must acknowledge that the problem of biodiversity loss is closely connected to "the ever-growing resource demands of [citizens of the First World and the Third World elite] . . . and their willingness to permit resource degradation in tracts outside their domain of concern."

Finally, the valuation of biodiversity has become a major issue not only because of the established connection between biodiversity loss and the loss of ecosystem resilience, but more narrowly, because of its close connection to "biodiversity prospecting," and therefore to the probable discovery of new pharmaceutical products. Polasky and Solow (1995), Simpson *et al.* (1996) and others have analyzed this valuation issue. These authors have shown that by deriving a demand curve for native genetic resources, one can ascertain the marginal willingness to pay for the marginal species and the marginal hectare of threatened habitat.

Although this body of research has certainly advanced our understanding of many facets of the biodiversity conservation question, it is still true that the extant literature has *not* analyzed the effects that alternate policies have on the decision to conserve biodiversity and on a social planner's expected utility from conservation. Consequently, our chapter has three objectives. However, before we discuss the objectives themselves, it is necessary to first comment on the relationship between natural habitats and biodiversity. The essential point is this: The conversion of natural habitats invariably leads to a loss of biodiversity. For instance, Smith *et al.*

---

3. Readers should also consult Swanson (1995a) and the papers in Perrings *et al.* (1995a).

(1995, p. 134) have remarked that overexploitation, the introduction of exotic species, and habitat conversion are "the three primary causes of . . . extinctions and endangerments . . ."[4]

The problems associated with habitat conversion are grave. Consider the case of tropical forests, generally acknowledged to be an important source of biodiversity. As noted in Myers (1992, pp. 175–176), commercial logging, fuelwood gathering, cattle raising, and forest farming operations collectively result in the conversion of approximately 200,000 square kilometers of primary forest every year. This massive conversion of tropical forests has given rise to the following two disturbing statistics: First, the tropical forests of West Africa, the Greater Antilles, India, Madagascar, the Philippines, and Atlantic Brazil have already been reduced to less than 10% of their original areas (Terborgh and van Schaik, 1997). Second, as pointed out in Terborgh (1992), outside of protected areas, tropical forests are expected to endure for only about 35 to 40 more years. Regrettably, despite the increased global attention to the loss of tropical forests, it does not appear as though the rate of forest conversion is slowing down. Recent studies by Whitmore and Sayer (1992) and by Aldhous (1993) suggest that this conversion rate is actually increasing in a number of nations.

With these sobering statistics in mind, let us now discuss the three objectives of this chapter. First, we construct a dynamic and stochastic model of decision making in the context of biodiversity conservation. Next, we use our model to shed light on a question that, to the best of our knowledge, has not been studied previously in the literature on the conservation of biodiversity. This question concerns the expected utility of a social planner when this individual is able to choose between autonomous (time independent) and non-autonomous (time dependent) conservation policies. Finally,

---

4. For more on the relationship between habitat conversion and biodiversity loss, see Myers (1992), Wilson (1992), Ehrlich (1994), Hartwick (1995), and Krautkraemer (1995). In particular, Myers (1992, pp. 379–383) provides a country by country review of conversion rates in tropical forests.

we compare and contrast the attributes of autonomous and non-autonomous policies and then we discuss the magnitude of the flexibility premium arising from the maintenance of temporal flexibility in decision making.

To see why the distinction between autonomous and non-autonomous policies is salient, note the following: Autonomous policies are rigid and they do not permit a social planner to alter his or her policy when new information is acquired. Put differently, new information about the consequences of habitat conversion cannot be incorporated into the policy. In contrast, non-autonomous policies are flexible and they permit the incorporation of new information about the effects of habitat conversion into the policy. Therefore, intuitively one expects to observe a flexibility premium associated with the use of a non-autonomous policy. Indeed, we explore the existence and the magnitude of this flexibility premium in Section 4 of this chapter.

The theory of optimal stopping (see Ross (1983), Dixit and Pindyck (1994), and Batabyal (1998; 2000)) can be used to shed light on the objectives of this chapter. Consequently, our chapter can also be thought of as an application of this theory to the problem of habitat conversion and biodiversity conservation over time and under uncertainty. The papers that are most closely related to our chapter are Batabyal (1998; 2000). Both these papers study biodiversity conservation over time and under uncertainty. However, the objective of Batabyal (1998) is exclusively on characterizing the optimal time at which a habitat conversion process ought to be halted. In Batabyal (2000), the focus is on studying the link between a social planner's optimal conservation policy and the length of his or her planning horizon. Neither paper has analyzed the properties of autonomous and non-autonomous policies in the context of biodiversity conservation over time and under uncertainty.

The rest of this chapter is organized as follows: Section 2 presents the theoretical framework. Section 3 uses this framework and provides a detailed analysis of the effects of autonomous and non-autonomous policies on the expected utility of a social planner contemplating the conservation of biodiversity. Section 4 discusses the properties of autonomous and non-autonomous conservation policies and then comments on the magnitude of the premium arising from the maintenance of temporal flexibility in decision making. Section 5 concludes and offers suggestions for future research on the subject of this chapter.

2. The Theoretical Framework

In order to keep things from getting unduly complicated, in the rest of this chapter we shall choose units so that the numerical values of all the pertinent variables and the distribution functions are drawn from the interval (0,1]. Now, consider a country such as Indonesia in which the conversion of natural habitat into developed land is taking place over time.[5] As Wilson (1992) and Krautkraemer (1995) have pointed out, estimates of the rate of species loss are generally based on the rate of habitat loss. Therefore, we shall interpret the area of natural habitat as a measure of the stock of biodiversity.[6] The conversion of natural habitat yields information about the consequences of development and the existing stock of biodiversity. This link between habitat conversion and information acquisition has been documented in the extant literature. For instance, Swanson (1995b, p. 247) has noted that sequential "decision making regarding . . . conversions implies the passage of time, and one component of time is the accumulation of information."

---

5. We have posed the decision making problem at the level of a country. However, a change of scale — to a region within a country or to a region encompassing more than one country — does not affect the analysis qualitatively.

6. This interpretation has been used previously in the literature. For more details, see Barrett (1995, p. 285). However, note that for some "hot spot" habitats (see Myers, 1992, pp. xxi–xxii), the use of the area of natural habitat as a measure of the stock of biodiversity will need to be augmented to account for the fact that these "hot spot" habitats contain species that are at risk and are found nowhere else. This augmentation can be accomplished by letting the social planner's utility function depend on both the information packets and on a second variable that is an indicator of biodiversity quality.

A social planner who is interested in conserving the scarce biological resources in his or her country receives this information sequentially over time and in packets. This planner has a strictly monotonic and one-to-one utility function defined over these information packets. Because these packets provide information about the consequences of development (habitat conversion) and the existing stock of biodiversity, the resultant utility to the social planner is also about these two things. Now, a policy that involves waiting indefinitely and never stopping the natural habitat conversion process is a policy that results in the complete destruction of the existing stock of biodiversity. In most practical instances, such a policy will be inadmissible. Consequently, we account for this by imposing a constraint on the social planner's optimization problem. This constraint says that the social planner would like to stop the habitat conversion process by time $T = 1.$[7] This means that if the planner fails to stop the habitat conversion process by time $T = 1$, then his or her utility is zero.

Our social planner receives information packets about the consequences of habitat conversion over time. These packets P_1, P_2, $P_3, \ldots$ are received in accordance with a Poisson process[8] with a fixed rate $\lambda = 1$. The packets themselves are independent random variables that are uniformly distributed on the interval $(0,1]$. The receipt of a packet generates a certain level of utility by means of the social planner's utility function. In other words, this utility function maps information about the effects of stopping conversion to utility from stopping conversion. Moreover, because the information packets are uniformly distributed on $(0,1]$ and because the utility

---

7. The specific value of T is not terribly important. Given our earlier assumption about the choice of units and the interval $(0,1]$, the value $T = 1$ makes our subsequent computations tractable. However, the reader should note that by an appropriate choice of units and interval, an analysis of the sort conducted in this chapter can be carried out for *any* finite T. Also, observe that by employing this constraint, we are ensuring that our social planner will stop the habitat conversion process. The germane question is: "When?"

8. For lucid discussions of the Poisson process, see Ross (1996, pp. 59–97) and Taylor and Karlin (1998, pp. 267–331).

function is strictly monotonic and one-to-one, the utility levels U_1, U_2, U_3,... themselves are also uniformly distributed random variables on the interval (0,1]. Upon receipt of an information packet and the corresponding utility, the social planner decides whether to stop the conversion of natural habitat or to permit conversion and wait for additional information. In this chapter, stopping the natural habitat conversion process should be viewed as an action that results in the creation of a protected area. Examples of such protected areas include Corbett National Park in India and the Pico da Neblina National Park in Brazil. The reader will note that in essence, it is information that is the driving force behind the social planner's decision about when to stop the habitat conversion process.

In order to accomplish his or her objective of stopping the conversion of natural habitat by time $T = 1$, our social planner will need to use a policy. In this chapter, we shall consider two types of policies. The first policy is the autonomous one and this policy is of the following type: The social planner decides on some threshold level of utility $\hat{U}$ that is independent of time. With this policy, our social planner will stop the stochastic habitat conversion process (create a protected area) upon receipt of the first information packet whose utility exceeds $\hat{U}$. For example, using this autonomous policy, if our social planner creates a protected area upon receipt of the fourth information packet, then it must be true that $U_1 \leq \hat{U}$, $U_2 \leq \hat{U}$, $U_3 \leq \hat{U}$, and $U_4 > \hat{U}$. The second policy is the non-autonomous policy and in this case the threshold level of utility is a function of time t. In other words, instead of working with a constant $\hat{U}$, our social planner will now work with a time dependent threshold $\hat{U}(t)$, where $\hat{U}(t) = (1 - t)/(3 - t)$.

There are five reasons for working with the time dependent threshold function $\hat{U}(t) = (1 - t)/(3 - t)$. First, the use of this function enables us to capture the dependence of the threshold on time in a simple manner and it permits us to obtain an analytical solution to the problem described in Section 3.2. Second, even though the specified function is relatively straightforward, the use of this function permits us to model and study the non-linear dependence of time on the threshold. Third, the use of the above function lets us compare the merits of autonomous and non-autonomous policies directly. Fourth, the above specified function is consistent with our intuition that the social planner's decision making threshold ought to decline over time. Finally, there is a precedent (see Batabyal (2004)) in the economics literature for studying this kind of threshold function. We now proceed to our analysis of the autonomous policy.

3. Alternate Policies and Their Effects

3.1. *The autonomous policy*

Our objective in this section is to compute the expected utility of our social planner when (s)he uses an autonomous policy with utility threshold $\hat{U}$. To this end, let us first compute the probability of creating a protected area by time $T = 1$ when this policy is used. Because the utility stochastic process deriving from the stochastic information packet process is a Poisson process with rate $\lambda = 1$, we can tell that the probability we seek is

$$\text{Prob}\{\text{creating protected area by } T = 1\} = 1 - \exp\{-(1 - \hat{U})\}.$$

$$(1)$$

Our next task is to ascertain the expected utility of the information packet that results in our social planner agreeing to create a protected area by time $T = 1$. Now, recall that these utilities are uniformly distributed on the interval $(0,1]$. Hence, given that our social planner creates a protected area by time $T = 1$, the expected utility of the information packet that results in the stopping of the natural habitat conversion process is $(1 + \hat{U})/2$. We can now ascertain our social planner's expected utility EU_A from the creation of a protected area with an autonomous policy. This is given by multiplying $(1 + \hat{U})/2$ by the probability on the right hand side (RHS) of Equation (1). We get

$$EU_A = \left[\frac{1 + \hat{U}}{2}\right][1 - \exp\{-(1 - \hat{U})\}]. \qquad (2)$$

Equation (2) tells us that when an autonomous policy is used, the expected utility to the social planner from the creation of a protected area is the product of two terms in square brackets. Both these terms in the square brackets contain the utility threshold $\hat{U}$. Note that Equation (2) is also our social planner's objective function. Consequently, with this information in mind, we can now ask the following question: What value of the utility threshold $\hat{U}$ should our social planner pick to maximize his or her expected utility from the creation of a protected area? This question can be answered by letting our social planner solve

$$\max_{\hat{U}} \left[\left[\frac{1 + \hat{U}}{2}\right][1 - \exp\{-(1 - \hat{U})\}]\right]. \qquad (3)$$

This is a straightforward but laborious maximization problem. Simplifying the maximand in Equation (3), we can rewrite it as $\max_{\hat{U}}[1/2 - (1/2)\exp\{-(1 - \hat{U})\} + \hat{U}/2 - (\hat{U}/2)\exp\{-(1 - \hat{U})\}]$. The first-order necessary condition to this expected utility maximization problem is $\exp\{-(1 - \hat{U})\} + (\hat{U}/2)\exp\{-(1 - \hat{U})\} - 1/2 = 0$. It is possible to rewrite this first-order necessary condition. This gives us $\log_e(2 + \hat{U}) - (1 - \hat{U}) = 0$. Finally, this last equation can be expressed as

$$\hat{U} + \log_e(2 + \hat{U}) = 1. \qquad (4)$$

Because $\hat{U} \epsilon (0, 1]$, it is easy to see that the solution to Equation (4) is $\hat{U}^* = 0.2079$. This means that if our social planner sets the value of the utility threshold $\hat{U}^* = 0.2079$, then (s)he will have maximized his or her expected utility from stopping the natural habitat conversion process.

What is the maximized value of our social planner's expected utility? This query can be answered by substituting $\hat{U}^* = 0.2079$ into Equation (2). This tells us that our social planner's maximized expected utility from the creation of a protected area is

$$EU_A^* \left[\frac{1 + \hat{U}^*}{2} \right] [1 - \exp\{-(1 - \hat{U}^*)\}] = 0.330425. \quad (5)$$

Equation (5) tells us that the expected utility to our social planner when (s)he uses the optimal autonomous policy is 0.330425. In other words, this is the highest level of expected utility that our social planner can hope to attain with an autonomous policy. This state of affairs naturally leads to the following question: Can our social planner do better by using a non-autonomous policy? We now proceed to answer this question.

3.2.   The non-autonomous policy

Our goal now is to calculate the social planner's expected utility from the creation of a protected area when (s)he uses the non-autonomous policy $\hat{U}(t) = (1 - t)/(3 - t)$. Continuing in the same manner as in the previous section, let us first ascertain the probability of stopping the habitat conversion process by time $T = 1$ when the above non-autonomous policy is used. Because the policy being used now is time dependent, the probability that we are interested in can be determined by computing the likelihood of creating a protected area in a small time interval $[t, t + dt]$. To compute this likelihood, we shall use two facts and the cumulative distribution function (cdf) for an exponentially distributed random variable (see Ross (1996, p. 35)). The two facts are (i) the relevant utility stochastic process is a Poisson process with rate $\lambda = 1$ and (ii) the interarrival times for this Poisson process are exponentially distributed random variables with mean equal to $1/\lambda = 1/1 = 1$ (see Ross (1996, p. 64) and Taylor and Karlin (1998, p. 292) for additional details). Using these two facts and the cdf for an exponentially distributed random variable, the likelihood we seek is

$$\text{Prob}\{\text{creating protected area within } [t, t + dt]\}$$

$$= \exp\left\{-\int_0^t (1 - \hat{U}(s))ds\right\} \{1 - \hat{U}(t)\}dt. \qquad (6)$$

Comparing Equations (1) and (6), we see that the time depen-dence of the non-autonomous policy complicates the computation of the probability of creating a protected area. We now need to cal-culate the expected utility of the information packet that results in our social planner stopping the habitat conversion process by time $T = 1$. Once again, continuing as in the previous section, we obtain a similar expression for this expected utility. Consequently, we can now determine our social planner's expected utility EU_N from the creation of a protected area with a non-autonomous policy. This is given by multiplying $(1 + \hat{U}(t))/2$ by the probability on the RHS of Equation (6) and then integrating the resulting expression between 0 and 1. Mathematically, we have

$$EU_N = \int_0^1 \left[\frac{1 + \hat{U}(t)}{2}\right] \exp\left\{-\int_0^t (1 - \hat{U}(s))ds\right\} \{1 - \hat{U}(t)\}dt.$$

$$(7)$$

Equation (7) tells us that when a non-autonomous policy is used, the expected utility from the creation of a protected area is the product of two terms. As in the previous section, both these terms contain the utility threshold $\hat{U}(\cdot)$. Also, observe that Equation (7) is our social planner's objective function. However, because of the time dependent nature of our social planner's non-autonomous pol-icy, we cannot now calculate an optimal $\hat{U}^*$ as we did in the previous section.

This notwithstanding, we can still ask: What is the maximized value of our social planner's expected utility when (s)he uses a non-autonomous policy? To answer this question, we will need to com-plete the integrations in Equation (7). Let us first complete the

integration in the expression for the probability of creating a protected area in the interval $[t, t + dt]$, i.e., in the second term on
the RHS of Equation (7). Integrating, we get

$$\exp\left\{-\int_0^t (1 - \hat{U}(s))ds\right\}\{1 - \hat{U}(t)\}dt$$

$$= \frac{1}{9}\left(\frac{2}{3-t}\right)\exp\{2\log_e(3-t)\}dt. \tag{8}$$

Using Equation (8), we can greatly simplify the objective function
delineated by Equation (7). This simplification yields

$$EU_N = \frac{2}{9}\int_0^1 (2-t)dt. \tag{9}$$

Now completing the integration in Equation (9), we get

$$EU_N^* = \frac{2}{9}\int_0^1 (2-t)dt = 0.333333. \tag{10}$$

Equation (10) tells us that the expected utility of our social planner when (s)he uses a non-autonomous policy is 0.333333. In
other words, this is the highest level of expected utility that our
social planner can hope to achieve with the non-autonomous policy
$\hat{U}(t) = (1-t)/(3-t)$. We now compare and contrast the properties
of autonomous and non-autonomous policies and then we discuss
the magnitude of the premium arising from the maintenance of
temporal flexibility in decision making.

4. Autonomous Versus Non-autonomous Policies

In principle, for reasons given in Section 1, we expect autonomous
and non-autonomous policies to yield very different payoffs to our
social planner. Our analysis thus far allows us to shed light on this
and associated issues. In particular, we can use Table 1 to compare
and contrast the properties of these two distinct policies. Reading
horizontally, the second row of Table 1 reveals the basic difference
in the two policies. In the autonomous case, the optimal value of

Table 1. A comparison of autonomous and non-autonomous conservation policies.

Criterion of interest	Autonomous conservation policy	Non-autonomous conservation policy
Optimal value of utility threshold	$\hat{U}^* = 0.2079$	$\hat{U}(t) = \dfrac{1-t}{3-t}$
Maximal expected utility from creation of protected area	$EU_A^* = 0.330425$	$EU_N^* = 0.333333$
Premium from the maintenance of temporal flexibility	$EU_N^* - EU_A^* = 0.002908 > 0$	

the utility threshold $\hat{U}$ is fixed at 0.2079 and this value does not change with the passage of time. In contrast, when our social planner uses a non-autonomous policy, the utility threshold is continually a function of time and hence its optimal value varies with the passage of time.

The third row of Table 1 gives us exact values of the expected utility from the creation of a protected area when these two policies are used by our social planner. Relative to an autonomous policy, a non-autonomous policy allows a social planner to be flexible in the face of changing conditions. In particular, the reader should note the nexus between this flexibility and the constraint describing our social planner's desire to stop the conversion of natural habitat by a certain time. To see this connection plainly, consider the following example: We have chosen units so that the time by which our social planner would like to create a protected area is $T = 1$. For the purpose of this example, let us measure time in years and suppose that the time constraint is $T = 40$ years. Then, it is reasonable to say that the optimal value of $\hat{U}$ for our social planner at $T = 10$ years will most likely be different from the optimal value of $\hat{U}$ at $T = 35$ years. Now, in contrast with an autonomous policy, the use of a non-autonomous policy allows our social planner to alter the value of $\hat{U}$ over time and hence, in general, this policy is more flexible and therefore more desirable. The third row of Table 1 shows that this reasoning is right because $EU_N^* = 0.333333 > 0.330425 = EU_A^*$.

How much more desirable is the non-autonomous policy? The simple answer is: Not much more. As shown in the fourth row of Table 1, the premium associated with the maintenance of temporal flexibility in decision making is positive but only 0.002908. Consequently, in the theoretical framework of this chapter, our social planner does almost as well by using an autonomous policy.

To summarize, we obtain the following five insights from our analysis thus far: First, the time dependence of the threshold in Section 3.2 permits our social planner to be flexible. Second, when making habitat conversion stoppage decisions (biodiversity conservation decisions) over time and under uncertainty, it pays to be flexible. Third, although the use of more complex non-autonomous policies will most likely increase the magnitude of the flexibility premium, these more complex non-autonomous policies often do not admit closed-form solutions. Fourth, we can view the decision to create a protected area as a decision to invest in biodiversity. Finally, if we view the decision to create a protected area as a decision to invest in biodiversity, then, the result depicted in the second row of Table 1 — that it is optimal to wait a while before investing — is consistent with the "value of waiting to invest" result in the investment under uncertainty literature (see Dixit and Pindyck (1994)).

5. Conclusions

In this chapter, we provided a theoretical analysis of the effects of alternate policies on the decision to stop the conversion of natural habitat in a dynamic and stochastic framework. To the best of our knowledge, this is the first chapter to provide a comparative analysis of the properties of autonomous and non-autonomous policies in the context of the conservation of biodiversity. After pointing out the basic difference between autonomous and non-autonomous policies, our analysis showed that non-autonomous policies are generally more desirable than autonomous policies because the expected utility from the creation of a protected area when a non-autonomous policy is used exceeds the expected utility from the creation of a protected area with an autonomous policy. In other words, there is a positive flexibility premium associated with the use of a non-autonomous policy.

The analysis in this chapter can be extended in a number of directions. In what follows, we suggest two possible extensions. First, note that the social planner's optimal policy is of an "all or nothing" type. In other words, the social planner either stops all conversion or permits all conversion to continue. Following recent developments in the literature on the development of land over time and under uncertainty (see Miller and Lad (1984) and Batabyal (1999)), it would be useful to examine the social planner's decision problem when partial stopping is a possibility.

Second, the time dependent decision rule that we have studied in this chapter involves altering the value of the utility threshold. However, the form of the policy itself does not change. Accordingly, it would be useful to compare and contrast the properties of the non-autonomous policy of this chapter with a different policy that involves the temporal modification of the form of the policy. An analysis of these aspects of the problem will allow richer analyses of the nexuses between alternate policies and the decision to conserve biodiversity over time and under uncertainty.

References

Aldhous, P. (1993). Tropical Deforestation: Not Just a Problem in Amazonia. *Science* 259:1390.

Barbier, E.B. and Rauscher, M. (1995). Policies to Control Tropical Deforestation: Trade Intervention versus Transfers. *In* C. Perrings, K.-G. Maler, C. Folke, C.S. Holling and B.-O. Jansson (eds.), *Biodiversity Loss*. Cambridge, UK: Cambridge University Press.

Barrett, S. (1995). On Biodiversity Conservation. *In* C. Perrings, K.-G. Maler, C. Folke, C.S. Holling and B.-O. Jansson (eds.), *Biodiversity Loss*. Cambridge, UK: Cambridge University Press.

Batabyal, A.A. (1998). An Optimal Stopping Approach to the Conservation of Biodiversity. *Ecological Modelling* 105:293–298.

Batabyal, A.A. (1999). On Some Aspects of Land Development when the Decision to Develop is Divisible. *Resources Policy* 25:173–177.

Batabyal, A.A. (2000). Habitat Conversion, Information Acquisition, and the Conservation of Biodiversity. *Journal of Environmental Management* 59:195–203.

Batabyal, A.A. (2004). Alternate Decision Rules, the Flexibility Premium, and Land Development over Time and under Uncertainty. *Stochastic Environmental Research and Risk Assessment* 18:141–146.

Dixit, A.K. and Pindyck, R.S. (1994). *Investment Under Uncertainty*. Princeton, New Jersey: Princeton University Press.

Ehrlich, P.R. (1994). Energy Use and Biodiversity Loss. *Philosophical Transactions of the Royal Society, London, B* 344:99–104.

Gadgil, M. (1995). Prudence and Profligacy: A Human Ecological Perspective. *In* T.M. Swanson (ed.), *The Economics and Ecology of Biodiversity Decline*. Cambridge, UK: Cambridge University Press.

Hartwick, J.M. (1995). Decline in Biodiversity and Risk-adjusted Net National Product. *In* T.M. Swanson (ed.), *The Economics and Ecology of Biodiversity Decline*. Cambridge, UK: Cambridge University Press.

Krautkraemer, J.A. (1995). Incentives, Development, and Population: A Growth-theoretic Perspective. *In* T.M. Swanson (ed.), *The Economics and Ecology of Biodiversity Decline*. Cambridge, UK: Cambridge University Press.

Miller, J.R. and Lad, F. (1984). Flexibility, Learning, and Irreversibility in Environmental Decisions: A Bayesian Approach. *Journal of Environmental Economics and Management* 11:161–172.

Myers, N. (1992). *The Primary Source*. New York: W.W. Norton.

Perrings, C., Maler, K.-G., Folke, C., Holling, C.S. and Jansson, B.-O. (eds.). (1995a). *Biodiversity Loss*. Cambridge, UK: Cambridge University Press.

Perrings, C., Maler, K.-G., Folke, C., Holling, C.S. and Jansson, B.-O. (1995b). Introduction: Framing the Problem of Biodiversity Loss. *In* C. Perrings, K.-G. Maler, C. Folke, C.S. Holling and B.-O. Jansson (eds.), *Biodiversity Loss*. Cambridge, UK: Cambridge University Press.

Polasky, S. and Solow, A.R. (1995). On the Value of a Collection of Species. *Journal of Environmental Economics and Management* 29:298–303.

Ross, S.M. (1983). *Introduction to Stochastic Dynamic Programming*. San Diego, California: Academic Press.

Ross, S.M. (1996). *Stochastic Processes*, 2nd edn. New York: Wiley.

Simpson, R.D., Sedjo, R.A. and Reid, J.W. (1996). Valuing Biodiversity for Use in Pharmaceutical Research. *Journal of Political Economy* 104: 163–185.

Smith, F.D.M., Daily, G.C. and Ehrlich, P.R. (1995). Human Population Dynamics and Biodiversity Loss. *In* T.M. Swanson (ed.), *The Economics and Ecology of Biodiversity Decline.* Cambridge, UK: Cambridge University Press.

Solow, A.R., Polasky, S. and Broadus, J. (1993). On the Measurement of Biological Diversity. *Journal of Environmental Economics and Management* 24:60–68.

Solow, A.R. and Polasky, S. (1994). Measuring Biological Diversity. *Environmental and Ecological Statistics* 1:95–103.

Southgate, D. (1995). Economic Progress and Habitat Conservation in Latin America. *In* T.M. Swanson (ed.), *The Economics and Ecology of Biodiversity Decline.* Cambridge, UK: Cambridge University Press.

Swanson, T.M. (ed.) (1995a). *The Economics and Ecology of Biodiversity Decline.* Cambridge, UK: Cambridge University Press.

Swanson, T.M. (1995b). The International Regulation of Biodiversity Decline: Optimal Policy and Evolutionary Product. *In* C. Perrings, K.-G. Maler, C. Folke, C.S. Holling and B.-O. Jansson (eds.), *Biodiversity Loss.* Cambridge, UK: Cambridge University Press.

Taylor, H.M. and Karlin, S. (1998). *An Introduction to Stochastic Modeling,* 3rd edn. San Diego, California: Academic Press.

Terborgh, J. (1992). *Tropical Deforestation.* Burlington, North Carolina: Carolina Biological Supply.

Terborgh, J. and van Schaik, C. (1997). Minimizing Species Loss: The Imperative of Protection. *In* R. Kramer, C. van Schaik and J. Johnson (eds.), *Last Stand.* New York: Oxford University Press.

Weitzman, M.L. (1992). On Diversity. *Quarterly Journal of Economics* 107:363–406.

Weitzman, M.L. (1993). What to Preserve: An Application of Diversity Theory to Crane Conservation. *Quarterly Journal of Economics* 108:157–184.

Weitzman, M.L. (1995). Diversity Functions. *In* C. Perrings, K.-G. Maler, C. Folke, C.S. Holling and B.-O. Jansson (eds.), *Biodiversity Loss.* Cambridge, UK: Cambridge University Press.

Whitmore, T.C. and Sayer, J.A. (1992). *Tropical Deforestation and Species Extinction.* London, UK: Chapman and Hall.

Wilson, E.O. (1992). *The Diversity of Life.* Cambridge, Massachusetts: Harvard University Press.

Part IV

Ecological Economics

Chapter 9

ON THE OPTIMAL MANAGEMENT OF A CLASS OF AQUATIC ECOLOGICAL-ECONOMIC SYSTEMS[1]

with H. Beladi

This chapter studies aquatic ecological-economic systems such as the Chesapeake Bay. The stability of such ecological-economic systems depends on the successful functioning of a small number of generalist species in a wide range of ecological and economic conditions. We first characterize the persistence of such systems. We then analyze the dynamic and the stochastic aspects of the resource allocation problem faced by the manager of an aquatic ecological-economic system. This manager wishes to allocate his scarce financial resources optimally among economic activities and the maintenance of the generalist species of the aquatic ecological-economic system.

1. Introduction

Economists and ecologists now agree that the problems associated with desertification, habitat loss, and species extinction, are global in scope. As well, researchers also concur that the solutions to these problems that have been proposed by scholars working within the

1. We thank Jyrki Wallenius, two anonymous referees, and seminar participants at the University of Tennessee-Knoxville for their comments on a previous version of this chapter. Batabyal acknowledges financial support from the Faculty Research Grant program at Utah State University and from the Utah Agricultural Experiment Station, Utah State University, Logan, UT 84322-4810, by way of grant UTA 024. The usual disclaimer applies.

confines of economics and ecology are not working because these solutions are, *inter alia*, narrow in scope. This recognition has led to a considerable amount of interdisciplinary research between economists and ecologists.[2] This body of research has emphasized the fact that ecological and economic systems are *jointly determined*. The clear implication of this is that if we are to truly comprehend the many *interdependencies* between such systems, then we must study these systems jointly.

Despite the significance of this implication, a number of issues relating to the functioning of jointly determined ecological-economic systems remain poorly understood. Consequently, the objective of this chapter is to study aspects of the stability and the optimal management of a class of aquatic ecological-economic systems; examples include coastal and estuarine ecological-economic systems such as the Chesapeake Bay in the USA. As Costanza *et al.* (1995) have noted, the distinguishing feature of these ecological-economic systems is that their stability depends on the successful functioning of a *small* number of generalist species in a wide range of ecological and economic conditions. In the Chesapeake Bay, for instance, the various species of submerged aquatic vegetation[3] make up an important part of this set of generalist species.

There are many ways in which one can think of the stability of an ecological-economic system. Indeed, as Stuart Pimm (1991, pp. 13–14) has noted, ecologists have used the word stability to refer to a number of different concepts. These concepts include the notions of persistence, resistance, and variability. Because of the many meanings of stability, the question as to which specific meaning one should use in a given situation depends greatly on the context that the researcher is interested in studying. In this chapter, we are interested in studying the optimal management of aquatic, i.e., coastal

---

2. For more on this research, see Perrings *et al.* (1995a), Swanson (1995), Dasgupta and Maler (1997), Batabyal (1998a; 1998b; 1998c), and Levin *et al.* (1998).

3. An example of such a species is epiphytic algae. See Costanza *et al.* (1995, p. 101) for additional details.

and estuarine ecological-economic systems like the Chesapeake Bay. For these ecological-economic systems, it is essential that management focus on how long the composition of the small number of generalist species (in the Chesapeake Bay the various species of submerged aquatic vegetation), that collectively determine the stability of the ecological-economic system, lasts. Now, persistence refers to "how long a variable lasts before it is changed to another value" (Pimm, 1991, p. 21).[4] This tells us that the stability concept that we should be concentrating on is persistence. This is the reason for focusing on persistence in this chapter.

Although ecologists and economists have been interested in the management of ecological-economic systems, they have gone about the task of managing such systems in their separate ways, each behaving as if the other did not exist. For instance, O'Neill and Kahn (2000) point out that the current paradigm in ecology views humans as an external disturbance on the natural ecosystem and that the current paradigm in economics sees ecosystems as external to human societies. This way of viewing the world has led economists to think of "the environmental resource-base as an *indefinitely* large and adaptable capital stock" (Dasgupta, 1996, p. 390, emphasis in original). Similarly, this isolationist attitude to the management of ecological-economic systems has led ecologists to view "the human presence as an inessential component of the ecological landscape. This has enabled them to ignore the character of human decisions and, so, of economics" (Dasgupta, 1996, p. 390).[5]

Fortunately, this unhappy state of affairs has begun to change. In particular, recent research in ecological economics has led to a number of new insights into the management of ecological-economic systems.[6] However, this research and the attendant insights into management that this research has yielded, have both been very

---

4. An implication of this definition is that persistence is measured in time units.

5. For more on these issues, see the April 2000 issue of *BioScience*.

6. For more on this research, see Perrings *et al.* (1995b), Perrings (1998), Batabyal (1999a; 1999b; 2000), and Dasgupta *et al.* (2000).

recent. Consequently, there are a number of outstanding research questions about the optimal management of jointly determined ecological-economic systems. In this chapter, we shall study the following hitherto unanswered question: How should the manager of an ecological-economic system allocate his scarce financial resources so as to optimally manage coastal and estuarine ecological-economic systems whose persistence is determined by the successful functioning of a small number of generalist species in a wide range of ecological and economic conditions?

The rest of this chapter is organized as follows. Section 2 provides a mathematical characterization of persistence for coastal and estuarine ecological-economic systems such as the Chesapeake Bay. Section 3 analyzes the above described resource allocation problem faced by the manager of an aquatic ecological-economic system. Finally, Section 4 concludes and offers suggestions for future research.

2.   Persistence of Coastal and Estuarine Ecological-economic Systems

Consider a stylized coastal or estuarine ecological-economic system (CEE) that consists of a finite number of species. As indicated in Section 1, the stability of such ecological-economic systems depends on the ability of a small number of generalist species to operate under a wide range of ecological and economic conditions.[7] As such, in what follows, we shall abstract away from the other species of this CEE. Instead, we shall focus on the small number of generalist species. To this end, suppose that our CEE consists of two generalist species called species 1 and species 2, respectively. Further, let n_1 and n_2 denote the total number of members in each of these two species.

---

7. As indicated previously, in the Chesapeake Bay, the various species of submerged aquatic vegetation make up an important part of this small number of generalist species.

We suppose that each of these n_1 and n_2 members are substitutes in the performance of ecological functions.[8] By this we mean that each member of species 1 (2) can substitute for other members of species 1 (2). We are not saying that species 1 members can substitute for species 2 members. As a result of this substitutability, our ecological-economic system is stable, i.e., persistent, if and only if at least one member of each of the two species is alive. In other words, when at least one member of each of these two species is alive, the composition of the all important generalist species is maintained, and hence the CEE is persistent.[9] Further, note that the ecological functions performed by any one member of a species can be performed equally well by some other member of that species. This means that if a particular member of species $i, i = 1, 2$, dies, then the ecological functions performed by that member will now be performed by some other member of the remaining $(n_i - 1)$ members.

Natural events such as hurricanes and winter freezes and economic activities such as fishing and water sports have an uncertain impact on the lives of the members of these two generalist species. Consequently, the lifetimes of the members of these two species are stochastic. To this end, we shall say that a member of species $i, i = 1, 2$, lives for an exponential[10] amount of time with rate $\beta_i, i = 1, 2$. Our task now is to determine the persistence of this CEE. Mathematically, this involves computing the mean length of time during which the generalist species composition of this CEE remains unchanged.[11] In other words, we want to compute $E[\min(\sum_{i=1}^{i=n_1} U_i, \sum_{i=1}^{i=n_2} V_i)]$ where $E[\cdot]$ denotes the

---

8. Generally speaking, one can expect this kind of intra-species substitutability in the performance of ecological functions. For more on this, see Perrings (1996) and Batabyal (1999a).

9. Recall the Section 1 discussion of the rationale for focusing on persistence as the relevant stability concept.

10. The use of the exponential distribution to study ecological-economic systems is not without precedent. Batabyal (1996; 1998a) and Batabyal and Beladi (1999; 2004) have used the exponential distribution to model and analyze various aspects of ecological-economic systems.

11. For textbook discussions of these kinds of problems, see Ross (1996), Chapter 2 and Ross (2000), Chapter 5.

expectation operator, and U_i and V_i are exponentially distributed random variables that represent the lifetimes of the two generalist species.

Note that this approach to computing the persistence of an ecological-economic system is quite general. For instance, if the persistence of a given ecological-economic system depended on four and not two species, then we would compute $E[\min(\sum_{i=1}^{i=n_1} U_i, \sum_{i=1}^{i=n_2} V_i, \sum_{i=1}^{i=n_3} W_i, \sum_{i=1}^{i=n_4} X_i)]$. Here, W_i and X_i are exponentially distributed random variables that represent the lifetimes of the third and the fourth species of the ecological-economic system, and n_3 and n_4 denote the total number of members of the third and the fourth species.

Let us now compute the persistence of this CEE. In order to compute the appropriate expectation, we will first determine $E[N]$, where N denotes the number of species 1 and 2 members that actually die as a result of natural events and the continuance of economic activities. Using the properties of the exponential distribution — see Ross (1996, pp. 35–39; 2000, pp. 242–294) — we find that

$$E[N] = \sum_{j=\min(n_1,n_2)}^{n_1+n_2-1} j \left[\binom{j-1}{n_1-1} \left(\frac{\beta_1}{\beta_1+\beta_2}\right)^{n_1} \left(\frac{\beta_2}{\beta_1+\beta_2}\right)^{j-n_1} \right.$$
$$\left. + \binom{j-1}{n_2-1} \left(\frac{\beta_1}{\beta_1+\beta_2}\right)^{j-n_2} \left(\frac{\beta_2}{\beta_1+\beta_2}\right)^{n_2} \right], \quad (1)$$

where $\binom{j-1}{i} = 0$ for $i > j-1$. Now, dividing the expected number of species members that die, $E[N]$, by the sum of the rates of the two exponential distributions, we get an expression for the persistence of the CEE. That expression is

$$\text{Persistence} \equiv E\left[\min\left(\sum_{i=1}^{i=n_1} U_i, \sum_{i=1}^{i=n_2} V_i\right) \right] = \frac{E[N]}{\beta_1+\beta_2}, \quad (2)$$

where $E[N]$ is given by Equation (1).

Equations (1) and (2) tell us that the persistence of this CEE depends on the number of members in each species (n_1, n_2) and on the rates of the two exponential lifetime distributions (β_1, β_2). Further, because of our assumption of intra-species substitutability in the performance of ecological functions, persistence varies directly with $E[N]$, the expected number of species members that die as a result of natural events and the continuance of economic activities. Finally, inspection of Equation (2) tells us that because β_1 and β_2 enter the numerator and the denominator of the expression for persistence, in general, the effect on persistence of an increase in the rates of the two exponential lifetime distributions is ambiguous.

Note that in addition to serving as a measure of the stability of an aquatic ecological-economic system, persistence can also be thought of as a measure of an aquatic ecological-economic system's well-being. This is because a persistent CEE will maintain the composition of its salient generalist species for a long time. Consequently, such ecological-economic systems will be able to provide a flow of services to society for extended periods of time. To shed light on some of the use aspects of this flow of services to society, we now adapt the theoretical framework in Merton (1969) and study the resource allocation problem faced by the manager of an aquatic ecological-economic system. Generally speaking, this individual's task is to manage the CEE in a way that takes the ecological and the economic aspects of the problem into account.

3. Optimal Management of Coastal and Estuarine Ecological-economic Systems

Consider the resource allocation problem faced by a manager who wishes to manage a CEE optimally. Suppose that a legislative authority has appropriated $\$B$ for the management of the CEE of Section 2. In other words, $\$B$ is the budget of the manager of our ecological-economic system. This manager's specific problem is to select a rule for allocating this budget optimally. In selecting this rule, the manager will want to ensure that the composition of the two generalist species is maintained, i.e., the ecological-economic system is persistent, and that society is able to enjoy the flow of services that this CEE provides.

Let us pose the manager's problem as one of allocating his budget among species 1, 2, and the cost of economic activities. To keep the problem tractable, suppose that the benefit to society from the manager's actions designed to protect species 1 is certain. Denote this certain dollar benefit per member of species 1 by s. In contrast, managerial actions designed to protect species 2 result in an uncertain benefit to society. Let u denote the expected dollar benefit to society per member of species 2 and let σ^2 denote the variance per unit time of benefit from species 2. Let $b \in [0, 1]$ be the fraction of the budget that the manager allocates to actions designed to protect the members of species 2. Finally, let c denote the cost of economic activities. We suppose that this cost is a strictly increasing function of the level of economic activity. Note that the level of economic activity affects the persistence of the CEE.[12] Consequently, by choosing c, the manager is selecting the optimal level of economic activity. In turn, this optimal level of economic activity determines the persistence of the CEE. So, although the persistence of the CEE (Equation (2)) does not enter the management problem directly, it does so indirectly, in the manner just described.

As a result of managerial actions, the budget B evolves over time. We suppose that the evolution of this budget can be described by a stochastic differential equation. Specifically, that equation is

$$dB = [n_1 s(1 - b)B + n_2 u b B - c]dt + bB\sigma dz, \qquad (3)$$

where dz is the increment of a standard Brownian motion process. Observe that the deterministic component of the change in the

---

12. To see this in a specific instance, consider the case of the Chesapeake Bay. As noted by Kemp *et al.* (1983) and Costanza *et al.* (1995), during the 1960s and the early part of the 1970s, pollutants arising from human activities had an adverse impact on the various species of submerged aquatic vegetation that are responsible for maintaining the persistence of the Chesapeake Bay. As a result, "there was a dramatic shift in the Bay's ecosystem trophic structure from a system of balanced production via benthic and planktonic food chains to one dominated by plankton" (Costanza *et al.*, 1995, p. 101).

budget is given by the certain total dollar benefit from protecting species 1, plus the uncertain total dollar benefit from protecting species 2, less the cost incurred by the manager to support economic activities. The manager's objective is to minimize, over an infinite horizon,[13] the expected discounted social loss from the continuance of economic activities. To this end, let $L(c) = c^w/w, w > 1$ be the social loss function that the manager wishes to minimize.

The reader should note the manner in which we have accounted for the ecological and the economic aspects of the management problem. The ecological aspect of the problem is accounted for by the first two terms in the deterministic component of Equation (3). These two terms capture the benefit to society from managerial actions designed to ensure the persistence, and hence the well-being, of the CEE. The economic aspects are accounted for by the presence of a finite budget, the focus on the costs of economic activities in Equation (3), and by the managerial objective of minimizing the social loss from the costs of these economic activities.

The manager's optimization problem can now be stated. This manager solves

$$\min_{\{b,c\}} E\left[\int_0^\infty e^{-rt}\frac{c^w}{w}dt\right], \tag{4}$$

subject to Equation (3), with the initial condition $B(0) = B_0$. In Equation (4), $E[\cdot]$ is the expectation operator and is r the discount rate. The dynamic programming equation for this problem is

$$rV(B) = \min_{\{b,c\}}\left[\frac{c^w}{w} + V'(B)\{n_1 s(1-b)B + n_2 ubB - c\}\right.$$

$$\left. + \frac{1}{2}b^2 B^2 \sigma^2 V''(B)\right], \tag{5}$$

---

13. The solution to the finite horizon problem is "messy." Further, as compared to the solution to the cleaner infinite horizon problem, this messy solution does not provide any additional insights. Consequently, we have decided to focus on the infinite horizon problem.

where $V(B)$ is the unknown current value function. The first-order necessary conditions to this problem are[14]

$$b = \frac{(n_1 s - n_2 u) V'(B)}{\sigma^2 B''(V)} \tag{6}$$

and

$$c = \{V'(B)\}^{1/(w-1)}. \tag{7}$$

An aspect of Equation (6) deserves some comment. We see that if $n_1 s = n_2 u$, then it is optimal for the manager to allocate zero dollars to the protection of the second generalist species. Although this is a theoretical possibility, from a practical perspective, this knife-edge case is not particularly interesting.

Now substituting Equations (6) and (7) into Equation (5), we get

$$rV(B) = \left[\frac{1 - w}{w} \{V'(B)\}^{w/(w-1)} + n_1 s B V'(B) \right.$$

$$\left. - \frac{(n_1 s - n_2 u)^2 \{V'(B)\}^2}{2\sigma^2 V''(B)} \right]. \tag{8}$$

Equation (8) is a non-linear, second order, ordinary differential equation. To solve this equation, let us attempt a solution of the form

$$V(B) = AB^w, \tag{9}$$

where A is a positive constant that needs to be determined. The relevant derivatives of $V(B)$ are $V'(B) = AwB^{w-1}$, $\{V'(B)\}^2 = (Aw)^2 B^{2(w-1)}$, and $V''(B) = Aw(w - 1)B^{w-2}$. Substituting these three expressions into Equation (8) and then simplifying, we get an equation for A. That equation is

$$Aw = \left[\frac{r - n_1 sw - ((n_1 s - n_2 u)^2 w)/(2\sigma^2(1 - w))}{1 - w} \right]^{w-1}. \tag{10}$$

---

14. We suppose that the second-order conditions are satisfied.

We conclude that the optimal current value function is indeed given by Equation (9), with A as in Equation (10). Now to determine the optimal values of the choice variables b and c, we can use Equations (9) and (10) in Equations (6) and (7). This gives

$$b = \frac{n_1 s - n_2 u}{(w - 1)\sigma^2} \tag{11}$$

and

$$c = (Aw)^{1/(w-1)} B, \tag{12}$$

where Aw is given by Equation (10). Note that in order for Equation (11) to make sense, we must have $n_1 s > n_2 u$.

Equation (11) tells us three significant things about the nature of the management function. First, the optimal division of the manager's budget between the two generalist species of the CEE is constant. In particular, this constant is *independent* of the manager's budget. This means that increasing or decreasing the size of the manager's budget will have no impact on the optimal division of this budget between the two species. Second, the portion of the budget that the manager spends on actions to protect species 2, i.e., the species for which managerial actions result in uncertain social benefits, varies directly with the number of species members n_2, the expected dollar benefit per member u, and inversely with the variance of this benefit. Third, Equation (11) tells us that as s, the certain social dollar benefit per member of species 1, or n_1, the number of species 1 members increases, the manager ought to allocate a larger fraction of his budget to the upkeep of generalist species 1.

Equations (10) and (12) provide additional useful information about the optimal management of CEEs. First, these two equations tell us that the manager should permit economic activities to continue up to the point where the cost of economic activities equals the right hand side of Equation (12). Second, Equations (10) and (12) tell us that the optimal cost is a *constant* fraction of the manager's budget, and that this cost depends on *all* the parameters of the problem. For instance, inspection of these two equations tells us that the optimal cost level varies directly with the discount rate r, and that it is an increasing function of the variance parameter σ^2.

4. Conclusions

In this chapter, we studied the optimal management of jointly determined CEEs. The distinguishing feature of these ecological-economic systems is the fact that their stability (persistence) depends on the successful functioning of a small number of generalist species in a wide range of ecological and economic conditions. We first provided a mathematical characterization of the persistence of CEEs. To the best of our knowledge, this task has not been undertaken previously in the literature. We then studied the dynamic and the stochastic aspects of the resource allocation problem faced by a manager who is interested in the ecological and the economic aspects of the management problem.

Our analysis leads to three salient policy conclusions. First, when considering the management of CEEs, it is important to take those steps which ensure that the composition of the small number of generalist species is maintained. In the context of a CEE such as the Chesapeake Bay, this means that it is salient to ensure the well-being of the various species of submerged aquatic vegetation. This is because the communities comprising the submerged aquatic vegetation are essential feeding and refuge areas for a number of species. Moreover, these communities have "been shown to play a significant role in modulating nutrient and sediment cycling in littoral regions of the Bay" (Costanza *et al.*, 1995, p. 107).

Second, in determining the optimal division of the exogenously given budget between the generalist species of the CEE, the manager should not consider the magnitude of the available budget. In other words, the decision rule for allocating this budget between the generalist species of the CEE is invariant to fluctuations in the actual level of the budget.

Finally, the manager of a CEE should permit economic activities to continue up to a point *and no further*. At this point, the cost of economic activities equals the right hand side of Equation (12). To see the merits of this kind of an approach to the management of CEEs, consider the effects of mismanagement in a particular CEE, namely, the Chesapeake Bay. The economic importance of this Bay stems primarily from the presence of species such as the American oyster, the striped bass, the American shad, and the blue crab (Cumberland, 1990). In recent times, the numbers of these species have declined dramatically. As noted by Costanza *et al.* (1995, pp. 118–119), this is because of "a combination of overfishing and mismanagement of . . . submerged aquatic vegetation . . . "

The analysis of this chapter can be extended in a number of directions. In what follows, we suggest three possible extensions. First, this chapter analyzed the case of uncertainty associated with the effects of managerial actions for a single species only. A more general approach would involve working with two stochastic differential equations, corresponding to the two sources of uncertainty in the management problem. Although it is unlikely that this more general formulation will lead to closed-form solutions, a numerical analysis of this more general model is likely to yield useful policy insights into the optimal management of jointly determined CEEs. Second, it might be useful to analyze a version of the CEE management problem in which the total number of members in each of the two generalist species, i.e., n_1 and n_2, vary over time. Finally, the analysis of this chapter can be made richer by studying the effects of specific price and quantity control instruments on the well-being of an ecological-economic system as measured by persistence or, depending on the context, an alternate stability concept such as resistance or variability. Analyses of these aspects of the problem will provide additional insights into the optimal management of jointly determined ecological-economic systems.

References

Batabyal, A.A. (1996). On Some Aspects of the Management of a Stochastically Developing Forest. *Ecological Modelling* 89:67–72.

Batabyal, A.A. (1998a). On Some Aspects of Ecological Resilience and the Conservation of Species. *Journal of Environmental Management* 52:373–378.

Batabyal, A.A. (1998b). The Concept of Resilience: Retrospect and Prospect. *Environment and Development Economics* 3:235–239.

Batabyal, A.A. (1998c). The Environment and Development: Which Way Now? *Development Policy Review* 16:433–439.

Batabyal, A.A. (1999a). Species Substitutability, Resilience, and the Optimal Management of Ecological-economic Systems. *Mathematical and Computer Modelling* 29:35–43.

Batabyal, A.A. (1999b). Aspects of the Optimal Management of Cyclical Ecological-economic Systems. *Ecological Economics* 30:285–292.

Batabyal, A.A. (2000). Quantifying the Transient Response of Ecological-economic Systems to Perturbations. *Environmental Impact Assessment Review* 20:125–133.

Batabyal, A.A. and Beladi, H. (1999). The Stability of Stochastic Systems: The Case of Persistence and Resilience. *Mathematical and Computer Modelling* 30:27–34.

Batabyal, A.A. and Beladi, H. (2004). Time Restrictions in Natural Resource Management: A Dynamic and Stochastic Analysis. *European Journal of Operational Research* 157:775–783.

Costanza, R., Kemp, M. and Boynton, W. (1995). Scale and Biodiversity in Coastal and Estuarine Ecosystems. *In* C. Perrings, K.-G. Maler, C. Folke, C.S. Holling and B.-O. Jansson (eds.), *Biodiversity Loss*. Cambridge, UK: Cambridge University Press.

Cumberland, J.H. (ed.) (1990). *Proceedings of the 5th Annual Conference on the Economics of Chesapeake Bay Management*. University of Maryland: Bureau of Business and Economic Research.

Dasgupta, P. (1996). The Economics of the Environment. *Environment and Development Economics* 1:387–428.

Dasgupta, P. and Maler, K.-G. (1997). The Resource Basis of Production and Consumption: An Economic Analysis. *In* P. Dasgupta and K.-G. Maler (eds.), *The Environment and Emerging Development Issues*, Vol. 1. Oxford, UK: Clarendon Press Oxford.

Dasgupta, P., Levin, S. and Lubchenco, J. (2000). Economic Pathways to Ecological Sustainability. *BioScience* 50:339–345.

Kemp, M., Boynton, W., Twilley, R.R., Stevenson, J.C. and Means, J.C. (1983). The Decline of Submerged Vascular Plants in Upper Chesapeake Bay: Summary of Results Concerning Possible Causes. *Marine Technological Society Journal* 17:78–89.

Levin, S., Barrett, S., Aniyar, S., Baumol, W., Bliss, C., Bolin, B., Dasgupta, P., Ehrlich, P., Folke, C., Gren, I., Holling, C.S., Jansson, A., Jansson, B.-O., Martin, D., Maler, K.-G., Perrings, C. and Sheshinsky, E. (1998). Resilience in Natural and Socioeconomic Systems. *Environment and Development Economics* 3:222–235.

Merton, R.C. (1969). Lifetime Portfolio Selection under Uncertainty: The Continuous-time Case. *Review of Economics and Statistics* 51:247–257.

O'Neill, R.V. and Kahn, J.R. (2000). Homo Economus as a Keystone Species. *BioScience* 50:333–337.

Perrings, C. (1996). Ecological Resilience in the Sustainability of Economic Development. *In* S. Faucheux, D. Pearce and J. Proops (eds.), *Models of Sustainable Development*. Cheltenham, UK: Edward Elgar.

Perrings, C. (1998). Resilience in the Dynamics of Economy-environment Systems. *Environmental and Resource Economics* 503–520.

Perrings, C., Maler, K.-G., Folke, C., Holling, C.S. and Jansson, B.-O. (1995a). Introduction: Framing the Problem of Biodiversity Loss. *In* C. Perrings, K.-G. Maler, C. Folke, C.S. Holling and B.-O. Jansson (eds.), *Biodiversity Loss*. Cambridge, UK: Cambridge University Press.

Perrings, C., Maler, K.-G., Folke, C., Holling, C.S. and Jansson, B.-O. (eds.) (1995b). *Biodiversity Loss*. Cambridge, UK: Cambridge University Press.

Pimm, S.L. (1991). *The Balance of Nature?* Chicago, Illinois: University of Chicago Press.

Ross, S.M. (1996). *Stochastic Processes*, 2nd edn. New York: John Wiley.

Ross, S.M. (2000). *Introduction to Probability Models*, 7th edn. San Diego, California: Academic Harcourt Brace.

Swanson, T.M. (ed.) (1995). *The Economics and Ecology of Biodiversity Decline*. Cambridge, UK: Cambridge University Press.

Chapter 10

NECESSARY AND SUFFICIENT CONDITIONS FOR THE EQUIVALENCE OF ECONOMIC AND ECOLOGICAL CRITERIA IN RANGE MANAGEMENT[1]

For rangelands managed with spatial and temporal controls, [a] the long run expected net cost of management operations, [b] the long run rate of moving grazing from one paddock to another, and [c] the long run rate of moving grazing between paddocks because of adverse environmental factors are salient criteria for a range manager. In this chapter, we provide the first theoretical analysis of the relationship between these three economic and ecological criteria. We first characterize these criteria mathematically. Then, we provide necessary and sufficient conditions under which criterion [a] (economic criterion) is equivalent to, in turn, criterion [b] (first ecological criterion) and criterion [c] (second ecological criterion).

1. Introduction

1.1. *The equivalence question in general*

All over the world, ecological systems are the settings for economic activities such as boating, fishing, grazing, and hunting. As a result of these and other economic activities, ecological systems are constantly being subjected to shocks. These shocks result in two interlinked sets of effects, one ecological and one economic. Just

1. We thank Barkley Rosser and two anonymous referees for their helpful comments on a previous version of this chapter. As well, we acknowledge financial support from the Gosnell endowment at RIT. The usual absolution applies.

as the ecological effects influence the evolution of the underlying ecological system(s), similarly, the economic effects shape the pertinent economic system(s).

For our purpose, what is relevant is that these two sets of effects collectively determine the kinds of economic activities that may be carried out on these ecological systems and the ability of the underlying ecological systems to support these activities. These interlinkages between ecological and economic systems have led ecologists (see Holling *et al.* (1995) and Levin (1999)), economists (see Perrings (1998) and Batabyal (2004)), and range scientists (see Anderies *et al.* (2002) and Walker and Janssen (2002)) to conclude that ecological and economic systems are *jointly determined*, a view that has been recognized *implicitly* in the literature at least since Clark (1973). Nevertheless, the *explicit* recognition of this point has been much more recent. Consequently, a number of salient issues in ecological economics remain inadequately understood.

Batabyal (1999) has pointed out that there are five outstanding issues in ecological economics on which significant additional research is needed. One of these five issues is the optimal management of jointly determined ecological-economic systems. Despite Batabyal's (1999) observation, for too long, ecologists and economists have approached the task of managing what are really "ecological-economic" systems in their separate ways, each behaving as if the other did not exist. As Dasgupta (1996) has noted, this separation has led economists to view the environmental resource base as a limitless stock of capital. Similarly, an isolationist attitude to the management of ecological-economic systems has led ecologists to view the human presence as an insignificant part of the ecological landscape. As a result, ecologists have typically tended to ignore the role that economic factors play in the management of ecological-economic systems. However, as we have noted in the previous two paragraphs, this non-cooperative state of affairs is fundamentally at odds with the recent explicit recognition that ecological-economic systems are jointly determined. Therefore, there is now overt interest in studying the management of ecological-economic systems from an expressly interdisciplinary perspective.

Given the past non-cooperative approach of ecologists and economists to the management of ecological-economic systems, one central question that arises in an interdisciplinary approach to the study of ecological-economic systems concerns the relationship between alternate economic and ecological management criteria. The basic issue here is this: under what circumstances are alternate economic and ecological criteria *equivalent*?[2] If these circumstances are general, then it does not really matter whether one adopts an economic or an ecological approach to the management problem because both approaches can be expected to yield approximately the same solution. On the other hand if these circumstances are very specific or if such circumstances do not exist, then the management problem is considerably more complicated, and managers will typically have to address the economic and the ecological aspects of the management problem concurrently.

This equivalence question was first analyzed explicitly and rigorously by Common and Perrings (1992) in the context of a general model of sustainable resource use. They showed that the economic and the ecological criteria they analyzed ("Solow-sustainability" and "Holling-sustainability") were largely disjoint. Although this is an important finding, the Common and Perrings paper is *not* concerned with the management of ecological-economic systems *per se*. Moreover, the analysis in this paper is deterministic. However, as Holling (1986), Westoby *et al.* (1989), Friedel (1991), Perrings and Walker (1995), and Batabyal and Godfrey (2002) have pointed out, it is uncertainty about, *inter alia*, the temporal behavior of ecological-economic systems that makes the management problem so difficult.

---

2. In what follows, we shall refer to this question as the equivalence question. Also, in the rest of this chapter, we shall use the terms "criteria" and "criterion function" interchangeably. The reader should note that this equivalence question has been addressed previously in the literature, albeit implicitly only. For more on this, see Gordon (1954) and Clark (1973; 1990).

Given this state of affairs, in this chapter we explicitly analyze — to the best of our knowledge, for the first time — the above mentioned equivalence question in the context of the management of ecological-economic systems.[3] To fix ideas, we focus on a particular ecological-economic system, namely rangelands for three reasons. First, rangelands are jointly determined ecological-economic systems that provide humans with a variety of important consumptive (food, fiber) and non-consumptive (recreation) services. Second, "rangelands are the primary land type in the world" (Holechek *et al.*, 2001, p. 9). Third, the salience of the equivalence question has been mentioned but *not* studied explicitly in the context of a formal theoretical model in the existing range science literature (see Huntsinger and Hopkinson (1996), Ward (1998), and Batabyal (2004)). We remind the reader that although the equivalence question studied in this chapter is formally in the context of rangelands, as indicated previously, similar equivalence questions have been implicitly addressed in the extant literature. We now discuss our equivalence question in more detail in the context of rangelands.

1.2.   *The equivalence question in the context of rangelands*

Rangelands today are routinely managed with specialized grazing systems. Examples of such systems include deferred rotation grazing (Sampson, 1913), the Merrill three herd and four pasture system (Merrill, 1954), rest rotation grazing (Hormay and Evanko, 1958), and short duration grazing (Savory and Butterfield, 1999).[4] Two key attributes typify all these specialized grazing systems. First, there are spatial and temporal control aspects to these systems. Second,

---

3. Clark (1973) studied the economics of overexploitation in the context of a specific ecological-economic system, namely, fisheries. In particular, Clark (1973) implicitly addressed the equivalence question that we analyze here. *Inter alia*, he pointed out that "overexploitation, perhaps even to the point of actual extinction, is a definite possibility under private management of renewable resources" (Clark, 1973, p. 630).

4. Short duration grazing is also known as cell grazing, rapid rotation grazing, and as time controlled grazing.

the concept of rotation is a "critical feature of all specialized grazing systems (Holechek *et al.*, 2001, p. 249). Rather than discuss all these grazing systems, for concreteness, in the rest of this chapter we shall focus on what is arguably the most prominent specialized grazing system, namely, short duration grazing.

As noted in Savory (1983) and in Savory and Butterfield (1999), in this form of grazing, rangelands are managed by controlling both the length of time during which animals graze a paddock[5] (a temporal control) and by controlling the area of this paddock (a spatial control). The basic idea in short duration grazing is threefold. First, the manager divides the rangeland under study into a number of fenced paddocks. Next, this manager allows his herd of animals to graze a particular paddock for a specific time period. Finally, the herd of animals is moved to the next paddock, and the manager continues this process in sequential fashion. For rangelands managed with short duration grazing, it has been said that "a well-managed cell permits stocking rates to be increased substantially ... compared to ... other grazing systems" (Holechek *et al.*, 2001, p. 271).

When range managers use specialized grazing systems such as short duration grazing to oversee rangelands, what economic and ecological criteria do they typically utilize? As noted in Workman (1986), the most common economic criterion is net return or net cost, where net return is the difference between total revenue and total cost and net cost is the difference between total cost and total revenue.[6] Consequently, the economic criterion we analyze in this chapter is [a] the long run expected net cost of management operations.

Many ecological criteria have been proposed for rangeland management. Two of the more noteworthy ones are the maintenance

---

5. In short duration grazing, the rangeland under study is the cell which is divided into a number of paddocks.

6. The reader will note that net return and net cost are two sides of the same coin. A rational manager will maximize net return and minimize net cost.

of rangeland productive capacity (McArthur *et al.*, 2000) and the maintenance of rangeland health (Joyce *et al.*, 2000). In short duration grazing, the rangeland under study is divided into a number of paddocks. Consequently, the productive capacity of an arbitrary paddock will be maintained if the range manager allows his animals to graze this paddock for time periods that are neither too long nor too short, and then he moves his animals to the next paddock. Put differently, the productive capacity of a paddock is intimately related to the rate at which grazing is moved from one paddock to another. Therefore, the first ecological criterion that we analyze is [b] the long run rate at which grazing is moved from one paddock to another.

Now, the health of an arbitrary rangeland paddock is very much a function of deleterious environmental events such as droughts, fires, pests, and soil erosion. Specifically, if any of these events affects a paddock particularly severely, then it may not be possible for a range manager to graze his animals on the affected paddock. In this case, the manager will be forced to move his animals to a different paddock. This tells us that the health of a paddock is dependent on the rate at which the range manager moves his animals from one paddock to another because of detrimental environmental factors. Consequently, the second ecological criterion that we study is [c] the long run rate at which grazing has to be moved from one paddock to another because of adverse environmental factors.

The rest of this chapter is organized as follows: Section 2 uses a renewal theoretic framework to derive [a] the long run expected net cost of management operations, [b] the long run rate at which grazing is moved from one paddock to another, and [c] the long run rate at which grazing has to be moved from one paddock to another because of adverse environmental factors. Next, this section specifies and then discusses the necessary and sufficient conditions under which criterion [a] is equivalent to, in turn, criterion [b] and criterion [c]. Section 3 concludes and offers suggestions for future research in range management.

2. The Renewal Theoretical Framework

2.1. *Criterion* [a]: *long run expected net cost*

In keeping with standard practice in short duration grazing (see Savory (1983) and Savory and Butterfield (1999)), suppose that the dynamic and stochastic rangeland (the cell) under study has been divided into a number of fenced paddocks of equal grazing capacity. During the relevant grazing season, one salient task performed by the range manager involves moving his herd of animals from one paddock to another in sequential fashion. The manager will generally move his animals from one paddock to the next when an appropriately defined economic criterion function has been optimized. In Section 1.2, we noted that the most common economic criterion function is net return or net cost. This leads us directly to criterion [a], the economic criterion of this chapter. In words, this criterion is the long run expected net cost of management operations. We now show how renewal theory can be used to derive this criterion function.

Without loss of generality, consider an arbitrary paddock of the rangeland under study. To keep the problem interesting, we suppose that forage *quality* in this paddock is a *random* variable. To be consistent with units (also see Footnote 7), suppose that the one-to-one and strictly monotone function $g(\cdot)$ maps the forage quality of a paddock to its "operative lifetime." The forage quality of an ungrazed paddock is a function of natural factors only. In other words, such a paddock has the highest operative lifetime. As this paddock is grazed for progressively longer periods of time, its forage quality and hence its operative lifetime declines. Because forage quality is a random variable and because operative lifetime is a one-to-one and strictly monotonic transformation of forage quality, operative lifetime itself is a *random* variable. We assume that these operative lifetime random variables are independent and identically distributed (i.i.d), and we denote the distribution and the density functions of operative lifetime by $F(\cdot)$ and $f(\cdot)$, respectively. In what follows, we shall not refer to the forage quality of a paddock; instead we shall speak of its operative lifetime. However, it should be clear to the reader that any specific value of operative lifetime refers unambiguously to a unique level of forage quality. Further, like all lifetimes, operative lifetime is measured in time units, and it is defined over the non-negative real numbers.

Our range manager will terminate grazing in this particular paddock and move his herd of animals to the next paddock either when T time periods have elapsed or when a stochastic and deleterious environmental event cuts down the operative lifetime of this paddock, thereby leading to a breakdown of this paddock as far as subsequent grazing is concerned.[7] Examples of such adverse environmental events include unusually high rainfall in an arid paddock that results in significant topsoil loss, a fire that kills plants on the paddock, the appearance of coyotes that kill sheep on the paddock (see Andelt (1996)), and the discovery of toxic agents such as alkaloids in paddock plants such as the western false hellebore, lupines, and locoweeds.

The completion of grazing in a particular paddock and the simultaneous movement of the herd of animals to the next paddock results in benefits and costs to our manager. The benefits stem from things such as animal weight gain and the costs arise from activities such as feeding and fencing. Let us denote the net cost to our manager from the completion of grazing on a paddock after T time periods (one grazing cycle) by $C(p)$. If grazing on a paddock has to be terminated because of the occurrence of a deleterious environmental event (a breakdown), then we suppose that in addition to $C(p)$, our manager incurs a net cost of $C(e)$. This additional net cost accounts for the fact that when a detrimental environmental event occurs, additional expenditure will typically be incurred by

---

7. The reason for speaking in terms of the operative lifetime — and not the forage quality — of a paddock should now be clear. In what follows, we wish to compare T (measured in time units) with another random variable that is also measured in time units. This comparative exercise cannot be undertaken by comparing T with forage quality directly.

our manager on things such as the repair of extant fences and the possible replacement of dead or diseased animals.

We now discuss and justify our assumption that the paddock operative lifetimes are independent and identically distributed random variables.[8] In actual instances of short duration grazing being used for management purposes, the length of the grazing period in a paddock (or its operative lifetime) is *short* in absolute terms and relative to the length of the non-use or idle period. As Fowler and Gray (1986) and others have noted, the absolute length of the grazing period in a paddock is often five days or fewer. Further, this five days or fewer grazing period is typically followed by a non-use period that is four weeks or more in length. In other words, a key idea in short duration grazing is that the grazed forage in a paddock will recover quickly relative to the time when this paddock will next be used. This is why paddocks receive "several periods of nonuse and grazing during the growing season" (Holechek *et al.*, 2001, p. 249). Under the circumstances that we have just described, we would expect the operative lifetimes of the individual paddocks to be nearly independent and identically distributed, explaining why we make this i.i.d. assumption in this chapter.

The reader should note that the fact that the paddock operative lifetimes are short in both absolute and in relative terms does not mean that a range manager does not have to contend with any environmental concerns. As discussed in Section 1.2, the environmental concerns typically stem from the occurrence of unpredictable events such as droughts, fires, and pest infestations that are exogenous from the standpoint of the manager. Moreover, these events are stochastic *and* they affect the health — and hence the usability — of the rangeland under study. This is precisely why they are of concern to the manager and why (see Section 1.2) we are studying the second ecological criterion, (i.e., criterion [c]), the long run rate at which

---

8. We thank an anonymous referee for his/her help in developing this justification.

grazing has to be moved from one paddock to another because of adverse environmental factors.

Our task now is to derive criterion [a], the range manager's long run average net cost function. To derive this cost function, we shall use renewal theory and specifically the renewal-reward theorem.[9] We begin by providing a brief description of this theorem. As Ross (1996, pp. 132–140) has noted, a stochastic process $\{W(t) : t \geq 0\}$ is said to be a counting process if $W(t)$ denotes the total number of events that have taken place by time t. Now, because $W(t-1)$, $W(t)$, $W(t+1)$, etc. are stochastic, the time between any two counts $W(t+1)$ and $W(t)$ is also stochastic. This time between any two counts is called the interarrival time. A counting process in which the interarrival times have an arbitrary distribution is a renewal process.

Now, consider the renewal process $\{W(t) : t \geq 0\}$ with interarrival times $X_w, w \geq 1$, that have a cumulative distribution function denoted by $H(\cdot)$. Further, assume that a monetary reward R_w is earned when the wth renewal is completed. Let $R(t)$, the total reward earned by time t, be given by $\sum_{w=1}^{W(t)} R_w$, and let the expectation of R_w, $E[R_w] = E[R]$, and similarly let $E[X_w] = E[X]$. The renewal-reward theorem — see Theorem 3.6.1 in Ross (1996, p. 133) — tells us that if $E[R]$ and $E[X]$ are finite, then with probability one,

$$\lim_{t \to \infty} \frac{E[R(t)]}{t} = \frac{E[R]}{E[X]}. \tag{1}$$

Equation (1) tells us that if we think of a cycle being completed every time a renewal occurs, then the long run average reward is simply the expected reward in a cycle divided by the expected amount of time it takes to complete that cycle. The reader should note that in our case, the relevant cycle is the grazing cycle on a paddock and the expected reward is the expected net cost (a negative reward) of management operations per grazing cycle.

---

9. Additional details on renewal theory and the renewal-reward theorem can be found in Ross (1996, pp. 132–140) and in Taylor and Karlin (1998, pp. 447–457).

We now provide an intuitive derivation of criterion [a], the range manager's long run average net cost function. Complete details of this derivation are provided in the Appendix. We first need to determine the expected net cost per grazing cycle (i.e., the numerator in the ratio on the right hand side (RHS) of Equation (1)). This cost expression has a deterministic component $C(p)$ and a stochastic component $C(e)F(T)$ to it. Putting these two components together, we get

$$E[\text{Cost per Grazing Cycle}] = C(p) + C(e)F(T). \qquad (2)$$

The next step in our derivation of the manager's average net cost function involves calculating the expected amount of time it takes to complete a grazing cycle (i.e., the denominator in the ratio on the RHS of Equation (1)). This expectation is given by

$$E[\text{Grazing Cycle Completion Time}]$$

$$= \int_0^T lf(l)\,dl + T\{1 - F(T)\}, \qquad (3)$$

where l is a realization of the operative lifetime random variable L. We can now state our manager's long run average net cost function. According to the renewal-reward theorem (Equation (1)), this function is given by dividing Equation (2) by Equation (3). Performing this division, we get

$$\text{Criterion } [a] = \frac{C(p) + C(e)F(T)}{\int_0^T lf(l)\,dl + T\{1 - F(T)\}}. \qquad (4)$$

This completes our derivation of the economic criterion of this chapter. Knowing Equation (4), one course of action for our range manager would be to choose T to minimize the long run expected net cost of management operations. We now proceed to the derivation of the ecological criteria of this chapter.

2.2. Criterion [b]: *long run rate at which grazing is moved from one paddock to another*

The paddocks in short duration grazing are generally of equal grazing capacity (see Holechek *et al.*, 2001, p. 269). Therefore, a question of some significance concerns the determination of the optimal temporal control. In other words, how long should the manager's herd of animals graze a particular paddock before they are moved to the next paddock? The reader will recall that this question formed the backdrop for our Section 1.2 discussion of the first ecological criterion, (i.e., criterion [b]). In words, criterion [b] is the long run rate at which grazing is moved from one paddock to another. We now derive this criterion. As in Section 2.1, a more detailed account of the derivation is provided in the Appendix.

To derive the long run rate at which grazing is moved from one paddock to another, note that the number of paddocks that are replaced by time t constitutes a renewal process. However, unlike the case analyzed in Section 2.1, we are now not interested in the average *reward* up to time t, as t tends to infinity. Instead, we want to determine the average renewal *rate* up to time t, as t approaches infinity. To determine this rate, we appeal to Proposition 3.3.1 in Ross (1996, p. 102). This proposition tells us that the long run average renewal rate is given by the reciprocal of the expected length of a grazing cycle. We already know that the expected length of a grazing cycle is given by Equation (3). Putting these two pieces of information together, we conclude that the long run rate at which grazing is moved from one paddock to another is

$$\text{Criterion } [b] = \frac{1}{\int_0^T lf(l)dl + T\{1 - F(T)\}}. \tag{5}$$

This completes our derivation of the ecological criterion [b]. As discussed earlier in Section 2.1, in short duration grazing, the time spent grazing a particular paddock is short (five days or less) relative to the length of the idle period (four weeks or more). In other words, the success of short duration grazing depends on the rapid rotation[10] of animals from one paddock to another. Consequently, given criterion [b], one course of action for our manager would be to choose T to maximize the function in Equation (5). We now derive ecological criterion [c], the long run rate at which grazing has to be moved from one paddock to another because of adverse environmental factors.

2.3. Criterion [c]: *long run rate at which grazing has to be moved due to environmental factors*

As Westoby *et al.* (1989), Friedel (1991), Laycock (1991), and Batabyal and Godfrey (2002) have noted, range management involves the performance of a number of functions in an inherently unpredictable or stochastic environment. Further, we have already commented (see Section 1.2) on the link between detrimental environmental events and the health of a rangeland. Consequently, we now provide a heuristic derivation of ecological criterion [c], the long run rate at which the range manager moves his animals from one paddock to another because of adverse environmental factors. Complete details of this derivation can be found in the Appendix.

Note that the number of paddocks that are in breakdown mode because of the occurrence of deleterious environmental events by time t constitutes a renewal process. Therefore, let us compute $E[B]$, the average time between breakdowns. This expectation can be expressed as

$$E[B] = \frac{\int_0^T lf(l)dl + T\{1 - F(T)\}}{F(T)}. \tag{6}$$

Now, as in Section 2.2, to determine the *rate* of interest to us, we appeal to Proposition 3.3.1 in Ross (1996, p. 102). This proposition, applied to the present case, tells us that the long run *rate* at which the range manager moves his animals from one paddock to

---

10. Recall that short duration grazing is also known as rapid rotation grazing.

another because of adverse environmental factors is given by the reciprocal of the expected time between breakdowns (i.e., the reciprocal of $E[B]$ in Equation (6)). So, we have

$$\text{Criterion } [c] = \frac{F(T)}{\int_0^T lf(l)\,dl + T\{1 - F(T)\}}. \tag{7}$$

This completes our derivation of the last criterion function of this chapter. We now specify and discuss the necessary and sufficient conditions under which the economic criterion (criterion [a]) is equivalent to the two ecological criteria (criteria [b] and [c]).

2.1. Necessary and sufficient conditions

Our first result concerns the equivalence of the long run expected net cost and the long run rate at which grazing is moved from one cell to another. Equations (4) and (5) together give us

Proposition 1. $C(p) = 1 - C(e)F(T) \Leftrightarrow \text{Criterion } [a] \Leftrightarrow \text{Criterion } [b]$. Also, $C(p) = 1$, $C(e) = 0 \Rightarrow \text{Criterion } [a] \Leftrightarrow \text{Criterion } [b]$.

Our second result concerns the equivalence of the long run expected net cost and the long run rate at which grazing has to be moved from one paddock to another because of adverse environmental factors. Equations (4) and (7) together give us this result. Specifically, we have

Proposition 2. $C(p) = F(T)\{1 - C(e)\} \Leftrightarrow \text{Criterion } [a] \Leftrightarrow \text{Criterion } [c]$. Further, $C(p) = 0$, $C(e) = 1 \Rightarrow \text{Criterion } [a] \Leftrightarrow \text{Criterion } [c]$.

In words, Proposition 1 tells us that the condition $C(p) = 1 - C(e)F(T)$ is necessary and sufficient for the economic criterion (long run expected net cost) to be equivalent to the first ecological criterion (long run rate at which grazing is moved from one paddock to another). Further, the conditions $C(p) = 1$, $C(e) = 0$ are sufficient but not necessary for the same two criteria to be equivalent.

Proposition 2 provides conditions under which the economic criterion and the second ecological criterion (i.e., the long run rate at which grazing is moved from one paddock to another because of adverse environmental factors), are equivalent. In this case, the condition $C(p) = F(T)\{1 - C(e)\}$ is necessary and sufficient for the equivalence of the economic and the ecological criteria under consideration. Furthermore, the conditions $C(p) = 0$, $C(e) = 1$ are sufficient but not necessary for the equivalence of these two criteria.

In the context of a *deterministic* model of sustainable resource use, Common and Perrings showed that economic and ecological criteria ("Solow-sustainability" and "Holling-sustainability") are largely disjoint. Our analysis shows that even in the context of the management of dynamic and *stochastic* ecological-economic systems such as rangelands, economic and ecological criteria are generally not equivalent. As such, our analysis lends additional support to the extant Common and Perrings finding.

Second, Propositions 1 and 2 collectively tell us that economic and ecological management criteria are equivalent only in exceptional circumstances. For instance, Proposition 1 tells us that $C(p) = 1$ and $C(e) = 0$ are sufficient to guarantee the equivalence of the long run expected net cost and the long run rate at which grazing is moved from one paddock to another. The reader will recall that $C(e)$ is the additional cost that a manager incurs when grazing on a paddock is terminated because of the occurrence of a deleterious environmental event (a breakdown). It should be clear to the reader that when an adverse environmental event does occur, the need to re-fence paddocks and/or the need to take care of dead or diseased animals make it practically impossible to avoid additional costs. Put differently, even the weaker sufficiency conditions are unlikely to hold in practice. This means that, in general, the optimization of an economic criterion function will *not* result in the simultaneous optimization of an ecological criterion function. Consequently, if a range manager wishes to adopt an integrated ecological-economic approach to range management, then this manager will have to address economic and ecological issues *simultaneously.*

Third, what are some ways that a range manager might address ecological and economic issues simultaneously? We believe that the answer to this question is *not* general but context dependent. In other words, the criteria that govern the management of a rangeland that is used primarily for consumptive purposes (food and fiber) will typically be different from the criteria that govern the management of a rangeland that is used principally for recreation and wildlife viewing. In the former case, a manager may want to optimize an economic criterion function subject to ecological considerations that affect the underlying optimization problem as constraints. In the latter case, this manager may wish to optimize an ecological criterion function subject to economic considerations that influence the underlying optimization problem as constraints.

Finally, Brunson and Steel (1994; 1996) and others have pointed out that most public rangelands in the United States are managed under a multiple use philosophy that makes an attempt to accommodate the economic and the ecological considerations demanded by society. Given our analysis thus far, one way to approach the multiple use case — in which economic and ecological considerations can be equally important — would be to optimize a criterion function that is partly economic and partly ecological in the sense that this function is a weighted sum of economic and ecological criteria. If this approach to management is adopted, then an outstanding task for a manager would be to determine the weights. In principle, these weights can be determined by surveying the citizenry on whose behalf public range managers typically act.[11]

3. Conclusions

We addressed an issue in this chapter that, to the best our knowledge, has *not* been addressed previously in the range management

---

11. For more on this, see Brunson and Steel (1994; 1996).

literature. Specifically, we used a renewal theoretic framework to provide necessary and sufficient conditions for the equivalence of economic and ecological criteria. We noted that, in general, economic and ecological criteria are not equivalent, and then we discussed the implications of this finding for practical range management.

The analysis contained in this chapter can be extended in a number of directions, and we have two suggestions for development. First, consistent with the discussion towards the end of Section 2.4, consider two approaches to the range management problem. In the first approach, the range manager optimizes an economic criterion function subject to one or more ecological constraints. In the second approach, this manager optimizes an ecological criterion function subject to one or more economic constraints. If we think of the first approach as the "primal" approach and the second approach as the "dual" approach, then it would be useful to study the mathematical relationship between the primal and the dual approaches to the range management problem. Second, on the empirical front, it would be helpful to collect data on the costs $C(p)$ and $C(e)$ and to determine which distribution functions are most useful in modeling the "operative lifetime" random variable. Studies of range management that integrate these aspects of the problem into the analysis will provide additional insights into the behavior of rangelands whose distinguishing feature is that they are jointly determined.

Appendix

A.1. *Derivation of criterion [a]*

We first determine the expected net cost per grazing cycle. To this end, let I be an indicator variable such that

$$I = \begin{cases} 1 & \text{if } L \leq T \\ 0 & \text{if } L > T, \end{cases} \tag{A.1}$$

and L is the operative lifetime of the paddock. With this definition in place we can see that the net cost incurred by our manager per grazing cycle on a paddock (i.e., when grazing is concluded either because of the adverse environmental event or because T time periods have expired) is

$$\text{Cost per Grazing Cycle} = C(p) + C(e)I. \tag{A.2}$$

Now taking the expectation of both sides of Equation (A.2), we get

$$E[\text{Cost Per Grazing Cycle}] = C(p) + C(e)F(T). \tag{A.3}$$

We now calculate the expected amount of time that it takes to complete a grazing cycle. To this end, note that the length of a grazing cycle on the paddock is L if $L \leq T$, and it is T if $L > T$. Using this information, we get

$$E[\text{Grazing Cycle Completion Time}]$$

$$= \int_0^T lf(l)\,dl + \int_T^\infty Tf(l)\,dl, \tag{A.4}$$

where l is a realization of the operative lifetime random variable L. The second integral on the RHS of (A.4) can be simplified, giving

$$E[\text{Grazing Cycle Completion Time}]$$

$$= \int_0^T lf(l)\,dl + T\{1 - F(T)\}. \tag{A.5}$$

By the renewal-reward theorem (equation (1) in the text), criterion [a], the manager's long run average net cost function, is given by dividing (A3) by (A5). This gives

$$\text{Criterion } [a] = \frac{C(p) + C(e)F(T)}{\int_0^T lf(l)\,dl + T\{1 - F(T)\}}. \tag{A.6}$$

A.2.   *Derivation of criterion [b]*

To derive the long run rate at which grazing is moved from one paddock to another, note that the number of paddocks that are replaced by time t constitutes a renewal process. Further, the length of a grazing cycle on the paddock is L if $L \leq T$ and T if $L > T$. Hence, the expected amount of time between paddock replacements is the same as the length of a grazing cycle, and the expected length of a grazing cycle is given by (A.5). Using this information and Proposition 3.3.1 in Ross (1996, p. 102), the long run rate at which grazing is moved from one paddock to another is

$$\text{Criterion } [b] = \frac{1}{\int_0^T lf(l)\,dl + T\{1 - F(T)\}}. \tag{A.7}$$

A.3. *Derivation of criterion [c]*

Note that the number of paddocks that are in breakdown mode by time t constitutes a renewal process. As such, the average time between breakdowns, $E[B]$, can be computed by conditioning on the operative lifetime of the first paddock grazed by the manager's animals. Thus, we have $E[B] = E[E[B/\text{operative lifetime of first paddock}]]$. Now observe that

$$E[B/\text{operative lifetime of first paddock is } L]$$

$$= \begin{cases} L & \text{if } L \leq T \\ T + E[B] & \text{if } L > T. \end{cases} \tag{A.8}$$

Some algebra and (A.8) together tell us that

$$E[B] = \frac{\int_0^T lf(l)\,dl + T\{1 - F(T)\}}{F(T)}. \tag{A.9}$$

Using (A.9) and Proposition 3.3.1 in Ross (1996, p. 102), the long run rate at which grazing has to be moved from one paddock to another because of adverse environmental factors is

$$\text{Criterion } [c] = \frac{F(T)}{\int_0^T lf(l)\,dl + T\{1 - F(T)\}}. \tag{A.10}$$

References

Andelt, W.F. (1996). Carnivores. In P.R. Krausman (ed.), *Rangeland Wildlife*. Denver, Colorado: Society for Range Management.

Anderies, J.M., Janssen, M.A. and Walker, B.H. (2002). Grazing Management, Resilience, and the Dynamics of a Fire Driven Rangeland System. *Ecosystems* 5:23–44.

Batabyal, A.A. (1999). Contemporary Research in Ecological Economics: Five Outstanding Issues. *International Journal of Ecology and Environmental Sciences* 25:143–154.

Batabyal, A.A. (2004). Contemporary Theoretical Research in Range Management: Four Outstanding Issues. In A.A. Batabyal, *Stochastic Modeling in Range Management*. Hauppauge, New York: Nova Science Publishers.

Batabyal, A.A. and Godfrey, E.B. (2002). Rangeland Management under Uncertainty: A Conceptual Approach. *Journal of Range Management* 55:12–15.

Brunson, M.W. and Steel, B.S. (1994). National Public Attitudes Towards Federal Rangeland Management. *Rangelands* 16:77–81.

Brunson, M.W. and Steel, B.S. (1996). Sources of Variation in Attitudes and Beliefs About Federal Rangeland Management. *Journal of Range Management* 49:69–75.

Common, M. and Perrings, C. (1992). Towards an Ecological Economics of Sustainability. *Ecological Economics* 6:7–34.

Clark, C.W. (1973). The Economics of Overexploitation. *Science* 181: 630–634.

Clark, C.W. (1990). *Mathematical Bioeconomics*, 2nd edn. New York: Wiley.

Dasgupta, P. (1996). The Economics of the Environment. *Environment and Development Economics* 1:387–428.

Fowler, J.M. and Gray, J.R. (1986). Economic Impacts of Grazing Systems During Drought and Non-drought Years on Cattle and Sheep Ranches in New Mexico. *New Mexico Agricultural Experiment Station Bulletin 725*, Las Cruces, New Mexico.

Friedel, M.H. (1991). Range Condition Assessment and the Concept of Thresholds: A Viewpoint. *Journal of Range Management* 44:422–427.

Gordon, H.S. (1954). The Economic Theory of a Common Property Resource: The Fishery. *Journal of Political Economy* 19:124–142.

Holechek, J.L., Pieper, R.D. and Herbel, C.H. (2001). *Range Management*, 4th edn. Upper Saddle River, New Jersey: Prentice-Hall.

Holling, C.S. (1986). The Resilience of Terrestrial Ecosystems: Local Surprise and Global Change. In W.C. Clark and R.E. Munn (eds.), *Sustainable Development of the Biosphere*. Cambridge, UK: Cambridge University Press.

Holling, C.S., Schindler, D.W., Walker, B. and Roughgarden, J. (1995). Biodiversity in the Functioning of Ecosystems: An Ecological Synthesis. *In* C. Perrings, K.-G. Maler, C. Folke, C.S. Holling and B.-O. Jansson (eds.), *Biodiversity Loss*. Cambridge, UK: Cambridge University Press.

Hormay, A.L. and Evanko, A.B. (1958). Rest-rotation Grazing: A Management System for Bunchgrass Ranges. *United States Department of Agriculture California Forest and Range Experiment Station Miscellaneous Paper 27*, Washington, District of Columbia.

Huntsinger, L. and Hopkinson, P. (1996). Viewpoint: Sustaining Rangeland Landscapes: A Social and Ecological Process. *Journal of Range Management* 49:167–173.

Joyce, L.A. Mitchell, J.E. and Loftin, S.R. (2000). Applicability of Montreal Process Criterion 3 — Maintenance of Ecosystem Health — to Rangelands. *International Journal of Sustainable Development and World Ecology* 7:91–99.

Laycock, W.A. (1991). Stable States and Thresholds of Range Condition on North American Rangelands: A Viewpoint. *Journal of Range Management* 44:427–434.

Levin, S. (1999). *Fragile Dominion*. Reading, Massachusetts: Perseus Books.

McArthur, E.D., Kitchen, S.G., Uresk, D.W. and Mitchell, J.E. (2000). Applicability of Montreal Process Criterion 2 — Productive Capacity — to Rangeland Sustainability. *International Journal of Sustainable Development and World Ecology* 7:81–90.

Merrill, L.B. (1954). A Variation of Deferred Rotation Grazing for use Under Southwest Range Conditions. *Journal of Range Management* 7:152–154.

Perrings, C. and Walker, B. (1995). Biodiversity Loss and the Economics of Discontinuous Change in Semiarid Rangelands. *In* C. Perrings, K.-G. Maler, C. Folke, C.S. Holling and B.-O. Jansson (eds.), *Biodiversity Loss*. Cambridge, UK: Cambridge University Press.

Perrings, C. (1998). Resilience in the Dynamics of Economy-environment Systems. *Environmental and Resource Economics* 11:503–520.

Ross, S.M. (1996). *Stochastic Processes*, 2nd edn. New York: Wiley.

Sampson, A.W. (1913). Range Improvement by Deferred and Rotation Grazing. *United States Department of Agriculture Bulletin 34*, Washington, District of Columbia.

Savory, A. (1983). The Savory Grazing Method or Holistic Resource Management. *Rangelands* 5:155–159.

Savory, A. and Butterfield, J. (1999). *Holistic Management*, 2nd edn. Washington, District of Columbia: Island Press.

Taylor, H.M. and Karlin, S. (1998). *An Introduction to Stochastic Modeling*, 3rd edn. San Diego, California: Academic Press.

Walker, B.H. and Janssen, M.A. (2002). Rangelands, Pastoralists, and Governments — Interlinked Systems of People and Nature. *Philosophical Transactions of the Royal Society B* 357:719–725.

Ward, N. (1998). Sustainable Ranching: A Rancher's Perspective. *Rangelands* 20:33–37.

Westoby, M., Walker, B. and Noy-Meir, I. (1989). Opportunistic Management for Rangelands not at Equilibrium. *Journal of Range Management* 42:266–274.

Workman, J.P. (1986). *Ranch Economics*. New York: Macmillan.

Chapter 11

ASPECTS OF THE MANAGEMENT OF ECOLOGICAL-ECONOMIC SYSTEMS WITH A SAFE MINIMUM STANDARD

Unless there is managerial intervention, the ability of an ecological-economic system to provide humans with key services will decline probabilistically. We model such an ecological economic system with a Brownian motion process with negative drift. The manager's goal is to prevent this system's ability to provide key services from declining to a level below the so-called safe minimum standard (SMS). We model this goal rigorously and then, on the assumption that the goal is met, we characterize the steady state probability distribution function of the ecological-economic system under study.

1. Introduction

A perusal of standard texts in natural resource and environmental economics such as Conrad and Clark (1987), Hartwick and Olewiler (1998), and Kahn (1998), shows that economists have generally used the term "renewable resource" to refer to, for instance, fisheries, forests, and rangelands. Even though there is no doubt that fisheries, forests, and rangelands are both renewable[1] and resources, the use of the term "renewable resource" obscures the salient fact emanating from contemporary research that the intertemporal behavior of practically all fisheries, forests, and rangelands is governed by forces that are partly ecological and partly economic in

---

1. Meaning that they are able to provide productive inputs to an economic system, in principle, indefinitely.

nature. Therefore, following Perrings (1996), we contend that a more useful way of thinking about fisheries, forests, and rangelands is to think of them as jointly determined *ecological-economic systems*. In addition, as noted by Mangel (1985), Batabyal (1999), and others, it is important to comprehend that the dynamic behavior of such coupled ecological-economic systems is a function of forces that are routinely *stochastic* in nature.

The significant role played by uncertainty in the management of ecological-economic systems has been recognized at least since Ciriacy-Wantrup (1952)[2] and there is now a sizable literature in economics that has attempted to shed light on the myriad ways in which uncertainty affects the management problem. Batabyal (2000) shows how to compute the stability notion of persistence for stochastic ecological-economic systems and he then uses this computation to study the problem of optimal species conservation. Batabyal (2002a) focuses on a stylized ecological-economic system and uses a simple, discrete-time Markov chain model to analyze the theoretical nexuses between human actions, the survival of the so-called keystone species,[3] and the resilience[4] of the aforementioned ecological-economic system. Distinguishing between the notions of transient and asymptotic resilience and focusing specifically on a rangeland, Batabyal (2002b) demonstrates how the theory of associated random variables can be used to compute an upper bound for the transient resilience of this rangeland.

---

2. Ciriacy-Wantrup did not use the term "ecological-economic system" in his 1952 book but the more traditional term "renewable resource." However, a perusal of his book leaves little doubt that he was, in fact, referring to what we have called "ecological-economic systems" in this chapter.

3. According to Krebs (1994, p. 554, emphasis in original), within a specific ecological-economic system, a "role may be occupied by a single species, and the presence of that role may be critical to the community. Such important species are called *keystone species* because their activities determine community structure."

4. The term resilience has two meanings in the ecology literature. The first meaning, due to Pimm (1984), focuses on stability near an equilibrium and emphasizes the speed of return to this equilibrium. In contrast, the second meaning (and the meaning we are using in this chapter) is due to Holling (1973) and it concentrates on conditions far from an equilibrium where perturbations can flip a system into an alternate stability domain.

Batabyal *et al.* (2003) were among the first to use the Ornstein–Uhlenbeck stochastic process to model an ecological-economic system. In this paper, the focus is on a lake that is characterized by two stable states and one unstable state. These researchers show how the Ornstein–Uhlenbeck process can be fruitfully used to not only characterize the resilience of the underlying lake but also to obtain a numerical scarcity value for the ecosystem service provided by this lake. Batabyal (2004) extends the human actions, keystone species, and resilience analysis in Batabyal (2002a) in two ways. First, the focus here is also on a discrete-time Markov chain model but with a larger number of states. Second, there are a greater number of keystone species. Using this more general model, Batabyal analyzes an important kind of interaction between the keystone species of the ecological economic system under study.

Higgins *et al.* (2007) study savanna rangelands and use a simulation model to show that conservative management strategies are superior to opportunistic strategies. Livestock grazing management in semi-arid rangelands is the subject of the paper by Baumgartner and Quaas (2009). These authors introduce the notion of "viability" and show that this notion is very useful in providing an operational criterion for strong sustainability in the context of semi-arid rangelands. Domptail and Nuppenau (2010) analyze commercial ranches in Namibia and point out that the incorporation of rainfall uncertainty in decision making is critical in comprehending land use strategies in arid, rain-fed rangelands. Wang and Ewald (2010) model the human exploitation of a two-species fishery as a stochastic differential game and then derive the Nash equilibrium, Markov feedback strategies. Specifically, these authors compare and contrast these strategies with alternate strategies that limit harvest to a single fish species. Finally, Crepin *et al.* (2011) present a method for studying non-convex dynamics in a coupled ecological-economic system and then contend that the "prices versus quantities" debate in environmental economics needs to be revisited using the lens of a complex adaptive system.

The literature that we have just reviewed clearly demonstrates that the optimal management of ecological-economic systems is challenging because of the presence of what Ready and Bishop (1991, p. 309) call "pure uncertainty." In addition, Margolis and Naevdal (2008) have pointed out that the management function is made even more challenging because managerial actions may result in irreversible change to some aspect of a managed ecological-economic system. Given this state of affairs, we contend that the studies discussed in the preceding three paragraphs have advanced our understanding of several aspects of the management of stochastic ecological-economic systems. Even so, it should be noted that the extant literature has paid insufficient *theoretical* attention to the management of ecological-economic systems in the presence of both *uncertainty* and potential *irreversibility.*

More than 50 years ago, Ciriacy-Wantrup (1952) suggested that when uncertainty and irreversibility are issues, the management function ought to pay attention to the establishment of what he called a "safe minimum standard" (SMS). The idea here is to manage an ecological-economic system so that this system's ability to provide humans with a flow of key ecosystem services[5] does not fall below a particular standard, namely, the SMS. We would like to point out that in addition to the claim made at the end of the previous paragraph, there are also very few theoretical analyses of the management of stochastic ecological-economic systems in which the manager explicitly incorporates a SMS in his decision making. Therefore, the central objective of this chapter is to conduct such a theoretical analysis.

The remainder of this chapter is organized as follows. Section 2 uses the theory of Brownian motion processes with drift to delineate our theoretical model of a stylized ecological-economic system. Next, this section shows the manner in which we incorporate a SMS in the manager's decision making. On the assumption that the manager is successful in keeping this ecological-economic system's

---

5. Examples of such services include food production, nutrient cycling, storm protection, and waste decomposition.

ability to provide key services above the SMS, Section 3 computes the steady state probability distribution function of the ecological-economic system under study and then discusses an implication of this computation. Finally, Section 4 concludes and then discusses ways in which the research described in this chapter might be extended.

2. The Theoretical Framework

Consider an arbitrary ecological-economic system such as a fishery, a forest, or a rangeland, whose evolution over time is determined by both deterministic and stochastic factors. We shall model this system with a Brownian motion process denoted by $\{X(t) : t \geq 0\}$. In other words, $X(t)$ represents this ecological-economic system's ability to provide humans with a flow of key ecosystem services at time t. Human use of this ecological-economic system commences at time $t = 0$ and hence this is also the time at which a manager is entrusted with the management of this system. At time $t = 0$, the ecological-economic system under study is devoid of any human influence and hence, moving forward in time, this system is able to provide humans with a flow of salient ecosystem services. We model this aspect of the problem by supposing that $X(0) = z > 0$.

Consistent with the discussion in Section 1, if there is human use of the ecological-economic system under study and there is no managerial intervention of any kind then the ability of the ecological-economic system to provide humans with key services will decline probabilistically. We model this feature of the problem by supposing that our Brownian motion process $\{X(t) : t \geq 0\}$ has a drift coefficient β where $\beta < 0$.[6] To model the potential irreversibility mentioned in Section 1, we contend that our ecological-economic system's ability to provide humans with a flow of key ecosystem

---

6. See Karlin and Taylor (1975, Chapter 7) and Ross (1996, Chapter 8) for textbook expositions of Brownian motion processes with drift.

services will be irreversibly impaired when the Brownian motion process $\{X(t) : t \geq 0\}$ becomes negative. Given this state of affairs, the use of a SMS to manage our ecological-economic system means that our manager's objective is to *never* allow $\{X(t) : t \geq 0\}$ to become negative. Our task now is to compute the steady state probability distribution function of the ecological-economic system under study when the above described SMS is used to manage it.

3.   The Steady State Probability Distribution Function

Let $\text{Prob}\{x, t : z\}$ be the probability distribution or density function that we seek to characterize. In words, $\text{Prob}\{\cdot\}$ is the density function of the state (the ability to provide humans with key ecosystem services) at time t given that the initial value of this state is $X(0) = z > 0$. Using Kolmogorov's forward diffusion equation or equation 8.5.2 in Ross (1996, p. 385), we get[7]

$$\frac{1}{2}\frac{\partial^2 \text{Prob}\{\cdot\}}{\partial x^2} = \beta\frac{\partial \text{Prob}\{\cdot\}}{\partial x} + \frac{\partial \text{Prob}\{\cdot\}}{\partial t}. \tag{1}$$

Note that in the steady state, the probability distribution function $\text{Prob}\{\cdot\}$ is independent of time. In symbols, this means that

$$\lim_{t \to \infty} \text{Prob}\{x, t : z\} = \text{Prob}\{x : z\}. \tag{2}$$

Now, using Equation (2) and taking the limit as time t goes to infinity, we can rewrite Equation (1) above. This gives us

$$\frac{1}{2}\frac{\partial^2 \text{Prob}\{x : z\}}{\partial x^2} = \beta\frac{\partial \text{Prob}\{x : z\}}{\partial x}. \tag{3}$$

Simplifying Equation (3), we get

$$\frac{\partial \text{Prob}\{x : z\}}{\partial x} = 2\beta \text{Prob}\{x : z\} + c_1, \tag{4}$$

---

7. See Ross (1996, pp. 383–393) for a more detailed discussion of the methodology we use in this chapter.

where c_1 is a constant. To determine the value of the constant c_1 in Equation (4), we use our previous contention that the SMS using manager is *successful* in ensuring that the ability of the ecological-economic system to provide humans with a flow of key ecosystem services is always maintained. This means that the potential irreversibility alluded to in Section 2 is avoided and hence the Brownian motion process $\{X(t) : t \geq 0\}$ under study never becomes negative. In symbols, this means that

$$\text{Prob}\{x : z\} = 0 \quad \text{when } x < 0. \tag{5}$$

Equation (5) tells us that the constant $c_1 = 0$.

Since the constant $c_1 = 0$, simplifying Equation (4), we infer that

$$\frac{\partial \text{Prob}\{x : z\}}{\partial x} = 2\beta \text{Prob}\{x : z\} \Rightarrow \frac{\partial \text{Prob}\{x : z\}/\partial x}{\text{Prob}\{x : z\}} = 2\beta. \tag{6}$$

Integrating the expression on the right hand side (RHS) of Equation (6) gives us

$$\log_e[\text{Prob}\{x : z\}] = 2\beta_x + c_2, \tag{7}$$

where c_2 is another constant.

Finally, simplifying Equation (7), we get

$$\text{Prob}\{x : z\} = 2\beta e^{2\beta x}. \tag{8}$$

Comparing the probability distribution function given in Equation (8) with Table 1.4.2 in Ross (1996, p. 18) it is clear that the steady state or limiting distribution of our ecological-economic system that is managed with a SMS is exponential with parameter or rate β.

It is well known that the exponential distribution is memoryless.[8] In the context of the management of this chapter's stochastic

---

8. See Ross (1996, pp. 35–39) or Tijms (2003, pp. 440–441) for a textbook discussion of this property.

ecological-economic system with a SMS, this feature has an interesting implication. Specifically, we see that the manager's success in ensuring that our ecological-economic system's ability to provide humans with a flow of key ecosystem services is *not* irreversibly impaired means that the steady state — and only the steady state — probabilistic behavior of this ecological-economic system is "history independent." This means that this system's limiting ability to provide key ecosystem services will not reflect the previous success of managerial actions in avoiding the irreversibility mentioned in Section 2.

4. Conclusions

This chapter studied aspects of the management of stochastic ecological-economic systems with a SMS. Specifically, we first used the theory of Brownian motion processes with negative drift to describe a stylized ecological-economic system. Second, we showed how to introduce a SMS in our manager's decision making. Third, on the assumption that the manager is successful in keeping the ecological-economic system's ability to provide key services above the so-called safe minimum standard, we computed the steady state or limiting probability distribution function of the ecological-economic system under study. Finally, we discussed an interesting implication of our computation of the steady state probability distribution function.

The analysis in this chapter can be extended in a number of different directions. Here are two examples of such extensions. First, it would be useful to study the probabilistic behavior of the ecological-economic system under study when, in addition to a SMS, the manager uses other policy instruments as well. Second, it would be helpful to investigate the stochastic behavior of our ecological-economic system when managerial actions are able to influence the magnitude of the drift coefficient β over time. Studies of the management of stochastic ecological-economic systems that incorporate these aspects of the problem into the analysis will permit a more nuanced understanding of these systems and hence provide valuable guidance about the desirability of alternate ways of managing such coupled systems.

References

Batabyal, A.A. (1999). Contemporary Research in Ecological Economics: Five Outstanding Issues. *International Journal of Ecology and Environmental Sciences* 25:143–154.

Batabyal, A.A. (2000). Aspects of Ecosystem Persistence and the Optimal Conservation of Species. *International Review of Economics and Finance* 9:69–77.

Batabyal, A.A. (2002a). Human Actions, the Survival of Keystone Species, and the Resilience of Ecological-economic Systems. *Resources Policy* 28:153–157.

Batabyal, A.A. (2002b). An Upper Bound for the Transient Resilience of a Rangeland that is Managed using Cell Grazing. *Journal of Economic Research* 7:151–160.

Batabyal, A.A. (2004). On the Links between Managerial Actions, Keystone Species, and the Resilience of Ecological-economic Systems. *Brazilian Journal of Business Economics* 4:51–58.

Batabyal, A.A., Kahn, J.R. and O'Neill, R.V. (2003). On the Scarcity Value of Ecosystem Services. *Journal of Environmental Economics and Management* 46:334–352.

Baumgartner, S. and Quaas, M.F. (2009). Ecological-economic Viability as a Criterion of Strong Sustainability Under Uncertainty. *Ecological Economics* 68:2008–2020.

Ciriacy-Wantrup, S.V. (1952). *Resource Conservation.* Berkeley, California: University of California Press.

Conrad, J.M. and Clark, C.W. (1987). *Natural Resource Economics.* Cambridge, UK: Cambridge University Press.

Crepin, A.S., Norberg, J. and Maler, K.-G. (2011). Coupled Ecological-economic Systems with Slow and Fast Dynamics — Modeling and Analysis Method. *Ecological Economics* 70:1448–1458.

Domptail, S. and Nuppenau, E.A. (2010). The Role of Uncertainty and Expectations in Modeling (Range) land Use Strategies: An Application of Dynamic Optimization Modeling with Recursion. *Ecological Economics* 69:2475–2485.

Hartwick, J.M. and Olewiler, N.D. (1998). *The Economics of Natural Resource Use*, 2nd edn. Reading, Massachusetts: Addison-Wesley.

Higgins, S.I., Kantelhardt, J., Scheiter, S. and Boerner, J. (2007). Sustainable Management of Extensively Managed Savanna Rangelands. *Ecological Economics* 62:102–114.

Holling, C. S. (1973). Resilience and Stability of Ecological Systems. *Annual Review of Ecology and Systematics* 4:1–23.

Kahn, J.R. (1998). *The Economic Approach to Environmental and Natural Resources*, 2nd edn. Fort Worth, Texas: Dryden Press.

Karlin, S. and Taylor, H.M. (1975). *A First Course in Stochastic Processes*, 2nd edn. San Diego, California: Academic Press.

Krebs, C.J. (1994). *Ecology*, 4th edn. Menlo Park, California: Addison-Wesley Longman.

Mangel, M. (1985). *Decision and Control in Uncertain Resource Systems*. San Diego, California: Academic Press.

Margolis, M. and Naevdal, E. (2008). Safe Minimum Standards in Dynamic Resource Problems: Conditions for Living on the Edge of Risk. *Environmental and Resource Economics* 40:401–423.

Perrings, C. (1996). Ecological Resilience in the Sustainability of Economic Development. *In* S. Faucheux, D. Pearce and J. Proops (eds.), *Models of Sustainable Development*. Cheltenham, UK: Edward Elgar.

Pimm, S.L. (1984). The Complexity and Stability of Ecosystems. *Nature* 307:321–326.

Ready, R.C. and Bishop, R.C. (1991). Endangered Species and the Safe Minimum Standard. *American Journal of Agricultural Economics* 73:309–312.

Ross, S. M. (1996). *Stochastic Processes*, 2nd edn. New York: Wiley.

Tijms, H.C. (2003). *A First Course in Stochastic Models*. Chichester, UK: Wiley.

Wang, W.K. and Ewald, C.O. (2010). A Stochastic Differential Fishery Game for a Two Species Fish Population with Ecological Interaction. *Journal of Economic Dynamics and Control* 34:844–857.

Part V

Invasive Species Management

Chapter 12

A THEORETICAL ANALYSIS OF RANDOM INSPECTIONS AND FINES IN INVASIVE SPECIES MANAGEMENT[1]

with S.J. Yoo

In this chapter, we conduct a theoretical analysis of inspections in a stochastic environment and we shed light on two hitherto unstudied issues concerning inspections in the context of invasive species management. First, given a particular port of entry in a country, we study the properties of a *random* inspection scheme. Second, we compute the average total *fines* that will be collected in the long run by an inspection agency that uses the above inspection scheme to screen arriving ships for the presence of one or more invasive species.

1. Introduction

There is no gainsaying the fact that we now live in an era of globalization. The phenomena of globalization in general and shocking recent events involving terrorism in the United States (US), Spain, and the United Kingdom have generated great interest in issues concerning security across the world. In the US in particular, this interest has manifested itself in the substantially increased interest in inspecting goods that are brought into the country from other parts of the world by means of airplanes, trucks, and, perhaps most

1. Batabyal acknowledges financial support from the Gosnell endowment at RIT. The usual disclaimer applies.

notably, ships. This concern with seaport security in particular is not misplaced. As *The Economist* (Anonymous, 2006) has recently noted, only about 5% of the containers that bring 2 billion tons of cargo to US seaports are actually inspected. Therefore, it is not difficult at all for all kinds of illegal goods and possibly detrimental animal and plant species to get into the US.

Batabyal (2004), Work *et al.* (2005) and DeAngelo *et al.* (2007) have clearly demonstrated that in addition to transporting goods between regions, airplanes, trucks, and ships have unwittingly also managed to carry all manner of invasive plant and animal species[2] from one part of the world to another. This inadvertent carriage has taken place in many different ways. Three examples follow. First, on occasion, invasive animal species have succeeded in lodging them-selves in the landing gear of airplanes and, in this way, they have trav-eled as stowaways from one part of the world to another. Second, a number of marine invasive species have been introduced inadver-tently into a particular part of the world by ships dumping their ballast water. Cargo ships often carry ballast water in order to boost vessel stability when they are not carrying full loads. When these ships come into a seaport, this ballast water must be discarded before cargo can be loaded. Finally, and perhaps most significantly, ships and trucks have introduced invasive species into a particular part of the world by means of the containers they routinely use to carry cargo from one part of the world to another. In this context, the reader should understand that invasive species can remain concealed in containers for extended periods of time. In addition, the mate-rial such as wood that is commonly used to pack the cargo in the containers may itself contain invasive species.

Biological invasions of new habitats by non-native species have frequently resulted in great losses to society. For the US alone, the extent of these losses is massive. In this regard, Keller and Lodge

---

2. Invasive species are also referred to as alien species, as exotic species, and as non-native species.

(2007) have noted that the state of Indiana spends more than $600,000 each year to control a particular invasive species, namely, the *Eurasian watermilfoil*. Similarly, Kolar and Lodge (2001) have pointed out that the total costs of all invasive species is around $137 billion per year. In addition to these economic costs, invasive species have also given rise to serious biological damage. For instance, Vitousek *et al.* (1996) have demonstrated that invasive species can change ecosystem processes, act as vectors of diseases, and diminish biological diversity. Cox (1993) has pointed out that out of 256 vertebrate extinctions with a known cause, 109 are the outcome of biological invasions. The implication of the discussion in this paragraph is clear. Invasive species have frequently been a great menace to society.

Broadly speaking, there are two kinds of managerial actions that one can take to control the spread of invasive species and their deleterious effects. These are *pre-invasion* and *post-invasion* actions. The purpose of pre-invasion actions is to preclude non-native species from invading a new habitat. In contrast, post-invasion actions are intended to control a non-native species, given that this species has already invaded a new habitat. In recent times, several researchers have analyzed a particular kind of pre-invasion action, namely, inspections. McAusland and Costello (2004) have shown that when one considers the future effects of current invasive species introductions, one is led to a course of action that may involve the use of higher or lower tariffs but certainly involves more stringent inspections. Batabyal and Nijkamp (2005) have shown that in an inspection cycle, the so-called "container policy" is preferable to the so-called "temporal policy" because the former policy leads to lower long run expected net costs from inspections. Using a model of seaport inspections, Batabyal (2006; 2008) has provided a rationale for and has developed aspects of the differential regulatory treatment of imports when invasive species are a potential problem. Batabyal and Yoo (2006) have analyzed the statistical properties of what they call a generic container inspection policy. Finally, DeAngelo *et al.* (2007) have used a queuing theoretic model of inspections to show that the question as to whether there is or is not a tension between the objectives of economic cost reduction and biological invasion damage control cannot be resolved unambiguously.

The papers discussed in the previous paragraph have surely advanced many aspects of our understanding of the role of inspections in invasive species management. Even so, there are two salient issues about inspections that have received *no* attention in the literature. Hence, in this chapter, we conduct a theoretical analysis of these two hitherto unstudied issues in a stochastic environment. Specifically, in Section 2.1, we describe a stylized model of inspections in which ships — possibly with injurious invasive species — arrive at a seaport in a country called Home. Next, in Section 2.2, we study the properties of a *random* inspection scheme. Then, in Section 2.3, we compute the average total *fines* that will be collected in the long run by an inspection agency that uses the above inspection scheme to screen arriving ships for the presence of invasive species. Finally, Section 3 concludes and then makes suggestions for extending the research described in this chapter.

2.   The Theoretical Model

2.1.   *Preliminaries*

Consider a port of entry such as a seaport in an arbitrary country called Home.[3] Our subsequent analysis is conducted from the perspective of an inspection agency that has been entrusted with the task of inspecting arriving ships in this seaport for the presence of one or more invasive species. The reader should note that as used in this chapter, the term "inspection" refers to the examination of the containers that are used by ships to transport cargo or to the

---

3. We stress that our subsequent analysis does *not* depend on the port of entry being a seaport. Our analysis would go through for land ports of entry — such as a border crossing or an airport — as well.

examination of the ballast water occasionally held by arriving ships or to the examination of both containers and ballast water.

Home engages in goods trade with a whole host of nations and hence ships from these various nations arrive in our seaport in Home to unload and/or to load cargo. Now, as noted in Batabyal (2006; 2008), the risk of inadvertent biological invasions in Home typically varies by trading partner. Therefore, consistent with the analysis in Batabyal (2006; 2008), we suppose that our seaport inspection agency has distinct protocols for inspecting the arriving ships from distinct nations. Put differently, ships arriving from country A are treated differently than ships arriving from country B, for any two arbitrary countries A and B. Let us now delineate the random inspection scheme that is the first of two key issues that we are studying in this chapter.[4]

2.2. *Random inspection scheme*

We focus on the ships coming into the seaport under study from some arbitrary country — say country A — that is also a trading partner of Home. These ships come into the Home seaport over time and sequentially. We suppose that on the basis of previously collected historical data, our seaport inspection agency has determined that there is a fixed probability p that a given arriving ship from country A will have one or more invasive species on it. Hence, such an arriving ship will fail to pass our agency's inspection. We also suppose that whether a particular ship from country A does or does not have a problem with invasive species does not depend on the status of any other ship arriving in the Home seaport from this same country A.

Our seaport inspection agency in Home proceeds as follows. Initially, it inspects every ship from country A until i consecutive

---

4. This random inspection scheme is based on the "continuous sampling" plan first formulated by Dodge (1943) and subsequently extended by White (1966) and by Bebbington *et al.* (2003).

ships are found not to have any invasive species on them. Once this happens, our agency then inspects only one out of every r ships from country A at *random* until another ship with one or more invasive species on it is discovered. When this happens, our agency reverts to 100% inspections until i consecutive ships with no invasive species on them are found. The agency's inspection continues in this way. The task before us now is to compute the average fraction of all country A ships that are and are not inspected. In what follows, we shall use the acronyms AFSI and AFSNI to refer to these two averages. Our computation proceeds in three steps.

In the first step, let state D_k ($k = 0, 1, 2, \ldots, i - 1$) denote the k consecutive country A ships with no invasive species that have been found during the one hundred percent inspection part of the scheme. Also, let state D_i denote the fact that the inspection scheme under study is in the second stage in which one out of every r country A ships is being inspected randomly. Time n follows the nth ship, whether or not it is inspected. Now, the reader should note that the above described sequence of states is a Markov chain.[5] The transition probability of this chain is given by $P_{jk} =$ Prob{state is D_k after $n{+}1$ ships/state is D_j after n ships}. Mathematically, we have

$$
P_{jk} = \begin{cases} p & \text{for } k = 0, \ 0 \le j \le i, \\ 1 - p & \text{for } k = j + 1 \le i, \\ p/r & \text{for } k = 0, \ j = i, \\ 1 - (p/r) & \text{for } k = j = i, \\ 0 & \text{otherwise.} \end{cases} \tag{1}
$$

In the second step, we specify the limiting probabilities for the Markov chain whose transition probabilities are given in Equation (1) and then we solve the equations that are satisfied by

---

5. For textbook accounts of Markov chains, the reader should consult Taylor and Karlin (1998, Chapter 4) or Ross (2003, Chapter 4).

these limiting probabilities. To this end, let π_k be the limiting probability that the stochastic system we are studying is in state D_k for $k = 0, 1, 2, \ldots, i$. To solve for these limiting probabilities, we have to specify the equations that these limiting probabilities satisfy. These equations are

$$p\pi_0 + p\pi_1 + \cdots + p\pi_{i-1} + (p/r)\pi_i = \pi_0, \tag{2}$$

$$(1 - p)\pi_0 = \pi_1, \tag{3}$$

$$(1 - p)\pi_1 = \pi_2, \tag{4}$$

and we keep going in this manner until we get to

$$(1 - p)\pi_{i-1} + \{1 - (p/r)\}\pi_i = \pi_i \tag{5}$$

and

$$\pi_0 + \pi_1 + \pi_2 + \cdots + \pi_i = 1. \tag{6}$$

Manipulating Equations (3) through (5) we can tell that $\pi_k = (1-p)^k \pi_0$ for $k = 0, 1, \ldots, i-1$. Similarly, simplifying Equation (5) we get $\pi_i = (r/p)(1-p)^i \pi_0$. Having ascertained π_k in terms of π_0 for $k = 0, 1, \ldots, i$, we can now use Equation (6) and then simplify the resulting expression to get

$$\pi_0 = \frac{p}{1 + (r-1)(1-p)^i}, \quad \pi_i = \frac{r(1-p)^i}{1 + (r-1)(1-p)^i},$$

$$\pi_k = \frac{p(1-p)^k}{1 + (r-1)(1-p)^i}, \quad k = 0, 1, \ldots i-1. \tag{7}$$

In the third step, we provide explicit closed-form expressions for the two averages of interest, that is, AFSI and AFSNI respectively. Because each ship is inspected when in states $D_0, D_1, \ldots, D_{i-1}$ but only one out of r ships is inspected in state D_i, we can infer that AFSI $= (\pi_0 + \pi_1 + \cdots + \pi_{i-1}) + (1/r)\pi_i$. Simplifying this last expression and then using the fact that AFSNI $= 1 -$ AFSI, we get

$$\text{AFSI} = \frac{1}{1 + (r-1)(1-p)^i} \quad \text{and} \quad \text{AFSNI} = \frac{(r-1)(1-p)^i}{1 + (r-1)(1-p)^i}. \tag{8}$$

Equation (8) tells us that in the random inspection scheme of this chapter, the average fraction of arriving ships from country A that are inspected depends fundamentally on the fixed probability p that a given arriving ship will have one or more invasive species on it and on the positive integer r describing the number of ships out of which one will be inspected at random in the second stage. It is straightforward to verify that when either $p = 1$ or $r = 1$, our random inspection scheme becomes a deterministic scheme in which all arriving ships from country A are inspected by the agency. Finally, when $p = 0$, the average fraction of ships that are inspected depends only on the positive integer r and as r increases (decreases), the average fraction of ships inspected decreases (increases). This completes the discussion of the first of two key issues that we are studying in this chapter. We now proceed to the second key issue. This involves computing the average total fines that will be collected in the long run by our inspection agency when it uses the random inspection scheme of this section to screen arriving ships for the presence of invasive species.

2.3. *Average total fines*

In the previous section, we described the way in which our random inspection scheme would work for ships arriving from a particular country A. However, it is clear that in addition to country A, ships from many other countries — with which Home trades — also arrive in the seaport under study. Further, there is an inspection protocol in place for the ships from every relevant country. Having said this, the next question that arises concerns the status of ships that fail our agency's inspection. In practice, agencies responsible for the management of invasive species in many countries such as Japan and the US levy fines on non-compliant entities.[6] Therefore, in the

---

6. For a more detailed corroboration of this claim, see Wanamaker (2008) and go to www.env.go.jp/en/nature/as/040427.pdf, www.state.hi.us/dlnr/Aliens3.html and www.aphis.usda.gov/lpa/pubs/fsheet_faq_notice/fs_ phcivilp.html.

remainder of this section, we suppose that ships — from all the pertinent countries — that fail our agency's inspection are fined and that the magnitude of these fines depends on the extent to which a particular ship is not in compliance with existing laws and regulations in Home. Put differently, the magnitude (dollar value) of the individual ship fines are *random* variables.

To model this feature of the problem, we proceed as follows. At the beginning of each time period, ships from the various countries with which Home trades arrive in the seaport under study at the times of a renewal process with distribution law given by $F(x)$. We suppose that for every arriving ship, there is an inspector available to inspect this ship. Upon the completion of the inspection process, each ship pays a random fine to our agency and the amounts of this fine are described by the distribution law $G(y)$ where $y > 0$.[7] Let $W(t)$ denote the total amount of all the fines from the various ships that have been collected by our inspection agency by time t. The outstanding task before us now is to provide an explicit stochastic characterization of the total amount $W(t)$.

To this end, let Υ_1, Υ_2, $\Upsilon_3,\ldots$ denote the successive individual ship fines and let $N(t)$ denote the total number of ships that arrive in the Home seaport in the time interval $(0, t]$. We can now express the fine total $W(t)$ as a particular sum and that sum is

$$W(t) = \Sigma_{k=1}^{N(t)+1}\ \Upsilon_k. \tag{9}$$

The reader will note that the sum $W(t)$ in Equation (9) is a random variable. Therefore, it makes sense to focus not on $W(t)$ *per se* but on its expectation $E[W(t)]$. Consistent with the discussion in Section 1, the most convenient way to compute the above expectation would

---

7. If we were to explicitly separate fine paying ships from non-fine paying ships then the under-lying mathematics would get unduly complicated. Therefore, to keep the subsequent mathematics straightforward, we are supposing that every ship pays a fine. The reader should *not* interpret this modeling feature literally. Put differently, the reader should interpret the "fines" paid by ships that pass inspection as a processing fee and not as a punitive measure. Having said this, the salient point to note here is that the individual ship fines are *random* variables and we are explicitly modeling this point.

be to take a long run view of inspections and fines and compute the limiting expectation given by $\lim_{t \to \infty} E[W(t)]/t$. Now, the theory of renewal processes[8] tells us that $\lim_{t \to \infty} E[W(t)]/t = E[Y]/E[X]$, where Y and X denote the fines and time respectively. The two expectations on the righthandside (RHS) of the previous expression can be simplified further. This simplification gives us the limiting expectation we seek in its simplest form. Specifically, we get

$$\lim_{t \to \infty} \frac{E[W(t)]}{t} = \frac{E[Y]}{E[X]} = \frac{\int_0^\infty \{1 - G(y)\} dy}{\int_0^\infty \{1 - F(x)\} dx}. \qquad (10)$$

Equation (10) gives us a closed-form expression for the average total fines that will be collected in the long run by our inspection agency when it uses the random inspection scheme of Section 2.2 to screen arriving ships for the presence of invasive species. The information contained in Equation (10) can be used to facilitate the general task of invasive species management in two ways. First, this equation can be used to determine whether it is feasible to make the conduct of inspections by our agency a revenue-neutral operation. Put differently, the objective here would be to ascertain whether it is possible to meet the agency's costs with the revenue from the collected fines. Second, Equation (10) can play the role of a constraint in an expected net social benefit from inspections maximization problem. The idea here would be to conduct ship inspections efficiently so that the net social benefit from inspections is maximized and, at the same time, the fine based revenue generated by these inspections does not fall below an exogenously given threshold. This concludes our discussion of the second key issue of this chapter.

3. Conclusions

In this chapter, we conducted a theoretical analysis of inspections in a stochastic environment and we shed light on two hitherto

---

8. For textbook expositions of renewal theory, the reader should consult Taylor and Karlin (1998, Chapter 7) or Ross (2003, Chapter 7).

unstudied issues concerning inspections in the context of invasive species management. First, given a particular port of entry, we analyzed the properties of a random inspection scheme. Second, we computed the average total fines that will be collected in the long run by an inspection agency that uses the above inspection scheme to screen arriving ships for the presence of one or more invasive species.

The analysis in this chapter can be extended in a number of directions. Here are two suggestions for extending the research described in this chapter. First, we treated the probability p that an individual ship from a particular country will have one or more invasive species on it as exogenous to the analysis. Therefore, it would be useful to formally study the estimation of this important probability. Second, following the discussion towards the end of Section 2.3, it would be useful to set up and solve an optimization problem involving the efficient allocation of inspection resources and the attainment of a threshold level of revenue from fines. Studies of inspections in invasive species management that incorporate these features of the problem into the analysis will provide further insights into a management function that has significant economic and ecological implications.

References

Anonymous. (2006). Trouble on the Waterfront. *The Economist*, February 23.

Batabyal, A.A. (2004). A Research Agenda for the Study of the Regulation of Invasive Species Introduced Unintentionally via Maritime Trade. *Journal of Economic Research* 9:191–216.

Batabyal, A.A. (2006). A Rationale for the Differential Regulatory Treatment of Imports When Invasive Species are a Potential Problem. *Studies in Regional Science* 36:179–187.

Batabyal, A.A. (2008). Two Theoretical Issues Concerning the Differential Treatment of Trading Partners in Alien Species Management. *Ecological Economics* 64:679–682.

Batabyal, A.A. and Nijkamp, P. (2005). On Container versus Time Based Inspection Policies in Invasive Species Management. *Stochastic Environmental Research and Risk Assessment* 19:340–347.

Batabyal, A.A. and Yoo, S.J. (2006). Some Statistical Properties of a Generic Container Inspection Policy in Invasive Species Management. *Ecological Economics* 60:1–4.

Bebbington, M., Lai, C. and Govindaraju, K. (2003). Continuous Sampling Plans for Markov-Dependent Production Processes Under Limited Inspection Capacity. *Mathematical and Computer Modelling* 38:1137–1145.

Cox, G.W. (1993). *Conservation Ecology*. Dubuque, Iowa: W.C. Brown Publishers.

DeAngelo, G.J., Batabyal, A.A. and Kumar, S. (2007). An Analysis of Economic Cost Minimization and Biological Invasion Damage Control. *Annals of Regional Science* 41:639–655.

Dodge, H.F. (1943). A Sampling Inspection Plan for Continuous Production. *Annals of Mathematical Statistics* 14:264–279.

Keller, R.P. and Lodge, D.M. (2007). Species Invasions from Commerce in Live Aquatic Organisms: Problems and Possible Solutions. *BioScience* 57:428–436.

Kolar, C.S. and Lodge, D.M. (2001). Progress in Invasion Biology: Predicting Invaders. *Trends in Ecology and Evolution* 16:199–204.

McAusland, C. and Costello, C. (2004). Avoiding Invasives: Trade-related Policies for Controlling Unintentional Exotic Species Introductions. *Journal of Environmental Economics and Management* 48:954–977.

Ross, S.M. (2003). *Introduction to Probability Models*, 8th edn. San Diego, California: Academic Press.

Taylor, H.M. and Karlin, S. (1998). *Introduction to Stochastic Modeling*, 3rd edn. San Diego, California: Academic Press.

Vitousek, P.M., D'Antonio, C.M., Loope, L.L. and Westbrooks, R. (1996). Biological Invasions as Global Environmental Change. *American Scientist* 84:468–478.

Wanamaker, T. (2008). New Rules Help Stop Invasive Species. *Watertown Daily Times*, May 25.

White, L.S. (1966). The Evaluation of H 106 Continuous Sampling Plans under the Assumption of Worst Conditions. *Journal of the American Statistical Association* 61:833–841.

Work, T.T., McCullough, D.G., Cavey, J.F. and Komsa, R. (2005). Arrival Rate of Nonindigenous Insect Species into the United States through Foreign Trade. *Biological Invasions* 7:323–332.

Chapter 13

TRADE, THE DAMAGE FROM ALIEN SPECIES, AND THE EFFECTS OF PROTECTIONISM UNDER ALTERNATE MARKET STRUCTURES[1]

We first construct three measures of the expected damage from the uninten-tional introduction of alien species into a country called Home. We then focus on four market structures. First, perfect competition prevails in both Home and Foreign, and Home is a small country. Second, the Home and the Foreign markets are both perfectly competitive, but Home is now a large country. Third, the exporter in Foreign is a monopolist and there are no import com-peting firms in Home. Finally, the Foreign exporter and the import competing firm in Home engage in Cournot competition. In all four scenarios, we ana-lyze the impact of small and optimal Home tariffs on prices, exports, imports, the damage from alien species, and social welfare in Home. *Inter alia*, our analysis identifies conditions under which it makes sense to use trade policy (tariffs) to regulate invasive species and conditions under which it does not.

1. We thank the Editor J. Barkley Rosser and three anonymous referees for their helpful comments on a previous version of this chapter. In addition, we thank participants at (i) the 2005 Midwest Economic Theory and International Economics meeting in Lawrence, Kansas, (ii) an IEFS session in the 2006 ASSA meeting in Boston, (iii) the 2006 WRSA meeting in Santa Fe, New Mexico, (iv) the 2006 NARSC meeting in Toronto and (v) the economics department in SUNY Binghamton, for their comments. Finally, Batabyal acknowledges financial support from USDA's PREISM program by means of Cooperative Agreement 43-3AEM-4-80100 and from the Gosnell endowment at RIT. The usual disclaimer applies.

1. Introduction

The fact that alien species (also known as invasive or non-native species) have been and continue to be introduced into one part of the world from another is not new. What is new is the realization that such introductions, particularly the unintentional ones, have often been very costly for the concerned nations. In this regard, consider the case of the United States. A report by the Office of Technology Assessment (OTA, 1993) declared that the annual monetary damage resulting from biological invasions is between $4.7 and $6.5 billion. More recent research by Pimentel *et al.* (2000) has concluded that the total annual monetary damage from invasive species is in fact over $100 billion.

Researchers now recognize that maritime trade in goods comprises a sizable proportion of the world's total international trade in goods. Ships are the primary vehicle in maritime trade, and consequently they are routinely used to carry goods of all kinds (often in containers) from one country to another. Now, international trade theorists have demonstrated that there are benefits to the nations involved in such voluntary trade. This notwithstanding, in recent times, natural resource and environmental economists have contended that these gains are likely to be smaller than what most researchers have believed thus far. Why? As Perrings *et al.* (2000), Costello and McAusland (2003), Batabyal (2004), Batabyal *et al.* (2005), and Margolis *et al.* (2005) have noted, this is because in addition to carrying goods between nations, ships have also managed to carry an assortment of deleterious non-native plant and animal species from one part of the world to another.

As far as unintentional introductions, the primary focus of this chapter, are concerned, there are two main ways in which alien species have been carried from one part of the world to another. First, many invasive species have been introduced into a country, often inadvertently, by ships discarding their ballast water. Cargo ships usually carry ballast water in order to increase vessel stability when they are not carrying full loads. When these ships come into a seaport, this ballast water must be jettisoned before cargo can be loaded. This manner of species introductions is important, and the problem of managing alien species that have been introduced into a particular nation by means of the discharge of ballast water has now received some attention in the economics literature (Nunes and Van den Bergh, 2004; Yang and Perakis, 2004; Batabyal and Beladi, 2006).

The second way in which alien species have been introduced into a particular country is by means of contaminated goods (agricultural goods readily come to mind) that may or may not be carried in containers. In this regard, the reader should note that invasive species can remain concealed in containers for long periods of time. In addition, material such as wood, which is often used to pack the cargo in the containers, may itself contain alien species. In fact, as pointed out by Costello and McAusland (2003), a joint report from the United States Department of Agriculture (USDA), the Animal and Plant Health Inspection Service (APHIS), and the United States Forest Service (USFS) has noted that nearly 51.8% of maritime shipments contain solid wood packing materials and that infection rates for solid wood packing materials are substantial (USDA, APHIS and USFS, 2000, p. 25). For example, inspections of wooden spools from China revealed infection rates between 22% and 24%, and inspections of braces for granite blocks imported into Canada were found to hold live insects 32% of the time (USDA, APHIS and USFS, 2000, pp. 27–28).

Economists and ecologists are both very interested in managing invasive species. This is because (see the first paragraph of this section) biological invasions can and often have proven to be very costly from an economic standpoint. In addition to these economic costs, the work of Vitousek *et al.* (1996), Simberloff *et al.* (1997), Costello and McAusland (2003), and others reminds us that alien species can alter ecosystem processes, act as vectors of diseases, and diminish biological diversity. In this regard, Cox (1993) has observed that out of 256 vertebrate extinctions with a known cause, 109 are the outcome of biological invasions. This discussion tells us that non-native species have been and continue to be a great menace to society.

It is only very recently that economists have begun to analyze questions pertaining to invasive species management. For instance, Eiswerth and Johnson (2002) have studied an intertemporal model of alien species stock management. They note that the optimal level of management effort is responsive to ecological factors that are not only species and site specific but also stochastic in nature. Second, Olson and Roy (2002) have used a stochastic framework to examine the circumstances under which it is optimal to wipe out an invasive species and the circumstances under which it is not optimal to do so. Third, Horan *et al.* (2002) have analyzed the properties of management approaches under full information and under uncertainty. Fourth, Batabyal *et al.* (2005) have observed that there is a tension between economic cost minimization and inspection stringency in invasive species management. Finally, Batabyal and Beladi (2006) have analyzed maximization problems stemming from the steady state analysis of two multi-person inspection regimes.

Despite the known connection between goods trade between countries and the damage from alien species, with the exception of Jenkins (1996), ecologists in general have paid *scant attention* to the role of trade policy in mitigating the damage from alien species introductions. Jenkins (1996) has contended that it may be necessary to use trade policy (bans and restrictions) to protect biological diversity. Very recently, a small number of papers have begun to analyze issues at the interface of international trade and invasive species management. Barbier and Shogren (2004) have analyzed a growth model in which a biological invasion occurs as a spillover effect from the importation of capital goods. They show that when a biological invasion diminishes the productivity of all firms in the economy, the government ought to impose an output tax to equate the private and the social desires for consumption growth and capital accumulation. Costello and McAusland (2003) and McAusland and Costello (2004) have studied the impact that tariffs have on the damage from invasive species introductions. Costello and McAusland

(2003) show that a tariff can either decrease or increase the damage from invasive species. McAusland and Costello (2004) show that although it is always optimal to use tariffs to control the damage from alien species, the same cannot be said about inspections. In particular, in their model, there are several circumstances in which it is optimal not to inspect imported goods at all. Prestemon *et al.* (2006) study international trade in forest products and show that trade liberalization will have a negligible effect on US imports of Siberian logs and on the risk of a biological invasion. Finally, using an integrated model with an international trade component, Zhao *et al.* (2006) demonstrate the consumer and the producer responses to livestock disease outbreaks and the welfare effects of alternate invasive species management policies.

Although the papers cited in the previous paragraph have cer tainly advanced our understanding of the impacts of trade policy on the damage from invasive species, three outstanding questions concerning the desirability of using trade policy to manage invasive species remain. Therefore, the purpose of this chapter is to analyze these three questions in detail. First, unlike the extant literature, we use a two-country model to study the efficacy of tariffs as an invasive species management tool under four *different market structures.*[2] Second, we focus not just on small tariffs but on *small and on optimal* tariffs. Finally, our emphasis is less on the impact that tariffs have on the damage from invasive species *per se* and more on the *impacts of tariffs on social welfare* when social welfare depends in part on the damage from alien species.[3]

The rest of this chapter is organized as follows. Section 2.1 briefly describes our two-country model. Sections 2.2–2.4 construct three

---

2. For analyses of tariffs in other contexts, see Parai (1999), Biswas and Marjit (2007), and Vishwasrao *et al.* (2007).

3. We are not suggesting that this chapter is the first to study the impacts of tariffs on social welfare when social welfare depends in part on the damage from alien species. This issue has also been looked at by McAusland and Costello (2004) and by Margolis *et al.* (2005). Instead, what we are suggesting is that, to the best of our knowledge, this chapter is the first to study the three questions stated earlier in this paragraph *collectively.*

measures of the expected damage in Home from the introduction of alien species. Section 3.1 continues the description of our two-country model. Then, this section derives a general expression for the change in Home social welfare as a function of a change in the Home tariff. Section 3.2 analyzes the impact of small and optimal tariffs imposed by Home on the damage from invasive species, on prices, exports and imports, and social welfare in Home for the case in which perfect competition prevails in both Home and Foreign and Home is a small country. Section 3.3 does the same for the case in which the Home and the Foreign markets are both perfectly competitive, but Home is now a large country. Section 3.4 conducts a similar analysis for the case in which the exporter in Foreign is a monopolist and there are no import competing firms in Home. Section 3.5 also conducts the same kind of analysis as the previous three sections, but now the Foreign exporter and the import competing firm in Home engage in Cournot competition. Section 3.6 first discusses the form of the dependence of all the tariff expressions on the expected total damage from alien species introductions in Home. Next, this section comments briefly on scenarios in which the above discussed form of dependence would be different. Section 4 concludes and offers suggestions for future research on the subject of this chapter.

2. Three Measures of Damage in Home from Stochastic Alien Species Introductions

2.1. *Preliminaries*

The world consists of two countries called Home and Foreign. Foreign exports and Home imports a specific good that could be either an agricultural good or a manufactured good. Over time, the import of this good also results in the *probabilistic* introduction of alien species from Foreign into Home. Initially, because of scientific uncertainty, citizens and the relevant authorities in Home do not realize that these unintentionally introduced alien species cause agricultural and/or ecological damage in Home. However, with the passage of time, scientific evidence implicating the alien species emerges, and then it becomes clear to the citizens and to the aforementioned authorities that the stochastic introductions of these alien species and the resulting monetary damage are *linked* to the import of the good in question from Foreign. With this realization come calls for the use of trade policies to restrict imports and thereby reduce the introduction of the deleterious alien species.

Given this temporal sequence of events, we now construct three measures of the expected damage in Home from the stochastic introduction of alien species. The measures in Sections 2.2 and 2.3 are monetary measures of damage, and the measure in Section 2.4 is a physical measure of damage. The damage measures in Sections 2.2 and 2.4 are based on the work of Batabyal and Nijkamp (2007), and the damage measure in Section 2.3 is based on the analysis in Batabyal and Beladi (2001). Why are we focusing on three measures of damage? This is because we would like to ascertain whether alternate specifications of the damage metric have a similar or a dissimilar qualitative impact on the various small and optimal tariff expressions that we derive in Sections 3.2–3.5.

2.2. *First measure of damage*

We model the stochastic nexus between the arrival of a possibly injurious alien species and the attendant monetary damage that results if this species is able to establish itself in the new habitat of Home. In this regard, we shall say that the monetary damages associated with the possibly successful introduction of alien species "arrive" at Home in accordance with a Poisson process with rate λ and $\lambda = \lambda(m)$. In other words, the arrival rate of the monetary damages stemming from the stochastic introduction of alien species is a function of the volume of imports m. Further, we suppose that as the volume of imports goes up, the arrival rate of the monetary damages also goes up. Therefore, we have $\lambda'(m) > 0$. The *amounts* of the successive monetary damages are independent random variables that are assumed to have the common discrete distribution $a_k = -\pi^k[k\log_e(1-\pi)]^{-1}$, where $k = 1, 2, 3, \ldots$ and the parameter $\pi \in (0, 1)$. Our task now is to ascertain the distribution of the total monetary damage in an interval $[0, t]$ and, without loss of generality, we suppose that this interval is a calendar year.

Let us now compute the generating function of the discrete probability distribution specified in the previous paragraph.[4] Because the common discrete distribution $a_k = -\pi^k[k\log_e(1-\pi)]^{-1}$, $k = 1, 2, 3, \ldots$ has the natural logarithm function in it, to make further progress, we want to work with a series expansion of the natural logarithm function. This series expansion is given by

$$-\log_e(1-x) = \sum_{k=0}^{\infty} \frac{x^k}{k}, \quad |x| < 1. \tag{1}$$

Further, Theorem 1.2.1 in Tijms (2003, p. 19) tells us that the generating function of the total monetary damage in a year can be written in terms of the exponential e. Now, using this result from Theorem 1.2.1, the series expansion in Equation (1), and some thought, we are able to conclude that the generating function of the total monetary damage in a year is given by

$$e^{-\lambda\{1-A(z)\}}, A(z) = \frac{\log_e(1-\pi z)}{\log_e(1-\pi)}, \quad |z| \le 1. \tag{2}$$

After several algebraic steps, the generating function in Equation (2) can be written as

$$\left[\frac{(1-\pi)}{(1-\pi z)}\right]^{-\lambda/\log_e(1-\pi)}, \quad |z| \le 1. \tag{3}$$

Consulting Kulkarni (1995, p. 584), it is clear that the generating function in Equation (3) is the generating function of a random variable that has a negative binomial distribution with parameters

---

4. See Kulkarni (1995, pp. 579–584) and Tijms (2003, pp. 449–455) for textbook accounts of the generating function.

$-\lambda/\log_e(1 - \pi)$ and $(1 - \pi)$. Therefore, we reason that the total monetary damage from biological invasions in a calendar year has a negative binomial distribution with the above specified parameters.

Using standard formulae for the negative binomial distribution, we can tell that the expected total monetary damage from biological invasions in a calendar year or $E[D_1]$ is

$$E[D_1] = \frac{-\pi\lambda}{\{(1 - \pi)\log_e(1 - \pi)\}}. \tag{4}$$

Equation (4) gives us our first measure of the damage from stochastic alien species introductions in Home. The right hand side (RHS) of Equation (4) is positive because the numerator and the denominator on the RHS are both negative. The reader will note that the expected total monetary damage from biological invasions in a calendar year is given by a particular ratio. The numerator of this ratio is the (negative) product of the rate λ of the Poisson arrival process of the monetary damages and the parameter π of the discrete distribution function of the amounts of the consecutive monetary damages. The denominator is the product of a simple function of the parameter π, for example, $(1 - \pi)$, and the natural logarithm of this same function. Inspection of the above expression for the expected value tells us that as the rate λ of the Poisson arrival process increases in magnitude, the expected total monetary damage from biological invasions goes up. We now compute our second measure of the monetary damage from alien species introductions.

2.3. *Second measure of damage*

As in Section 2.2, we wish to compute the *expected* total monetary damage in the interval $[0, t]$ which, without loss of generality, is a calendar year. Once again, we assume that alien species are introduced into Home in accordance with a Poisson process with rate λ, where $\lambda = \lambda(m)$ and $\lambda'(m) > 0$. In words, the rate of introduction of alien species into Home, λ, is a function of the volume of imports m, and this introduction rate is an increasing function of the volume of imports.[5] The ith introduction causes monetary damage M_i, $i \geq 1$. The M_i are assumed to be independent and identically distributed (i.i.d.), and they are also assumed to be independent of the total number of alien species introductions by time t, $N(t)$. As one might expect, the monetary damage from a specific introduction in the calendar year $[0, t]$ is typically not constant but variable. Therefore, we suppose that the monetary damage from a specific alien species introduction decreases exponentially over time. Mathematically, this means that if the initial damage from a particular species introduction is M, then at some later time t, the damage is $Me^{-\alpha t}$, where α is the parameter or the rate of the exponential distribution.

With the above description in place, we can now tell that the total monetary damage from invasive species introductions into Home in a calendar year is

$$D_2 = \Sigma_{i=1}^{N(t)} M_i e^{-\alpha(t-A_i)}, \tag{5}$$

where A_i is the arrival time of the ith introduction. Obviously, D_2 is a random variable. Therefore, let us now compute $E[D_2]$, the expected dollar damage from alien species introductions into Home in a calendar year. Conditioning on $N(t)$, the total number of introductions by time t, we get

$$E[D_2] = \sum_{j=0}^{\infty} E[D_2/N(t) = j]e^{-\alpha t} \left\{ \frac{(\alpha t)^j}{j!} \right\}. \tag{6}$$

Theorem 2.3.1 in Ross (1996, p. 67) tells us that conditioned on $N(t) = j$, the unordered arrival times $A_1, \ldots, A_j$ are distributed as independent, uniform random variables in the interval $[0, t]$. From this, we deduce that given $N(t) = j$, D_2 has the same distribution as $\Sigma_{i=1}^{j} M_i e^{-\alpha(t-G_i)}$, where the G_i, $i = 1, \ldots, j$ are independent and

---

5. These assumptions have also been made by Costello and McAusland (2003). For more on the Poisson process, the reader should consult Ross (1996, Chapter 2) or Tijms (2003, Chapter 1).

uniformly distributed random variables in $[0, t]$. Putting these last two pieces of information together, we get

$$E[D_2/N(t) = j] = jE[M]E[e^{-\alpha(t-G)}], \tag{7}$$

where $E[M]$ is the initial monetary damage caused by a particular introduction and G is a uniformly distributed random variable in $[0, t]$. To compute the last expectation on the RHS of Equation (7), observe that

$$E[e^{-\alpha(t-G)}] = \int_0^t \frac{1}{t} e^{-\alpha(t-g)} \, dg = \left(\frac{1 - e^{-\alpha t}}{\alpha t} \right). \tag{8}$$

Using Equation (8), we can now write

$$E[D_2/N(t)] = N(t)E[M] \left(\frac{1 - e^{-\alpha t}}{\alpha t} \right). \tag{9}$$

Finally, taking expectations and using the fact that $E[N(t)] = \lambda t$, we obtain

$$E[D_2] = \left(\frac{\lambda E[M]}{\alpha} \right) (1 - e^{-\alpha t}). \tag{10}$$

Equation (10) gives us our second measure for the expected monetary damage in Home from the stochastic introduction of invasive species in the interval $[0, t]$ that is a calendar year.

This expected monetary damage depends on the mean initial monetary damage from an introduction ($E[M]$), on the rate (α) of the exponential distribution, and most importantly for our purpose, on the rate (λ) at which alien species are being introduced into Home. Recall that because $\lambda = \lambda(m)$, the expected monetary damage metric given by Equation (10) also depends on the volume of imports (m) coming into Home. We now proceed to compute our third and final measure of the damage from alien species introductions. This metric is a physical measure of damage.

2.4. *Third measure of damage*

Upon arrival in Home, ships unload their containers carrying cargo. The arrival of these containers (and the possible discharge of ballast

water) coincides with the arrival of a whole host of potentially deleterious alien animal and plant species. Consistent with the approach
adopted in Sections 2.2 and 2.3, we suppose that the arrival process
of these alien species can be described with a Poisson process with
rate λ.[6] What's different in our construction of this third measure of
damage is that unlike most of the previous literature on this subject,
we suppose that this rate λ of the Poisson arrival process is a *random
variable* that follows a gamma distribution with shape parameter α
and scale parameter β.[7] As in Sections 2.2 and 2.3, we assume that
the time interval of interest $[0, t]$ is a calendar year. The task before
us now is to compute the total number of biological invasions in
this calendar year.

Let p_k denote the probability that there are k biological invasions
in a year. Then, using the law of conditional probabilities and the
fact that the rate λ of the alien species arrival process is gamma
distributed with parameters (α, β), we reason that

$$p_k = \int_0^\infty e^{-x} \left(\frac{x^k}{k!}\right) \beta^\alpha \left(\frac{x^{\alpha-1}}{\Gamma(\alpha)}\right) e^{-\beta x} dx, \qquad (11)$$

where $\Gamma(\alpha)$ is the gamma function.

Now, we know that the gamma density function $\gamma^\delta \{x^{\delta-1}/
\Gamma(\delta)\}e^{-\gamma - x}$ integrates to unity over the interval $(0, \infty)$ for any
$\gamma, \delta > 0$. Therefore, after several steps of algebra, we see that

$$p_k = \frac{\Gamma(\alpha + k)}{\Gamma(\alpha)\Gamma(k + 1)} \left(\frac{\beta}{1 + \beta}\right)^\alpha \left(\frac{1}{1 + \beta}\right)^k, \qquad k = 0, 1, 2, \ldots$$

$$(12)$$

---

6. See Costello and McAusland (2003), Batabyal and Nijkamp (2005), and Batabyal and Lee
(2006) for additional details on this point.

7. See Ross (1996, p. 18) and Tijms (2003, pp. 441–442) for more on the gamma distribution. We are using the gamma distribution to characterize the rate λ for four reasons. First, this
distribution has been used previously in the natural resource economics literature (see Batabyal
and Nijkamp (2009)) to study stochastic arrival processes. Second, the gamma distribution is a
general two-parameter distribution for positive random variables. Third, many other probability distribution functions are variants of the gamma distribution. Finally, in Bayesian inference,
the conjugate prior of the unknown rate parameter λ is commonly modeled with the gamma
distribution.

Consulting Ross (1996, p. 16), it is clear that Equation (12) describes the probability mass function of a negative binomial random variable with parameters α and $\beta/(\beta+1)$. Therefore, the total number of biological invasions in a calendar year has a negative binomial distribution with parameters α and $\beta/(\beta+1)$.

Using standard formulae for the negative binomial distribution, it is straightforward to confirm that the expected number of biological invasions in a calendar year or $E[D_3]$ is

$$E[D_3] = \alpha/\beta. \tag{13}$$

Equation (13) gives us our third and final measure of damage from stochastic alien species introductions in Home. Specifically, this equation tells us that the expected number of biological invasions in a calendar year is given by the ratio of the shape parameter α of the gamma distribution to the scale parameter β of this same distribution. As α increases in magnitude, the expected number of biological invasions goes up, and as β increases in magnitude, the expected number of biological invasions goes down. We now move on to analyze the effects of small and optimal tariffs imposed by Home on the expected damage from invasive species, on prices, on exports and imports, and on social welfare in Home for four alternate market structures.

3. Tariffs and Alien Species Management

3.1. *Tariffs and social welfare in Home*

Our two-country model is adapted from the standard two-country trade model discussed in Feenstra (2004, Chapter 7). Home imports a single (agricultural or manufactured) good from Foreign. The price of the import good in Home is p and its world price is p^*.[8] To keep the subsequent analysis straightforward and to avoid focusing on too many cases, we shall analyze the effects of a Home instituted

---

8. In the rest of this chapter we shall adopt the convention of denoting the relevant Foreign functions and variables with the * superscript.

specific import tariff τ.[9] Given τ, it is clear that $p = p^* + \tau$. In addition to the import good, we suppose that the second (numeraire) good is also traded at the fixed world price of unity. Labor (L) is the only factor of production, and we suppose that each unit of the numeraire good requires one unit of labor. Therefore, wages in Home are also unity, and hence total labor income in Home equals the fixed supply of labor L. The reader will note that we are in a partial equilibrium setting in which wages are fixed and trade is balanced through flows of the numeraire good.

The output of the good in question in Home is q, and the industry cost of producing this good is $c(q)$ where $c'(q) > 0$ and $c''(q) > 0$. Imports are denoted by the scalar $m = d(p) - q$, where $d(p)$ is the demand function for the good whose output is q, and we suppose that $d'(p) < 0$. The tariff revenue τm is returned to the citizens of Home, and these citizens also obtain the profits of the import competing industry $pq - c(q)$. Given this specification, we can now write the social welfare function in Home at time t as

$$W\{p, L + \tau m + pq - c(q), E[D_i]\} \equiv W(\tau), \quad i = 1, 2, 3. \quad (14)$$

We see that social welfare in Home depends on prices (p), income ($L + \tau m + pq - c(q)$), and the expected total damage (see Equations (4), (10), and (13)) from the probabilistic introduction of alien species ($E[D_i]$), $i = 1, 2, 3$. The social welfare function described by Equation (14) is like an indirect utility function for Home as a whole with one caveat[10]: Home's welfare at time t also depends *negatively* on the expected damage from the introduction of alien species.

We are now in a position to analyze the impact of the specific tariff on prices, quantities, mean damage, and social welfare under

---

9. Results for an *ad valorem* tariff can be expected to be qualitatively similar to that for a specific tariff.

10. For additional details on this point see Feenstra (2004, pp. 213–214).

alternate market structures. To this end, let us first derive a general expression for the change in social welfare when a tariff is put in place by Home. The derivation of this general expression will be helped by first noting that

$$\frac{dE[D_1]}{d\tau} = \frac{-\pi}{(1 - \pi)\log_e(1 - \pi)} \frac{d\lambda}{dm} \frac{dm}{dp} \frac{dp}{d\tau},$$

$$\frac{dE[D_2]}{d\tau} = \frac{E[M](1 - e^{-\alpha t})}{\alpha} \frac{d\lambda}{dm} \frac{dm}{dp} \frac{dp}{d\tau},$$

$$\frac{dE[D_3]}{d\tau} = 0. \tag{15}$$

Continuing with the derivation, we assume that p and q both depend on the tariff τ. Totally differentiating Equation (14) with respect to τ, we get

$$\frac{dW}{d\tau} = -d(p)\frac{dp}{d\tau} + m + \left\{\tau\frac{dm}{dp} + q + Z_i\frac{\partial W}{\partial(E[D_i])}\frac{d\lambda}{dm}\frac{dm}{dp}\right\}\frac{dp}{d\tau}$$

$$+ \{p - c'(q)\}\frac{dq}{d\tau}, \quad i = 1, 2, 3, \tag{16}$$

where

$$Z_1 = [-\pi/\{(1 - \pi)\log_e(1 - \pi)\}] > 0,$$
$$Z_2 = [\{E[M](1 - e^{-\alpha t})\}/\alpha] > 0, \tag{17}$$
$$Z_3 = 0,$$

and we have used the fact that $\partial W/\partial p = -d(p)$. Now note that $m = d(p) - q$, and because $p = p^* + \tau$, we have $\{1 - dp/d\tau\} = -dp^*/d\tau$. Using these two pieces of information, we can simplify Equation (16). This simplification yields

$$\frac{dW}{d\tau} = \left\{\tau\frac{dm}{dp} + Z_i\frac{\partial W}{\partial(E[D_i])}\frac{d\lambda}{dm}\frac{dm}{dp}\right\}\frac{dp}{d\tau} - m\frac{dp^*}{d\tau}$$

$$+ \{p - c'(q)\}\frac{dq}{d\tau}, \quad i = 1, 2, 3. \tag{18}$$

Let us examine the three terms on the RHS of Equation (18) in greater detail. The first term can be thought of as the efficiency effect of the tariff. The second term is the effect of the tariff on the foreign price p^* or the terms of trade effect. Finally, the third term is the price-cost margin multiplied by the change in the industry output. In the remainder of this chapter, we shall use Equation (18) repeatedly to study the effects of the specific tariff (τ) under alternate market structures. We begin with the case in which perfect competition prevails in both Home and Foreign and Home is a small country.

3.2. Perfect competition with Home a small country

When the Home economy is perfectly competitive and it is a small country, we have $p = c'(q)$, and because p^* is fixed, we also have $dp^*/d\tau = 0$ and $dp/d\tau = 1$. We now simplify Equation (18) using these three results. This gives us

$$\frac{dW}{d\tau} = \tau\frac{dm}{dp} + Z_i\frac{\partial W}{\partial(E[D_i])}\frac{d\lambda}{dm}\frac{dm}{dp}, \quad i = 1,2,3, \quad (19)$$

and the Z_i in Equation (19) are given in Equation (17). Now recall from the discussion in Section 3.1 that the expected damage from alien species introductions affects social welfare in Home negatively, and hence $\partial W/\partial(E[D_i]) < 0$. We have already noted in Section 2 that increasing the volume of imports increases the rate of introductions, and therefore $d\lambda/dm > 0$. Finally, $dm/dp = d'(p) - \{1/c''(q)\}$. Because the demand function slopes downward and the cost function is strictly convex, we have $d'(p) < 0$ and $c''(q) > 0$, and hence $dm/dp < 0$. We now use these three results and evaluate Equation (19) at $\tau = 0$. This gives us

$$\left.\frac{dW}{d\tau}\right|_{\tau=0} = Z_i\frac{\partial W}{\partial(E[D_i])}\frac{d\lambda}{dm}\frac{dm}{dp} > 0,$$

$$i = 1,2, \quad \left.\frac{dW}{d\tau}\right|_{\tau=0} = 0, \quad i = 3. \quad (20)$$

Equation (20) tells us that when the expected damage in Home from stochastic alien species introductions is *monetary* (i.e., when

Equations (4) and (10) are relevant), starting from a position of free trade ($\tau = 0$), a *small* tariff unambiguously raises social welfare in Home. In contrast, when the expected damage from stochastic alien species introductions is *physical* (i.e., when Equation (13) is pertinent), starting from a position of free trade, a small tariff does not raise welfare. This last result arises because the expected total physical damage (see Equations (13), (15), and (17)) is independent of the rate λ of the Poisson arrival process. Put differently, the small tariff has no impact on the expected total damage from alien species introductions, and hence this tariff also has no impact on social welfare in Home. Given these results, we now determine the impact of an *optimal* tariff on social welfare in Home. To compute the optimal tariff, we set the RHS of Equation (19) equal to zero and then simplify. This gives us

$$\tau_o = -Z_i \frac{\partial W}{\partial(E[D_i])} \frac{d\lambda}{dm} > 0, \quad i = 1, 2, \quad \tau_o = 0, \quad i = 3. \quad (21)$$

Equations (20) and (21) together tell us that when social welfare depends on the expected damage from the introduction of alien species, small and optimal tariffs both *raise* welfare in Home as long as the expected total damage in Home is monetary (i.e., when Equations (4) and (10) are relevant). In contrast, when the expected total damage is physical and independent of the rate λ, a tariff is incapable of affecting social welfare in Home, and hence, in this last case, it is optimal to not use a tariff to regulate alien species in Home. Even though Home is a small country, we have seen that in two out of the three cases that we are studying, tariffs have a positive impact on social welfare, and hence Home ought to have an activist trade policy in place in these two cases.

Stepping away from the criterion of social welfare for a moment, does a small tariff lower the expected total damage from the introduction of alien species? To answer this question, let us inspect Equation (15) carefully. This inspection tells us that $dE[D_1]/d\tau < 0$, $dE[D_2]/d\tau < 0$, and $dE[D_3]/d\tau = 0$. In this chapter, imports are the only means by which alien species are introduced into Home. As a result, because a small tariff reduces the volume of imports when the expected total damage is monetary (i.e., $dm/d\tau < 0$), this same tariff also *lowers* the expected monetary damage in Home from the introduction of alien species.[11] In contrast, when the expected total damage is physical and independent of the rate λ, a small tariff has no impact on the expected total damage. This is what the derivative $dE[D_3]/d\tau = 0$ in Equation (15) is telling us.

It is well known in international trade theory (see Feenstra (2004, p. 216)) that the optimal tariff for a small country is zero. However, our analysis thus far tells us that this result does not hold in *some cases* in which imports and invasive species go together. In fact, as we have just seen, when imports are the only means by which alien species are introduced into Home and the expected total damage from alien species is given by either Equation (4) or Equation (10), the optimal course of action for Home is to set a positive tariff. We now investigate the effects of a tariff when Home is a large country.

3.3. Perfect competition with Home a large country

We now write the world price of imports as $p^*(\tau)$. Therefore, because $p = p^*(\tau) + \tau$, $dp^*/d\tau \neq 0$ and $dp/d\tau \neq 1$. However, because the Home economy is perfectly competitive, we still have $p = c'(q)$. Using these three results to simplify Equation (18), we get

$$\frac{dW}{d\tau} = \left\{ \tau \frac{dm}{dp} + Z_i \frac{\partial W}{\partial(E[D_i])} \frac{d\lambda}{dm} \frac{dm}{dp} \right\} \frac{dp}{d\tau} - m \frac{dp^*}{d\tau}, \quad i = 1, 2, 3.$$

$$(22)$$

Now, because Home is a *large* country, $dp/d\tau \neq 1$, and we expect that the foreign exporter will absorb a part of the Home tariff. As noted in Feenstra (2004, pp. 218–219), this means that in general,

---

11. Using a different model, Costello and McAusland (2003) have obtained a similar result.

we expect $dp^*/d\tau < 0$ and $0 < dp/d\tau < 1$. Let us now use these two findings and the results stated in Section 3.2 to evaluate Equation (22) at $\tau = 0$. This gives us

$$\left.\frac{dW}{d\tau}\right|_{\tau=0} = Z_i \frac{\partial W}{\partial(E[D_i])} \frac{d\lambda}{dm} \frac{dm}{dp} \frac{dp}{d\tau} - m \frac{dp^*}{d\tau} > 0, \quad i = 1, 2,$$

$$\left.\frac{dW}{d\tau}\right|_{\tau=0} = -m \frac{dp^*}{d\tau} > 0, \quad i = 3. \tag{23}$$

Equation (23) tells us two things of note. First, as in Section 3.2, we see that when the expected total damage from alien species is monetary (Equations (4) and (10) apply), starting from a position of free trade, a small tariff, once again, *raises* social welfare in Home. Second, and unlike what we saw in Section 3.2, when the expected total damage from alien species is physical and independent of λ, the small tariff now is not zero but positive. This is because even though the small tariff is unable to affect the expected total damage from alien species, because Home is a large country, the small tariff is able to generate a beneficial terms of trade effect and hence, as shown by the $-m(dp^*/d\tau)$ term in Equation (23), this tariff is positive.

To compute the optimal tariff for Home, we set the RHS of Equation (22) equal to zero and then simplify the resulting expression. This gives us

$$\tau_0 = \frac{m \frac{dp^*}{d\tau}}{\frac{dm}{dp} \frac{dp}{d\tau}} - Z_i \frac{\partial W}{\partial(E[D_i])} \frac{d\lambda}{dm} > 0, \quad i = 1, 2,$$

$$\tau_0 = \frac{m \frac{dp^*}{d\tau}}{\frac{dm}{dp} \frac{dp}{d\tau}} > 0, \quad i = 3. \tag{24}$$

Equation (24) tells us that for the case of monetary expected total damage from alien species (i.e., for $i = 1, 2$), Home's optimal tariff is positive and is the sum of the terms of trade effect and the damage from alien species effect. In contrast, for the physical damage or the $i = 3$ case, there is no damage from alien species effect to contend with because $Z_3 = 0$ but, unlike the case studied in Section 3.2, there is still a beneficial terms of trade effect. This is why the optimal tariff in this $i = 3$ case is also positive. The reader will note that the optimal tariff in this $i = 3$ case is equivalent to the optimal import tariff for a large country in the *absence* of damage from alien species.[12] Equation (24) also tells us that when the damage from invasive species introductions *is* an issue (i.e., when $i = 1, 2$), the optimal tariff is not only positive but also larger in magnitude than the optimal tariff with no invasive species damage.

The impact of a small tariff on the expected total damage from alien species introductions into Home is, once again, given by Equation (15). Although $dp/d\tau \neq 1$ now, as discussed earlier, in general, we expect $dp/d\tau > 0$ to hold. Therefore, inspection of Equation (15) and some thought together tell us that $dE[D_1]/d\tau < 0$, $dE[D_2]/d\tau < 0$, and $dE[D_3]/d\tau = 0$. Since a small tariff reduces the volume of imports when the expected total damage is monetary (i.e., $dm/d\tau < 0$), this same tariff also *reduces* the expected monetary damage in Home from the introduction of alien species. In contrast, when the expected total damage is physical and independent of λ, a small tariff has no impact on the expected total damage, and therefore $dE[D_3]/d\tau = 0$. Let us now analyze the effects of tariffs when the exporter in Foreign is a monopolist and there are no import competing firms in Home.

3.4. *Monopolist in Foreign*

In this case we have a single exporter in Foreign, and we suppose that there are no import competing firms in Home. The purpose of a tariff is generally to protect domestic firms in Home, so if there are no domestic firms, then, in principle, there is no rationale for an import tariff. However, as we shall see, in our case it is the damage from alien species introductions that provides a rationale for protectionism.

---

12. See Feenstra (2004, p. 220) for more details on this point.

Let us denote the Foreign firm's exports to Home by x; this equals Home consumption and therefore we can write $x = d(p)$. Inverting this expression, we get the inverse demand function $p = p(x)$ where $p'(x) < 0$. Denote the price received by the Foreign exporter by $p^* = p(x) - \tau$, and let $c^*(x)$ denote this firm's cost function. We suppose that $c^{*'}(x) > 0$ and that $c^{*''}(x) > 0$. The Foreign exporter's profit function is $\pi^*(x) = xp^* - c^*(x) = x\{p(x) - \tau\} - c^*(x)$. Maximizing this function with respect to the volume of exports x gives us

$$\pi^{*'}(x) = p(x) + xp'(x) - \{c^{*'}(x) + \tau\} = 0, \tag{25}$$

where $p(x) + xp'(x)$ is the marginal revenue and $\{c^{*'}(x) + \tau\}$ is the tariff inclusive marginal cost. Now, totally differentiating Equation (25), we get

$$\frac{dx}{d\tau} = \frac{1}{2p'(x) + xp''(x) - c^{*''}(x)} = \frac{1}{\pi^{*''}(x)} < 0 \tag{26}$$

and

$$\frac{dp}{d\tau} = \frac{dp}{dx}\frac{dx}{d\tau} = \frac{p'(x)}{\pi^{*''}(x)} > 0. \tag{27}$$

Equation (26) tells us that the Foreign firm's exports decline as a result of the tariff, and Equation (27) tells us that the domestic price of the good in question inclusive of the tariff rises.

When $dp/d\tau = 1$ (as in Section 3.2), the so-called "pass-through" of the tariff is complete. In other words, the tariff inclusive price p rises by the same amount as the tariff τ. However, when Home is not a small country, the "pass-through" of the tariff will typically be incomplete. When this is the case, we will have $dp/d\tau < 1$. This also means that the foreign firm will absorb a part of the tariff. Mathematically, this means that $dp^*/d\tau < 0$. It should be clear to the reader that when the pass-through of a tariff is *incomplete*, there is a terms of trade *gain* for Home.

We would now like to derive a condition that tells us when there will be a terms of trade gain for Home. Equation (27) helps to provide us with the answer. Because the numerator and the denominator on the RHS of Equation (27) are both negative, we conclude that $dp/d\tau < 1$ if and only if

$$p'(x) > 2p'(x) + xp''(x) - c^{*''}(x). \qquad (28)$$

Now, following the discussion in Feenstra (2004, pp. 221–222), we can say that the LHS of the inequality in (28) is the slope of the inverse demand function, and the RHS of this inequality is the difference between the slopes of the marginal revenue and the marginal cost functions. To proceed further with the derivation, it will be helpful to suppose that the Foreign cost function $c^*(x)$ is linear. Then $c^{*''}(x) = 0$ and the inequality in (28) reduces to

$$p'(x) > 2p'(x) + xp''(x). \qquad (29)$$

The inequality in (29) and some thought together tell us that when the slope of the marginal revenue function *exceeds* that of the inverse demand function, $dp/d\tau < 1$ and $dp^*/d\tau < 0$.

We now determine the impact of the tariff on social welfare in Home. Because there are no import competing firms in Home, $q = 0$, and therefore $dq/d\tau = 0$. Using this result to simplify Equation (18), we get

$$\frac{dW}{d\tau} = \left\{ \tau \frac{dm}{dp} + Z_i \frac{\partial W}{\partial(E[D_i])} \frac{d\lambda}{dm} \frac{dm}{dp} \right\} \frac{dp}{d\tau} - m \frac{dp^*}{d\tau}, \quad i = 1, 2, 3.$$
$$(30)$$

From the discussion in the previous paragraph, we know that when the marginal revenue function is steeper than the inverse demand function, $dp/d\tau < 1$ and $dp^*/d\tau < 0$. Using these two results and other results from our earlier analysis, let us evaluate Equation (30) at $\tau = 0$. We get

$$\left. \frac{dW}{d\tau} \right|_{\tau=0} = Z_i \frac{\partial W}{\partial(E[D_i])} \frac{d\lambda}{dm} \frac{dm}{dp} \frac{dp}{d\tau} - m \frac{dp^*}{d\tau} > 0, \quad i = 1, 2,$$

$$\left. \frac{dW}{d\tau} \right|_{\tau=0} = -m \frac{dp^*}{d\tau} > 0, \quad i = 3. \qquad (31)$$

We see that when the expected total damage from alien species is monetary (i.e., when Equations (4) and (10) apply and $i = 1, 2$), starting from a position of free trade, a small tariff *raises* social welfare in Home. In addition, when the expected damage from alien species is physical and independent of the rate λ (i.e., when $i = 3$, as in Section 3.3), a beneficial terms of trade effect results from the small tariff and this explains why this tariff is, as shown by the last derivative in Equation (31), positive.

Does the optimal tariff also raise welfare? To answer this question, we set the RHS of Equation (30) equal to zero and then simplify the resulting expression. This gives us

$$\tau_0 = \frac{x\frac{dp^*}{d\tau}}{\frac{dx}{d\tau}} - Z_i \frac{\partial W}{\partial(E[D_i])} \frac{d\lambda}{dm} > 0, \quad i = 1, 2,$$

$$\tau_0 = \frac{x\frac{dp^*}{d\tau}}{\frac{dx}{d\tau}} > 0, \quad i = 3. \tag{32}$$

The optimal import tariff when the exporter in Foreign is a monopolist, when there are no import competing firms in Home, and when the expected total damage from alien species is physical and independent of the rate λ is given by the second expression in (32). This expression is the ratio of two negative quantities, and hence the optimal tariff described by this expression is positive. Equation (32) tells us that when the damage from invasive species introductions is monetary, we have $Z_i > 0$, $i = 1, 2$, and in these two instances, the optimal tariff, given by the first expression in (32), is not only positive but also larger in magnitude than the optimal tariff with physical alien species damage.

As in Sections 3.2 and 3.3, Equation (15) gives us the impact of a small tariff on the expected total damage from alien species introductions into Home. Equation (27) tells us that $dp/d\tau > 0$. Using this and our previous results in Equations (15) and (17) tells us that $dE[D_1]/d\tau < 0$, $dE[D_2]/d\tau < 0$, and $dE[D_3]/d\tau = 0$. Since a small tariff reduces the volume of imports when the expected total damage is monetary (i.e., $dm/d\tau < 0$), this same tariff also *reduces* the expected monetary damage in Home from the introduction of alien species. In contrast, when the expected total damage is physical and independent of λ, a small tariff has no impact on the expected total damage, and hence $dE[D_3]/d\tau = 0$. We now study the impact of a tariff when the Foreign exporter and an import competing firm in Home engage in Cournot competition.

3.5. *Cournot competition*

We now have a Home (domestic) firm competing with an exporting firm from Foreign in the domestic market. Let us denote the sales of the Foreign exporting firm by x and that of the Home import competing firm by q so that aggregate consumption of the good in question at Home is $y = q + x$. Following the logic of Section 3.4, the pertinent demand function now is $y = d(p)$, and therefore the relevant inverse demand function is $p = p(y)$ where $p'(y) < 0$.

Using the notation of Section 3.4, the profit functions of the Foreign exporter and the Home import competing firm are $\pi^*(x) = x\{p(y) - \tau\} - c^*(x)$ and $\pi(q) = qp(y) - c(q)$. Maximizing these two functions with respect to the choice variables x and q respectively, we get

$$\pi^{*'}(x) = p(y) + xp'(y) - \{c^{*'}(x) + \tau\} = 0 \qquad (33)$$

and

$$\pi'(q) = p(y) + qp'(y) - c'(q) = 0. \qquad (34)$$

The reader can confirm that the two second-order conditions for profit maximization are $\pi^{*''}(x) = 2p'(y) + xp''(y) - c^{*''}(x) < 0$ and $\pi''(q) = 2p'(y) + qp''(y) - c''(q) < 0.$[13] We now want to determine the impact of the Home tariff on the Foreign firm's exports. In other words, we want to determine the sign of the derivative $dx/d\tau$. To determine this sign, we totally differentiate Equation (33) and then

---

13. We assume that the stability condition $\pi^*_{xx}\pi_{qq} - \pi^*_{xq}\pi_{qx} > 0$ is satisfied.

use the second-order condition for $\pi^{*'}(x)$ given above. This gives us

$$\frac{dx}{d\tau} = \frac{1}{2p'(y) + xp''(y) - c^{*''}(x)} = \frac{1}{\pi^{*''}(x)} < 0. \qquad (35)$$

Equation (35) tells us that with the Home tariff in place, the Foreign exporter reduces the amount it wishes to export to Home.

To study the impact of the Home tariff on prices, it will be necessary first to compute the impact of the tariff on total sales $y = x + q$. To do this, let us now sum the two first-order necessary conditions given in Equations (33) and (34). This gives

$$2p(y) + yp'(y) = c'(q) + \{c^{*}(x) + \tau\}. \qquad (36)$$

Totally differentiating Equation (36) and then simplifying, we get

$$3p'(y)dy + yp''(y)dy = c''(q)dq + c^{*''}(x)dx + d\tau. \qquad (37)$$

Now, as in Section 3.4, to progress further it will help to make a simplifying assumption. Therefore, we assume that the cost functions of the two competing firms in Home and in Foreign are both linear. Then Equation (37) can be simplified to give us

$$\frac{dy}{d\tau} = \frac{1}{3p'(y) + yp''(y)}, \qquad (38)$$

and, because $dp/d\tau = (dp/dy)(dy/d\tau)$, we have

$$\frac{dp}{d\tau} = \frac{p'(y)}{3p'(y) + yp''(y)}. \qquad (39)$$

Inspecting the denominators on the RHSs of Equations (38) and (39) we see that the impact of the Home tariff on total output (y) and the price (p) depends significantly on the sign of $3p'(y) + yp''(y)$. When this expression is negative, we have $dy/d\tau < 0$ and $dp/d\tau > 0$. In words, total output with the tariff declines, and the price in Home with the tariff rises. Some thought will convince the reader that the condition $3p'(y) + yp''(y) < 0$ holds for some inverse demand functions (such as the linear function), but not for all such functions. This tells us that the imposition of a tariff by Home *may* lead to counterintuitive results. Specifically, total output with the tariff may rise ($dy/d\tau > 0$), and the domestic price of the good in question at Home may fall ($dp/d\tau < 0$).

We now focus on the "pass-through" of the tariff τ. We know that for there to be a terms of trade gain in Home, we must have $0 < dp/d\tau < 1$. Now, when $3p'(y) + yp''(y) < 0$ holds, from Equation (39) we can tell that for $dp/d\tau < 1$ to hold, we must have

$$p'(y) > 3p'(y) + yp''(y) \Leftrightarrow 0 > 2p'(y) + yp''(y). \qquad (40)$$

The expression $2p'(y) + yp''(y)$ on the RHS of (40) is the slope of the marginal revenue function $p(y) + yp'(y)$. Therefore, what (40) is really saying is that when the marginal revenue function is *downward* sloping $dp/d\tau < 1$ holds or, alternately, $dp^*/d\tau < 0$, and hence there is a terms of trade gain for Home.

We now ascertain the impact of the tariff on social welfare in Home. Because $m = x$ in equilibrium, we use this to rewrite Equation (18) as

$$\frac{dW}{d\tau} = \left\{ \tau \frac{dx}{dp} + Z_i \frac{\partial W}{\partial(E[D_i])} \frac{d\lambda}{dx} \frac{dx}{dp} \right\} \frac{dp}{d\tau} - x \frac{dp^*}{d\tau}$$

$$+ \{p - c'(q)\} \frac{dq}{d\tau}, \quad i = 1, 2, 3. \qquad (41)$$

From Equation (35) we know that $dx/d\tau < 0$. Further, as we have just discussed in the previous paragraph, when the inequality in (40) holds, the marginal revenue function is downward sloping, and hence $dp^*/d\tau < 0$. Finally, because $dq/d\tau = (dq/dp)(dp/d\tau)$, in general, we expect $dq/d\tau > 0$.[14] Using these three results we can evaluate Equation (41) at $\tau = 0$. This gives us

$$\left. \frac{dW}{d\tau} \right|_{\tau=0} = Z_i \frac{\partial W}{\partial(E[D_i])} \frac{d\lambda}{dx} \frac{dx}{d\tau} - x \frac{dp^*}{d\tau}$$

$$+ \{p - c'(q)\} \frac{dq}{d\tau} > 0, \quad i = 1, 2,$$

---

14. See Feenstra (2004, pp. 225–226) for a graphical explanation of this line of reasoning.

$$\left.\frac{dW}{d\tau}\right|_{\tau=0} = -x\frac{dp^*}{d\tau} + \{p - c'(q)\}\frac{dq}{d\tau} > 0, \quad i = 3. \quad (42)$$

Consider the cases in which the expected total damage from alien species introductions is monetary. These are the $i = 1, 2$ cases. In these two cases, Equation (42) tells us that when the inequality in (40) holds, a small tariff leads to a terms of trade gain ($dp^*/d\tau < 0$). In addition, when $dq/d\tau > 0$, there is an additional gain from this small tariff. These two positive effects along with the fact that the first term on the RHS of Equation (42) with Z_i in it is positive together tell us that a small tariff raises social welfare in Home. Next, consider the $i = 3$ case in which the expected total damage from alien species introductions is physical and independent of λ. In this case $Z_3 = 0$, but we still have a beneficial terms of trade effect and a general increase in domestic output as a result of the small tariff. These two positive effects explain why the small tariff in this $i = 3$ case is also positive. The reader should note that in this case of Cournot competition, it is *not* inevitable that a small tariff will lead to an increase in domestic output. It is certainly possible that $dq/d\tau < 0$, and when this happens, this negative effect will tend to offset the positive terms of trade effect; hence the impact of a small tariff on social welfare in Home may not be positive.

Does the optimal import tariff raise social welfare in Home? To answer this question, we set the RHS of Equation (41) equal to zero and then simplify the resulting expression. This gives us

$$\tau_0 = \frac{x\frac{dp^*}{d\tau}}{\frac{dx}{d\tau}} - \frac{\{p(y) - c'(q)\}\frac{dq}{d\tau}}{\frac{dx}{d\tau}} - Z_i\frac{\partial W}{\partial(E[D_i])}\frac{d\lambda}{dx} > 0, \quad i = 1, 2,$$

$$\tau_0 = \frac{x\frac{dp^*}{d\tau}}{\frac{dx}{d\tau}} - \frac{\{p(y) - c'(q)\}\frac{dq}{d\tau}}{\frac{dx}{d\tau}}, \quad i = 3. \quad (43)$$

Assuming that the inequality in (40) holds, let us first focus on the $i = 1, 2$ cases. There are three terms on the RHS of Equation (43) to discuss. The first term is positive because both $dp^*/d\tau$ and $dx/d\tau$ are negative. The second term is positive because the numerator is generally positive and the denominator is negative. Finally, the third term is positive because $Z_i > 0$, $i = 1, 2$, $\partial W/\partial(E[D(t)]) < 0$, and $d\lambda/dx > 0$. Therefore, the optimal tariff, which is the sum of three positive terms, is itself positive. Next, focus on the $i = 3$ case. In this case, the expected total damage from alien species introductions is independent of the rate λ, and hence this case is like the case in which there is Cournot competition between the exporting and the import competing firms and there is no damage from invasive species introductions. In this case, Home's optimal tariff is positive, and it is the sum of the first two terms as shown in the last derivative in Equation (43). Finally, Equation (43) tells us that the optimal tariff in the $i = 1, 2$ cases is the sum of three positive terms and hence larger in magnitude than the optimal tariff in the $i = 3$ case.

As in Sections 3.2–3.4, Equation (15) gives us the impact of a small tariff on the expected total damage from alien species introductions into Home. Using Equation (35), the fact that $m = x$ in equilibrium, and our previous analysis, we reason that $dE[D_1]/d\tau < 0$, $dE[D_2]/d\tau < 0$, and $dE[D_3]/d\tau = 0$. Since a small tariff diminishes the volume of exports when the expected total damage from alien species is monetary (i.e., $dx/d\tau < 0$), this same tariff also *reduces* the expected monetary damage in Home from the introduction of alien species. In contrast, when the expected total damage is physical and independent of λ, a small tariff has no impact on the expected total damage, and hence $dE[D_3]/d\tau = 0$. These results about the impact of the tariff on the expected total monetary damage from invasive species in Sections 3.2 to 3.5 are similar to and consistent with Proposition 1 in Costello and McAusland (2003, p. 967).

In the strategic trade theory literature of the 1980s, a considerable amount of emphasis was placed on the third term $\{p - c'(q)\}$ $(dq/d\tau)$ in Equation (41), and this third term was often thought of as a profit shifting rationale for the strategic use of tariffs.[15] While this interpretation makes sense when the derivative $dq/d\tau$

---

15. See Brander and Spencer (1984), Horstmann and Markusen (1986), and Helpman and Krugman (1989) for more on this literature.

is positive, we have already pointed out that this need not always be the case. Suppose for the moment that $dq/d\tau$ is positive. Then, what we have seen thus far in this chapter is that in addition to any profit shifting rationale, in the presence of monetary damage from alien species introductions, there is a second and arguably more important rationale for the use of import tariffs. Indeed, when tariffs are used as described in this chapter, it may be possible to "kill three birds with one stone." What we mean by this expression is that the Home government may be able to (i) obtain a terms of trade benefit, (ii) shift profits away from the Foreign exporter and toward the domestic import competing firm, and (iii) reduce the monetary damage from deleterious alien species. We now discuss the form of the dependence of all the tariff expressions in this chapter on the expected total damage from alien species introductions in Home. Then, we briefly talk about scenarios in which this form of dependence would be different.

3.6. *Form of dependence of tariffs on damage from alien species introductions*

We derived three measures of damage from alien species introductions in Sections 2.2–2.4 of this chapter. Of these three measures, the first two measures, Equations (4) and (10), are monetary, and the third measure, Equation (13), is physical. In our detailed analysis thus far, we have seen that tariffs are useful policies with which to control the deleterious effects of alien species introductions when Equations (4) and (10) are pertinent (i.e., when the damage measure is monetary). This is because in these two cases, the rate λ of the Poisson arrival process directly influences the two derived damage metrics. In contrast, tariffs have no role to play as an alien species control device when Equation (13) is germane because in this case, the derived damage metric is independent of λ.

We now note *two features* of our analysis thus far. First, even though Equations (4) and (10) are *dissimilar* damage measures, in both these equations, the rate λ enters the damage measure multiplicatively. Second, the three expected damage measures of this chapter enter the social welfare function in Home (see Equation (14)) in a *standard* manner. In other words, we have $W\{p, L + \tau m + pq - c(q), E[D_i]\}$, $i = 1, 2, 3$. Therefore, when we differentiate this social welfare function with respect to the tariff τ, we get the multiplicative term $(\partial W/\partial\{E[D_i]\})(d\{E[D_i]\}/d\tau)$. It is these two modeling features that together account for the fact that the Z_i term affects all our tariff expressions (see Equations (20), (21), (23), (24), (31), (32), (42) and (43)) multiplicatively.

We stress that the positivity of most of the tariffs that we have analyzed in this chapter is *not* the result of modeling the damage from alien species introductions in a particular way. In fact, as we have shown in this chapter, even for dissimilar damage measures, this positivity result largely holds. We conclude this section by pointing out that if the two modeling features delineated in the previous paragraph do not hold, then it is possible that the signs of some of the small and the optimal tariffs in the four different market structures that we have analyzed will become ambiguous.

4. Conclusions

In this chapter, we provided a theoretical perspective on the impacts of small and optimal specific tariffs when international trade in goods results in the stochastic introductions of alien species from one country to another as a byproduct. Conducting the analysis from the standpoint of the tariff imposing country (i.e., Home), we first derived three (two monetary and one physical) measures of the expected total damage from alien species introductions into Home. Next, we analyzed the effects of small and optimal tariffs under four alternate market structures. Our basic result is that there are several circumstances in which it makes sense to use trade policy (tariffs) to control the damage from alien plant and/or animal species.

The analysis in this chapter can be extended in a number of directions. In what follows, we suggest two possible extensions of this chapter's research. First, in our model the rate of alien species introductions depends only on the volume of imports. Therefore, it would be useful to determine the extent to which one can obtain results from a model in which, in addition to the volume of imports, the rate of species introductions depends also on the *number of previously successful* introductions. Second, it would be useful to analyze the impacts of import *quotas* to see if our basic result from the previous paragraph also holds in the case of quotas. Studies of alien species management that incorporate these aspects of the problem into the analysis will provide additional insights into a management problem that has considerable economic and ecological implications.

References

Barbier, E.B. and Shogren, J.F. (2004). Growth with Endogenous Risk of Biological Invasion. *Economic Inquiry* 42:587–601.

Batabyal, A.A. (2004). A Research Agenda for the Study of the Regulation of Invasive Species Introduced Unintentionally via Maritime Trade. *Journal of Economic Research* 9:191–216.

Batabyal, A.A. and Beladi, H. (2001). Aspects of the Theory of Financial Risk Management for Natural Disasters. *Applied Mathematics Letters* 14: 875–880.

Batabyal, A.A. and Beladi, H. (2006). International Trade and Biological Invasions: A Queuing Theoretic Analysis of the Prevention Problem. *European Journal of Operational Research* 170:758–770.

Batabyal, A.A. Beladi, H. and Koo, W.W. (2005). Maritime Trade, Biological Invasions, and the Properties of Alternate Inspection Regimes. *Stochastic Environmental Research and Risk Assessment* 19:184–190.

Batabyal, A.A. and Lee, D.M. (2006). The Infinitesimal, the Deterministic, and the Probabilistic: Alternate Container Inspection Policies in Invasive Species Management. *Biological Invasions* 8:1663–1671.

Batabyal, A.A. and Nijkamp, P. (2005). On Container versus Time Based Inspection Policies in Invasive Species Management. *Stochastic Environmental Research and Risk Assessment* 19:340–347.

Batabyal, A.A. and Nijkamp, P. (2007). The Stochastic Arrival of Alien Species and the Number of and the Damage from Biological Invasions. *Ecological Economics* 62:277–280.

Batabyal, A.A. and Nijkamp, P. (2009). Two Aspects of Waste Management from the Viewpoints of a Waste Generator and a Recipient. *Applied Economics Letters* 16:337–341.

Biswas, A.K. and Marjit, S. (2007). Preferential Trade and Mis-invoicing: Some Analytical Implications. *International Review of Economics and Finance* 16:130–138.

Brander, J.A. and Spencer, B. (1984). Tariff Protection and Imperfect Competition. *In* H. Kierzkowski (ed.), *Monopolistic Competition and International Trade*. Oxford, UK: Oxford University Press.

Costello, C. and McAusland, C. (2003). Protectionism, Trade, and Measures of Damage from Exotic Species Introductions. *American Journal of Agricultural Economics* 85:964–975.

Cox, G.W. (1993). *Conservation Ecology*. Dubuque, Iowa: W.C. Brown Publishers.

Eiswerth, M.E. and Johnson, W.S. (2002). Managing Nonindigenous Invasive Species: Insights from Dynamic Analysis. *Environmental and Resource Economics* 23:319–342.

Feenstra, R.C. (2004). *Advanced International Trade*. Princeton, New Jersey: Princeton University Press.

Helpman, E. and Krugman, P.R. (1989). *Trade Policy and Market Structure*. Cambridge, Massachusetts: MIT Press.

Horan, R.D., Perrings, C., Lupi, F. and Bulte, E.H. (2002). Biological Pollution Prevention Strategies Under Ignorance: The Case of Invasive Species. *American Journal of Agricultural Economics* 84:1303–1310.

Horstmann, I. and Markusen, J.R. (1986). Up the Average Cost Curve: Inefficient Entry and the New Protectionism. *Journal of International Economics* 20:225–247.

Jenkins, P. (1996). Free Trade and Exotic Species Introductions. *Conservation Biology* 10:300–302.

Kulkarni, V.G. (1995). *Modeling and Analysis of Stochastic Systems*. London, UK: Chapman and Hall.

Margolis, M., Shogren, J. and Fischer, C. (2005). How Trade Politics Affect Invasive Species Control. *Ecological Economics* 52:305–313.

McAusland, C. and Costello, C. (2004). Avoiding Invasives: Trade-related Policies for Controlling Unintentional Exotic Species Introductions. *Journal of Environmental Economics and Management* 48:954–977.

Nunes, P.A.L.D. and Van den Bergh, J.C.J.M. (2004). Can People Value Protection Against Invasive Marine Species? Evidence from a Joint TC-CV Survey in the Netherlands. *Environmental and Resource Economics* 28:517–532.

Office of Technology Assessment (OTA) (1993). *Harmful Non-indigenous Species in the United States. OTA-F-565.* Washington, District of Columbia: U.S. Government Printing Office.

Olson, L.J. and Roy, S. (2002). The Economics of Controlling a Stochastic Biological Invasion. *American Journal of Agricultural Economics* 84: 1311–1316.

Parai, A.K. (1999). Profit Tax and Tariff Under International Oligopoly. *International Review of Economics and Finance* 8:317–326.

Perrings, C., Williamson, M. and Dalmazzone, S. (2000). Introduction. *In* C. Perrings, M. Williamson and S. Dalmazzone (eds.), *The Economics of Biological Invasions.* Cheltenham, UK: Edward Elgar.

Pimentel, D., Lach, L., Zuniga, R. and Morrison, D. (2000). Environmental and Economic Costs of Nonindigenous Species in the United States. *BioScience* 50:53–65.

Prestemon, J.P., Zhu, S., Turner, J.A., Buongiorno, J. and Li, R. (2006). Forest Product Trade Impacts of an Invasive Species: Modeling Structure and International Trade-offs. *Agricultural and Resource Economics Review* 35:128–143.

Ross, S.M. (1996). *Stochastic Processes,* 2nd edn. New York: Wiley.

Simberloff, D., Schmitz, D. and Brown, T. (eds.) (1997). *Strangers in Paradise.* Washington, District of Columbia: Island Press.

Tijms, H.C. (2003). *A First Course in Stochastic Models.* Chichester, UK: Wiley.

USDA, APHIS and USFS (2000). Pest Risk Assessment for Importation of Solid Wood Packing Materials into the United States. Available at http://www.aphis.usda.gov/ppq/pra/swpm/complete.pdf [22 January 2013].

Vishwasrao, S., Gupta, S. and Benchekroun, H. (2007). Optimum Tariffs and Patent Length in a Model of North–South Technology Transfer. *International Review of Economics and Finance* 16:1–14.

Vitousek, P.M., D'Antonio, C.M., Loope, L.L. and Westbrooks, R. (1996). Biological Invasions as Global Environmental Change. *American Scientist* 84:468–478.

Yang, Z. and Perakis, A.N. (2004). Multiattribute Decision Analysis of Mandatory Ballast Water Treatment measures in the US Great Lakes. *Transportation Research Part D* 9:81–86.

Zhao, Z., Wahl, T. I. and Marsh, T. L. (2006). Invasive Species Management: Foot-and-mouth Disease in the U.S. Beef Industry. *Agricultural and Resource Economics Review* 35:98–115.

Chapter 14

AN ANALYSIS OF INSPECTIONS WHEN ECONOMIC COST REDUCTION MATTERS MORE THAN BIOLOGICAL INVASION DAMAGE CONTROL

with H. Beladi

DeAngelo *et al.* (2006; 2007) have shown that there are circumstances in which there is a tension between economic cost minimization and inspection stringency in invasive species management. We explore this issue further in this chapter by studying the behavior of a *risk loving* inspector in a seaport who is entrusted with the task of inspecting the container cargo on arriving ships for the presence of one or more deleterious invasive species. This inspector is risk loving in the sense that he is more concerned about economic cost reduction than he is about biological invasion damage control. Specifically, we first use the theory of continuous time Markov chains (CTMCs) to delineate a probabilistic inspection regime. Next, we mathematically explain the sense in which our inspector is risk loving. Finally, we use the stochastic features of the problem to compute the long run expected amount of time (LRET) an arriving ship that is inspected by the risk loving inspector spends in the seaport under study.

1. Introduction

It is now well known that in addition to carrying goods between regions, airplanes, trucks, and particularly ships have also managed to carry a whole host of invasive plant and animal species from one geographical region of the world to another. There are many ways in which airplanes, trucks, and ships have transported invasive plant and animal species from one region of the world to another. Invasive animal species have sometimes succeeded in lodging themselves in the landing gear of airplanes and in this way they have traveled as stowaways from one country to another. Similarly, a number of marine invasive species have been introduced unintentionally into a region by ships dumping their ballast water. Cargo ships commonly carry ballast water in order to augment vessel stability when they are not carrying full loads. When these ships come into a seaport, this ballast water must be released before cargo can be loaded. This means of species introductions is important and Yang and Perakis (2004), Batabyal *et al.* (2005), Batabyal and Beladi (2006), and others have now studied the problem of managing invasive species that have been introduced into a particular region by means of the dumping of ballast water.

Ships routinely use containers to carry cargo from one nation to another and these containers are often the source for the introduction of one or more invasive species. Such introductions take place because invasive species can remain hidden in containers for long periods of time. In addition, substances such as wood — often used to pack cargo in containers — may themselves contain invasive species. In fact, as noted by Batabyal and Nijkamp (2005), a joint report from the United States Department of Agriculture (USDA), the Animal and Plant Health Inspection Service (APHIS), and the United States Forest Service (USFS) has shown that nearly 51.8% of maritime shipments contain solid wood packing substances and that infection rates for solid wood packing substances are noteworthy (USDA, APHIS and USFS, 2000, p. 25). To see this clearly, consider the following case. Inspections of wooden spools from China revealed infection rates between 22% and 24% and inspections of braces for granite blocks imported into Canada were found to hold live insects 32% of the time (USDA, APHIS and USFS, 2000, pp. 27–28).

Successful invasions of new habitats by deleterious invasive species give rise to immense costs in the nations in which these novel habitats are located. In this regard, the Office of Technology Assessment (OTA, 1993) has established that the Russian wheat aphid caused $600 million worth of crop damage between 1987 and

1989. As a second example, Pimentel *et al.* (2000) have calculated the total costs of all invasive species to be around $137 billion per year. Economic costs are not the end of the story. In fact, in addition to these economic costs, invasive species have caused a lot of ecological damage as well. For example, Vitousek *et al.* (1996) have noted that invasive species can change ecosystem processes, act as vectors of diseases, and diminish biological diversity. In addition, Cox (1993) has observed that out of 256 vertebrate extinctions with a known cause, 109 are the result of the actions of invasive species. Because of these reasons, the management of invasive species is a subject that interests both economists and ecologists.

From the vantage point of a manager, there are a number of actions that this individual can take to address the problem of biological invasions. These actions are typically *pre-invasion* or *post-invasion* in nature. The objective of pre-invasion actions is to prevent invasive species from invading a new habitat. In contrast, post-invasion actions involve the optimal control of an invasive species, given that this species has already invaded a new habitat. *Inspections* are a basic pre-invasion tool that is available to managers interested in precluding biological invasions. They are routinely used at airports, land border crossings, and in seaports to screen humans, the cargo carried by humans, and the cargo carried in containers. Given the salience of inspections, several researchers have now begun to formally study inspections in the context of invasive species management.

In this regard, McAusland and Costello (2004) show that when one takes an intertemporal view and considers the future effects of current species introductions, one is naturally led to favor more stringent inspections. Batabyal and Yoo (2006) have studied the statistical properties of what they call a generic container inspection policy. Ameden *et al.* (2007) study border enforcement and firm responses in a theoretical model of invasive species management. They demonstrate that increased inspections are likely to result in a decrease of both shipments and due care by importers. Batabyal and Yoo (2008) analyze a random inspection scheme and compute the expected total fines that will be collected by an inspector who uses this scheme to screen arriving ships for the presence of one or more invasive species.

Batabyal (2008) studies inspections in a scenario in which a seaport inspector places equal weight on biological invasion damage control and on economic cost reduction. Specifically, he notes that the optimal dependability and speed of inspections is the solution to a particular long run expected net cost (LRENC) minimization problem. Merel and Carter (2008) show that the import risk from invasive species is usefully handled with inspections. In particular, when inspection costs are relatively low, a penalty on contaminated imports is likely to be superior to a simple tariff designed to reduce the overall volume of trade. Sanchirico *et al.* (2010) point to the ways in which inspections are useful in managing invasive species when these inspections are a single policy tool in a package consisting of other policy tools as well.

The two papers that are closest to the present chapter are DeAngelo *et al.* (2006; 2007). These two papers focus on the twin objectives of reducing the economic cost associated with inspections and on diminishing the likelihood of one or more biological invasions. In these two papers, greater (lesser) inspection stringency reflects an enhanced (decreased) concern for the potential damage from a biological invasion. Therefore, an inspector who places a relatively big (small) weight on invasion damage control will, all else being equal, want to inspect ships more (less) stringently. We explore this relatively little studied issue further in this chapter by studying the behavior of a *risk loving* inspector in a seaport who is entrusted with the task of inspecting the container cargo on arriving ships for the presence of one or more damaging invasive species. In the setting of this chapter, risk loving means that our inspector is *more* concerned about reducing the economic cost associated with inspections than he is about biological invasion damage control. Specifically, we first use the theory of continuous time

Markov chains (CTMCs)[1] to delineate a probabilistic inspection regime. This delineation is based on Lin and Kumar (1984). Next, we mathematically explain the sense in which our inspector is risk loving. Finally, we use the stochastic features of the problem to compute the long run expected amount of time (LRET) an arriving ship that is inspected by the risk loving inspector spends in the seaport under study.

The rest of this chapter is arranged as follows. Section 2 first uses the theory of CTMCs to provide a detailed description of the stochastic inspection regime that is the subject of this chapter. Next, this section explains the sense in which our inspector is risk loving. Section 3 calculates the LRET an arriving ship that is inspected by the risk loving inspector spends in the seaport under study. Section 4 concludes and offers suggestions for future research on the subject of this chapter.

2. A Probabilistic Inspection Regime

Ships carrying container cargo arrive at the seaport in a particular geographical region of a nation in accordance with a stationary Poisson process with time independent rate $\lambda > 0$. We suppose that there is space in this seaport where each arriving ship can temporarily wait until it is to be inspected by our seaport inspector. Consistent wih the discussion in DeAngelo *et al.* (2006; 2007), in conducting his inspections, our inspector can follow one or both of the following two protocols. First, he can inspect arriving ships relatively slowly and "relatively slowly" here is a proxy for more stringent inspections. More stringent inspections will be conducted by our inspector if preventing one or more biological invasions is *more* important

---

to him than is reducing the economic cost from conducting inspections. Second, this same inspector can inspect arriving ships relatively quickly and "relatively quickly" in this chapter is a proxy for less stringent or more lax inspections. More lax inspections will be conducted by the inspector if he is *more* concerned about reducing the economic cost associated with inspections than he is about reducing the damage to society from one or more biological invasions.

Let us denote the faster (slower) inspection protocol by 1 (2). We suppose that the time it takes to inspect a ship using the faster (slower) inspection protocol is exponentially distributed with mean $1/\beta_i$ where $i = 1, 2$. Because inspection protocol 1 is faster than inspection protocol 2, we have $1/\beta_1 < 1/\beta_2$. For reasons of mathematical tractability, we assume that $\beta_1 + \beta_2 > \lambda$. Our inspector is risk loving because he generally uses the faster and less stringent inspection protocol to inspect an arriving ship, independent of this arriving ship's country of origin. The slower and more stringent inspection protocol is used by our inspector only when the number of ships waiting to be inspected exceeds a critical threshold denoted by T.

The use of each inspection protocol results in the inspection of a single ship at any particular point in time. Given that our inspector is risk loving in the sense described earlier in this section, we suppose that he would like to *minimize* the LRET a ship spends being inspected at the seaport before its cargo is cleared for transport to various inland destinations. To this end, our inspector uses the following decision rule to determine when only the fast inspection protocol is to be used and when both protocols are to be used to inspect arriving ships. The slower or more stringent protocol is used only when the number of ships waiting to be inspected in the seaport exceeds the critical threshold T. When the number of waiting ships in the seaport is either at or lower than the threshold T, our inspector reverts back to using the fast inspection protocol only. Given this description of the probabilistic inspection regime, our next task is to use the theory of CTMCs to compute the LRET an arriving ship that is inspected spends in the seaport under study.

3. The Expected Inspection Time

Let $X(t)$ denote the number of ships present at time t in the seaport under study. Let the random variable $Y(t) = 1$ if the slow or the second inspection protocol is being used by our inspector to conduct inspections and let $Y(t) = 0$ if only the fast protocol is being used. Then, recalling the definition of a CTMC from either Ross (1996, pp. 231–294) or from Tijms (2003, pp. 141–186), it is clear that the stochastic process $\{X(t), Y(t)\}$ is a CTMC whose state space I is given by the union of two specific sets. In symbols, we have

$$I = \{(i,0) : i = 0,1,2,\ldots T\} \cup \{(i,1) : i = 1,2,3,\ldots\}. \quad (1)$$

With this specification of the state space out of the way, let us denote the so-called equilibrium probabilities of the above described CTMC by $p(i,\alpha)$ where α takes on any one of the two values described above.

To proceed further, it will be necessary to use the so called flow rate equation method — see Tijms (2003, pp. 147–154) for additional details — to equate the rate out of the set of states with i or more ships present in our seaport to the rate into this set. Undertaking this exercise, we get four equations. These are given by

$$\beta_1 p(1,0) + \beta_2 p(1,1) = \lambda p(0,0) \quad (2)$$

$$\beta_1 p(i,0) + (\beta_1 + \beta_2) p(i,1)$$
$$= \lambda \{p(i-1,0) + p(i-1,1)\}, \quad i = 2,3,\ldots,T, \quad (3)$$

$$(\beta_1 + \beta_2) p(T+1,1) = \lambda \{p(T,0) + p(T,1)\}, \quad (4)$$

and

$$(\beta_1 + \beta_2) p(i,1) = \lambda p(i-1,1), \quad i = T+2, T+3,\ldots \quad (5)$$

In addition, by equating the rate out of state $(i,0)$ to the rate into state $(i,0)$, we get

$$(\lambda + \beta_1) p(i,0) = \beta_1 p(i+1,0) + \beta_2 p(i+1,1)$$
$$+ \lambda p(i-1,0), \quad i = 1,2,\ldots,T. \quad (6)$$

The reader should note that in writing Equations (2)–(6), it is understood that the probability $p(T+1,0) = 0$.

Equations (2)–(6) can be solved using the procedure discussed in Tijms (2003, pp. 147–154). To this end, we first calculate the $2T+2$ unknowns given by $p(i,0)$, $i = 0,1,2,\ldots,T$ and $p(i,1)$, $i = 1,2,\ldots,T+1$ by solving a system of $2T+2$ linear equations. In order to undertake this last task, we use Equations (2)–(4), (6), and an equation that tells us that the expected number of ship arrivals in our seaport per unit time must equal the expected number of inspections completed per unit time. This last equation is given by

$$\lambda = \beta_1 \sum_{i=1}^{T} p(i,0) + \beta_2 p(1,1) + (\beta_1 + \beta_2) \sum_{i=2}^{\infty} p(i,1). \tag{7}$$

Manipulating Equation (7), we get

$$\lambda = \beta_1 \sum_{i=1}^{T} p(i,0) + \beta_2 p(1,1) + (\beta_1 + \beta_2)$$

$$\times \left\{ 1 - p(0,0) - \sum_{i=1}^{T} p(i,0) \right\}. \tag{8}$$

We can now use Equations (2)–(4), (6), and (8) to solve for the above mentioned $2T+2$ unknowns. Once we have solved for $p(i,0)$ where $i = 0,1,2,\ldots,T$ and $p(i,1)$ where $i = 1,2,\ldots,T+1$, we can recursively calculate the other probabilities $p(i,1)$ where $i > T+1$ by using the recurrence relation given by Equation (5). Once this has been done, by adapting an equation in Tijms (2003, p. 153), we deduce that the long run expected number of ships in the seaport under study or LRENS is given by

$$\text{LRENS} = \sum_{i=1}^{T} i\{p(i,0) + p(i,1)\} + \sum_{i=T+1}^{\infty} ip(i,1). \tag{9}$$

Finally, using Little's formula — see Tijms (2003, p. 153) for more details — it follows that the LRET spent by inspected ships in the seaport is given by $(1/\lambda)$(LRENS) or

$$\text{LRET} = \frac{1}{\lambda} \left[\sum_{i=1}^{T} i\{p(i,0) + p(i,1)\} + \sum_{i=T+1}^{\infty} ip(i,1) \right]. \quad (10)$$

Given that our inspector is risk loving in the sense explained in Section 2, if he were to solve an optimization problem then he would like to choose apposite control variables and minimize the right hand side (RHS) of Equation (10). We suppose that the arrival rate of ships or λ is exogenous to our inspector. This means that the only control variables available to him are the parameters β_1 and β_2 of the two exponentially distributed fast and slow inspection protocol times. By selecting β_1 and β_2 optimally, our inspector will be able to minimize the time spent by arriving ships undergoing inspections in the seaport under study. This completes our characterization and discussion of the probabilistic inspection regime that is marked by risk loving behavior on the part of the inspector.

4. Conclusions

In this chapter, we analyzed a stochastic inspection regime which, consistent with previous literature on this subject, accounted for the fact that there is a tension between economic cost minimization and inspection stringency in invasive species management. We explored this issue further by examining the behavior of a *risk loving* inspector in a seaport who is responsible for inspecting the container cargo on arriving ships for the presence of one or more damaging invasive species. In particular, we first used the theory of CTMCs to describe the stochastic inspection regime. Next, we mathematically explained the sense in which our inspector is risk loving. Finally, we used the stochastic features of the problem to compute the LRET an arriving ship — inspected by our risk loving inspector — spends in the seaport.

The analysis in this chapter can be extended in a number of directions. We now suggest two possible extensions. First, to account for the fact that ships are more likely to arrive at the seaport under study at certain times than at others, one could model the ship arrival process with a non-stationary Poisson process with a time dependent intensity function given by, for instance, $\lambda(t) \geq 0$. Second, from the standpoint of the efficient allocation of inspection resources, it would be useful to set up — possibly with one or more constraints — and then solve the optimization problem discussed briefly towards the end of Section 3. Research on inspections as a tool for managing deleterious invasive species that incorporate these aspects of the problem into the analysis will provide additional insights into a management problem that has considerable economic and ecological ramifications.

References

Ameden, H.A., Cash, S.B. and Zilberman, D. (2007). Border Enforcement and Firm Response in the Management of Invasive Species. *Journal of Agricultural and Applied Economics* 39:35–46.

Batabyal, A.A. (2008). A Theoretical Note on the Optimal Dependability and Speed of Container Inspections in Invasive Species Management. *Studies in Regional Science* 38:199–204.

Batabyal, A.A., Beladi, H. and Koo, W.W. (2005). Maritime Trade, Biological Invasions, and the Properties of Alternate Inspection Regimes. *Stochastic Environmental Research and Risk Assessment* 19:184–190.

Batabyal, A.A. and Beladi, H. (2006). International Trade and Biological Invasions: A Queuing Theoretic Analysis of the Prevention Problem. *European Journal of Operational Research* 170:758–770.

Batabyal, A.A. and Nijkamp, P. (2005). On Container versus Time Based Inspection Policies in Invasive Species Management. *Stochastic Environmental Research and Risk Assessment* 19:340–347.

Batabyal, A.A. and Yoo, S.J. (2006). Some Statistical Properties of a Generic Container Inspection Policy in Invasive Species Management. *Ecological Economics* 60:1–4.

Batabyal, A.A. and Yoo, S.J. (2008). A Theoretical Analysis of Random Inspections and Fines in Invasive Species Management. *Economics Bulletin* 17:1–9.

Cox, G.W. (1993). *Conservation Ecology*. Dubuque, Iowa: W.C. Brown Publishers.

DeAngelo, G., Batabyal, A.A. and Kumar, S. (2006). On Economic Cost Minimization versus Biological Invasion Damage Control. *In* A. Oude Lansink (ed.), *New Approaches to the Economics of Plant Health*. Heidelberg, Germany: Springer-Verlag.

DeAngelo, G., Batabyal, A.A. and Kumar, S. (2007). An Analysis of Economic Cost Minimization and Biological Invasion Damage Control Using the AWQ Criterion. *Annals of Regional Science* 41:639–655.

Lin, W. and Kumar, P. (1984). Optimal Control of a Queuing System with Two Heterogeneous Servers. *IEEE Transactions on Automatic Control* 29:696–703.

McAusland, C. and Costello, C. (2004). Avoiding Invasives: Trade-related Policies for Controlling Unintentional Exotic Species Introductions. *Journal of Environmental Economics and Management* 48:954–977.

Merel, P.R. and Carter, C.A. (2008). A Second Look at Managing Import Risk from Invasive Species. *Journal of Environmental Economics and Management* 56:286–290.

Office of Technology Assessment (OTA) (1993). *Harmful Non-Indigenous Species in the United States*. OTA-F-565, Washington, District of Columbia.

Pimentel, D., Lach, L., Zuniga, R. and Morrison, D. (2000). Environmental and Economic Costs of Nonindigenous Species in the United States. *BioScience* 50:53–65.

Ross, S.M. (1996). *Stochastic Processes*, 2nd edn. New York: Wiley.

Sanchirico, J.N., Albers, H.J., Fischer, C. and Coleman, C. (2010). Spatial Management of Invasive Species: Pathways and Policy Options. *Environmental and Resource Economics* 45:517–535.

Tijms, H.C. (2003). *A First Course in Stochastic Models*. Chichester, UK: Wiley.

USDA, APHIS and USFS (2000). Pest Risk Assessment for Importation of Solid Wood Packing Materials into the United States. Available at http://www.aphis.usda.gov/ppq/pra/swpm/complete.pdf [accessed on 22 January 2013].

Vitousek, P.M., D'Antonio, C.M., Loope, L.L. and Westbrooks, R. (1996). Biological Invasions as Global Environmental Change. *American Scientist* 84:468–478.

Yang, Z. and Perakis, A.N. (2004). Multiattribute Decision Analysis of Mandatory Ballast Water Treatment Measures in the US Great Lakes. *Transportation Research Part D* 9:81–86.

Part VI

Environmental Regulation

Chapter 15

CONSISTENCY AND OPTIMALITY IN A DYNAMIC GAME OF POLLUTION CONTROL II: MONOPOLY

This chapter continues a line of research begun and shown in Batabyal (1996) [Consistency and Optimality in a Dynamic Game of Pollution Control I: Competition. *Environmental and Resource Economics* 8: 205–220]. I model the interaction between a regulator and a monopolistic, polluting firm as a Stackelberg differential game in which the regulator leads. The firm creates pollution, which results in a stock externality. I analyze the intertemporal effects of alternate pollution control measures. The principal issue here concerns the dynamic inconsistency of the optimal solution. *Inter alia*, I compare the steady state levels of pollution under optimal and under dynamically consistent policies.

1. Introduction[1]

As is well known,[2] the static Pigouvian approach to environmental regulation involves setting a corrective tax equal to the marginal social damage caused by the externality. Unfortunately, this approach overlooks the fact that most contemporary regulatory problems in environmental economics are *dynamic* in nature. As such, any reasonable analysis of environmental regulation must

---

1. I thank Larry Karp, Maury Obstfeld, and seminar participants at the University of Massachusetts-Amherst for useful comments. The USDA and the Giannini Foundation provided financial support. The usual disclaimer applies.
2. See Bator (1958), Baumol and Oates (1988), and Cropper and Oates (1992) among others.

explicitly account for four features which are germane owing to the dynamic nature of the underlying problem. The first feature concerns the inherent *conflict* in the objectives of the regulator and the polluter. The second feature pertains to the *ongoing* nature of the interaction between the regulator and the polluter. Third, the question of the dynamic effects of *alternate* regulatory instruments is relevant. Fourth, because the interaction between the regulator and the polluter is ongoing, the parties are forward looking, i.e., the future affects the present. As a result, analyses of environmental regulation must address the problem of *dynamic inconsistency* of the adopted regulatory policies. While the significance of the first feature is generally well understood, analyses of environmental regulation which explicitly incorporate all four features have been few and far between.[3]

Given this state of affairs, in this chapter, I study environmental regulation in a dynamic context, explicitly incorporating all four features mentioned in the above paragraph. An important part of my analysis will consist of studying the effects of alternate price control instruments. While there exists a large literature on the effects of price versus quantity control instruments,[4] a literature of similar magnitude on the properties of alternate price control measures does not exist. As such, in focusing on the properties of alternate price control instruments, I hope to contribute to this nascent literature on "prices versus prices."

I shall model the interaction between a regulator and a monopolistic, polluter as a deterministic Stackelberg differential game in which the regulator leads.[5] The differential game incorporates two significant aspects of the regulator/polluter interaction; first, it explicitly considers the dynamic nature of the interaction and

---

3. For more on this aspect, see the discussion in Batabyal (1996).

4. See Weitzman (1974). See Batabyal (1995) for a recent survey of many of the important issues.

5. A companion paper — Batabyal (1996) — analyzes the competitive industry case.

second, it recognizes that the game being played by the regulator and the polluting firm at each instant in time is different owing to the evolution of the state.

The first part of the analysis considers dynamically inconsistent policies in a game in which the state, i.e., the stock of pollution, evolves in a manner known to both the players. In every case analyzed, the *production* of a certain good causes pollution. The informational costs of taxing pollution directly are assumed to be prohibitive. As a result, the regulator taxes the production of the polluting good. The regulator's objective is to maximize the sum of net benefits and tax revenues.[6] The two kinds of policies available to the regulator include a unit tax an *ad valorem* tax. Depending on the industry structure, as compared to a unit tax, an *ad valorem* tax often leads to different (a) levels of revenue and (b) welfare effects. For these reasons, I have chosen to study the dynamic effects of these two policy instruments. *Inter alia*, my study will involve a comparison of the outcomes of the different games resulting from the use of these two price control instruments.

As I shall show, an important part of this comparative exercise will turn on the intertemporal consistency of the policies employed by the regulator. Further, the effectiveness of regulatory action will depend fundamentally on whether the firm's production costs are related to the stock of pollution. Finally, if the regulator's policy instrument set is sufficiently large, distortions stemming from market imperfections can be dealt with effectively.

Section 2 describes the Stackelberg differential game. Section 3 derives and compares the various open loop policies. In Section 4, I derive time consistent policies and then compare them to the time inconsistent policies of Section 3. Section 5 offers concluding comments and discusses directions for future research.

---

6. See Van der Ploeg and de Zeeuw (1992, p. 121) for a similar objective.

2. The Stackelberg Differential Game

My model is a variant of one analyzed by Karp (1984). A monopolistic polluter maximizes profits. $P(q)$ is the thrice differentiable inverse demand function faced by the firm. Let $P'(q) < 0$, where q is the production rate of the firm. Associated with production at rate q are two kinds of costs. The first kind of cost depends on the current stock of pollution.[7] Only a portion of this cost is internalized by the firm. Let $c(x)$ be the internalized average cost of producing unit output at time t when the stock of pollution is $x(t)$. Then $c(x)q$ represents the instantaneous, internalized pollution dependent cost of producing at rate q. I assume that $c'(x) > 0$, $c''(x) > 0$, and that $c(0) = 0$.

The second kind of cost is independent of the level of pollution. Let w denote the constant marginal cost of producing at rate q; then wq represents the pollution independent cost of producing at rate q. Let τ_u and ζ_a denote the unit and the *ad valorem* tax, respectively. Then the firm's payoff in an infinite horizon game in which the regulator uses a unit tax and where r denotes the interest rate is

$$J_F = \int_0^\infty e^{-rt}\{P(q)q - wq - \tau_u q - c(x)q\}dt. \tag{1}$$

When the regulator employs an *ad valorem* tax, the corresponding payoff for the firm is

$$J_F = \int_0^\infty e^{-rt}\{\tau_a P(q)q - wq - c(x)q\}dt, \tag{2}$$

where $\tau_a = 1/(1 + \zeta_a)$.

There are three components to the regulator's payoff. A twice differentiable function $B(q)$ measures social benefit when production is at rate q. $D(x)$ is a twice differentiable function which measures the damage from pollution. Alternately put, the firm creates pollution;

---

7. See Batabyal (1996) for an example of such stock dependent costs.

the level of this pollution at time t is $x(t)$. The function $D(\cdot)$ maps pollution to a measure of environmental damage for society.[8] Let $B'(q) > 0$, $B''(q) < 0$, $D'(x) > 0$, and let $D''(x) > 0$. When the regulator uses a unit tax to control pollution, his payoff is

$$J_R = \int_0^\infty e^{-rt}\{B(q) + \tau_u q - D(x)\}dt. \tag{3}$$

When he uses an *ad valorem* tax, his corresponding payoff is

$$J_R = \int_0^\infty e^{-rt}\{B(q) + (1 - \tau_a)P(q)q - D(x)\}dt. \tag{4}$$

The regulator controls $\tau_u(t)$ and $\tau_a(t)$ and the firm controls $q(t)$. As the leader, the regulator announces a trajectory for the tax which the firm treats parametrically. The regulator and the firm are constrained by the evolution of the stock of pollution which is given by

$$dx/dt = \dot{x} = q(t), \tag{5}$$

where $x(0) = x_0 > 0$ is given. Equation (5) tells us that the evolution of the stock of pollution is a function of the flow of production. In my model there is no way to "naturally" reduce pollution.[9]

Depending on the policy employed by the regulator, different steady state levels of output and pollution emerge. One can think of these levels as the outcomes of different games. I shall say that game 1 results in less pollution than game 2 if and only if $x_1^* < x_2^*$, where x_i^* refers to the steady state pollution level in game i, $i = 1, 2$. Similarly, I shall say that game 1 results in less output than game 2 if and only if $q_1^* < q_2^*$ where q_i^* refers to the steady state output level in game i, $i = 1, 2$. In many cases it will not be possible to obtain general results. In such cases my analysis will concentrate on special functional forms.

---

8. Also see Batabyal (1996).

9. See Batabyal (1996) for a discussion of the implications of using a state equation $\dot{x} = q(t) - f(x)$, where $f(x)$ is the regenerative capacity of the environment.

3. Open Loop Taxes

In this section I shall derive the optimal open loop unit and *ad valorem* taxes for the regulatory objectivs described in Section 2. These taxes are dynamically inconsistent except when the stock dependent cost function is constant. In other words, if the stock dependent cost function is not constant and the regulator is able to alter — at some time $t > 0$ — the trajectory of taxes he set at $t = 0$, then he will choose to do so. This is an extremely important fact and I shall have more to say about dynamic inconsistency in Section 4.

3.1. *The open loop unit tax*

I shall solve the regulator's problem using a method due to Chen and Cruz (1972) and Simaan and Cruz (1973a; 1973b). This method clearly brings out the connection between dynamic inconsistency and the pollution dependent cost function. The basic idea is as follows. The regulator treats the firm's first-order condition as an ordinary constraint and the firm's costate variable as a state variable. These two conditions along with the requirement that the optimal solution approach a steady state converts the differential game into a control problem for the regulator.

When the regulator levy's a unit tax on the firm, the firm's first-order necessary conditions are

$$P'(q)q + P(q) - w - \tau_{\mathrm{u}} - c(x) + \lambda(t) = 0 \qquad (6)$$

and

$$\dot{\lambda} = r\lambda + c'(x)q, \qquad (7)$$

where $\lambda(t)$ is the costate variable associated with (5). The reader should note that (7) represents a jump state constraint.[10] That is, $\lambda(0)$ is free and the value of $\lambda(t)$ is determined by current

---

10. For more on jump state constraints, see Karp and Newbery (1993).

and/or future events. In other words, (7) is not a fixed initial state constraint for the regulator. This makes the regulator's problem a non-standard control problem. Solving for τ_u from (6) and substituting in (3) I get

$$J_R = \int_0^\infty e^{-rt}\{B(q) + P'(q)q^2 + P(q)q$$
$$- wq - c(x)q + \lambda q - D(x)\}dt. \tag{8}$$

Equation (8) gives the regulator's payoff. Of particular interest is the term λq. Since λ is the shadow value of pollution to the firm, λq can be thought of as the firm's implicit value of polluted air gained by production at rate q. I have now converted the regulator's problem from one of maximizing (3) over τ_u subject to (5), to one of maximizing (8) over q subject to (5) and (7). The first-order necessary conditions to the regulator's problem are

$$B'(q) + P''(q)q^2 + 3P'(q)q + P(q)$$
$$- w - c(x) + \lambda + \sigma_1 + \sigma_2 c'(x) = 0, \tag{9}$$

$$\dot{\sigma}_1 = r\sigma_1 + c'(x)q + D'(x) - \sigma_2 c''(x)q, \tag{10}$$

and

$$\dot{\sigma}_2 = -q, \tag{11}$$

where σ_1 and σ_2 are the costate variables associated with (5) and (7). The key equation here is (11). Since $\lambda(0)$ is free, as Simaan and Cruz (1973b) have noted, the boundary condition for σ_2 is $\sigma_2(0) = 0$. Using this last condition, (11) can be written as

$$\sigma_2(t) = x_0 - x(t). \tag{12}$$

Equation (12) tells us that the regulator's marginal value of the firm's shadow value of pollution can be expressed as the difference between the initial stock of pollution and the current stock of pollution. Using $q(t) \geq 0$, (12) implies that $\sigma_2(t) < 0$. This means that

$\forall t \in (0,\infty)$, the regulator will want to decrease the firm's marginal value of pollution. Hence, this solution is dynamically inconsistent. Since the firm does not completely internalize the impact of the pollution it causes, the regulator will want to deviate from the policy trajectory he announced at $t = 0$, and decrease the firm's marginal value of pollution to the socially optimal level. The reader will note that the constancy of the pollution dependent cost function is necessary and sufficient to eliminate the inconsistency of the above solution.

A comment on (7) is in order. I have already noted that optimality requires that the regulator set $\sigma_2(0) = 0$. Once he has done so, (7) is a binding constraint on the regulator's subsequent actions. In other words, (7) acts as a rational expectations constraint for the regulator. The rational expectations nature of this constraint stems from the fact that the firm's problem is dynamic.

3.2.   *The open loop ad valorem tax*

I shall now derive the solution when the regulator uses an *ad valorem* tax. The first-order necessary conditions to the firm's problem are

$$\tau_a\{P(q) + P'(q)q\} - w - c(x) + \lambda(t) = 0, \qquad (13)$$

and (7). Solving for τ_a from (13) and substituting into (4), I get

$$J_R = \int_0^\infty e^{-rt}[B(q) + P(q)q - \Psi(q)\{w + c(x) - \lambda\} - D(x)]dt,$$

$$(14)$$

where $\Psi(q) = \phi(q)q$, $\phi(q) = 1/\{\alpha(q) + 1\}$, $|\alpha(q)| < 1$, and $\alpha(q)$ is the price flexibility, i.e., the reciprocal of the demand elasticity. The first-order necessary conditions to the regulator's problem are

$$B'(q) + P(q) + P'(q)q - \Psi'(q)\{w + c(x) - \lambda\} + \sigma_1 + \sigma_2 c'(x) = 0,$$

$$(15)$$

$$\dot{\sigma}_1 = r\sigma_1 + \Psi(q)c'(x) + D'(x) - \sigma_2 c''(x)q, \qquad (16)$$

and

$$\dot{\sigma}_2 = \Psi(q), \tag{17}$$

where σ_1 and σ_2 are the costate variables associated with (5) and (7).

Equations (8) and (14) tell us that — unlike the competitive case studied in Batabyal (1996) — the use of these two policy instruments leads to different outcomes. This is because these two taxes affect the shape of the inverse demand function differently.

3.3. *Analysis*

I shall denote steady state values by "*". When the regulator uses a unit tax, I get $q^* = 0$ from (5), $\lambda^* = 0$ from (7), $\sigma_1^* = D'(x^*)/r$ from (10), and $\sigma_2^* = x_0 - x^*$ from (12). Substituting these values in (9), I get an equation for the steady state level of pollution, x^*. This equation is

$$B'(0) + P(0) - w - c(x^*) - \{D'(x^*)/r\} + c'(x^*)(x_0 - x^*) = 0. \tag{18}$$

Comparing (18) with the corresponding equation for a competitive industry in Batabyal (1996), I note that the *steady state* level of pollution is the same irrespective of whether the industry is competitive or monopolistic. When the regulator uses an *ad valorem* tax, the expressions for q^* and λ^* remain the same as above. However, now $\sigma_1^* = [\{-\Psi(0)c'(x^*) - D'(x^*)\}/r]$, and σ_2^* can be obtained by integrating (17) and then evaluating the resulting expression at $t = \infty$, using $\sigma_2(0) = 0$. Substituting these values for q, λ, σ_1, and σ_2 into (15) gives me an equation for x^*. This is

$$B'(0) + P(0) - \Psi'(0)\{w + c(x^*)\}$$

$$- \Psi(0)c'(x^*)/r - \{D'(x^*)/r\} + c'(x^*)\sigma_2^* = 0. \tag{19}$$

Inspecting (18) and (19), I find that in both cases the steady state pollution effects of the two taxes are fundamentally affected by the initial level of pollution as long as the stock dependent cost function is non-constant.[11] In other words, history matters.

From (6) and (13), I can compute expressions for the open loop unit and *ad valorem* taxes at $t = 0$ and at $t = \infty$. With these expressions, I can now state.

Proposition 1. *The optimal ad valorem tax is nonzero at $t = 0$ and at $t = \infty$ assuming that $\{P(\cdot) + P'(\cdot)q\} \neq 0$ at $t = 0$ and at $t = \infty$. The same is true of the optimal unit tax as long as $\{P(q) + P'(q)q\} \neq \{w + c(x) - \lambda\}$.*

Proof.   Recall that $\tau_a(0) = [\{w+c(x_0)-\lambda(0)\}]/[P\{q(0)\}+P'\{q(0)\} q(0)] \neq 0$ and that $\tau_a^* = [\{w + c(x^*)\}/\{P(0)\}] \neq 0$. Further, observe that $\{P(q) + P'(q)q\} \neq \{w + c(x) - \lambda\} \Rightarrow \tau_u(0) = [P\{q(0)\} + P'\{q(0)\}q(0) - w - c(x_0) + \lambda] \neq 0$ and that $\tau_u^* = [P(0) - w - c(x^*)] \neq 0$. $\square$

Proposition 1 describes the conditions — with perfect regulatory commitment — under which an optimal program does not involve setting zero taxes either at the beginning or at the end of the game. Note that because these solutions are inconsistent, as time progresses, the regulator will want to decrease the firm's valuation of pollution. Finally, observe that if the conditions stated in the proposition are not satisfied, it is possible for these optimal open loop taxes to be temporarily zero.

I can now compare the steady state output and pollution levels that arise from the use of the two open loop taxes. Since a general analysis of this condition cannot be conducted, the subsequent analysis will concentrate on special cases. Recall that in every case $q^* = 0$. Hence, the variable of interest is x^*. I shall use (18) and (19). Let $B(q) = \gamma q - (1/2)q^2$, $D(x) = (1/2)\delta x^2$, $c(x) = \alpha_1 x$, $P(q) = q^{-\alpha}$, $\alpha \in (0,1)$, and let $(1 - \alpha)\gamma > w$. Substituting

---

11. For the *ad valorem* tax case, the dependence of x^* on $x(0)$ can be verified in certain special cases. One such case is when the inverse demand function is isoelastic.

these functions into (18) and (19) I find that as compared to the *ad valorem* tax, the unit tax leads to a higher (lower) level of pollution as $\alpha\gamma/\{2\alpha_1 + (1 - \alpha)\delta/r\} > (<) [[\{\gamma - w + \alpha_1 x_0\}/\{2\alpha_1 + (1 - \alpha)\delta/r\}] - [\{\gamma - w + \alpha_1 x_0\}/\{2\alpha_1 + \delta/r\}]]$. Next, consider the case in which the damage function is linear, i.e., $D(x) = \delta x$. The functional forms for benefit, inverse demand, and the stock dependent cost are as above. Substituting these equations into (18) and (19), I note that as compared to the *ad valorem* tax, the unit tax leads to lower (higher) pollution as $\alpha\{(\delta/r) - \gamma\} > (<)0$. While it is difficult to interpret these parametric restrictions along economic lines, the reader will note that the key parameter is the price flexibility $-\alpha$.

I now use (18) to compare the steady state levels of pollution that arise under alternate specifications of the benefit and inverse demand functions when the regulator uses a unit tax. Let $P(q) = a - bq$, $D(x) = \delta x$, and let $c(x) = \alpha_1 x$. Then, irrespective of whether $B(q) = \gamma q - (1/2)q^2$ or $B(q) = \gamma q$, the unit tax leads to the same level of pollution. Next, let $B(q) = \gamma q - (1/2)q^2$, $D(x) = (1/2)\delta x^2$, $c(x) = \alpha_1 x$. If $\gamma > w$, then the unit tax leads to a lower level of pollution when $P(q) = a - bq$, as opposed to when $P(q) = q^{-\alpha}$, $\alpha \in (0, 1)$.

Note that the results of the above analysis depend in a fundamental way on the properties of the pollution dependent cost function. If this function is constant then the open loop and the consistent solutions of Section 4 coincide. As such, the regulator's policy — set at the beginning of the game — is credible and the question of forward looking firms thwarting the intended objective of a particular plan of action does not arise.

Given that the unit tax and the *ad valorem* tax lead to different outcomes, I now ask at what level each tax should be set when the regulator wishes to use both taxes simultaneously. The answer is contained in Proposition 2.

Proposition 2. *When the regulator uses both taxes simultaneously, it is optimal for him to set $\zeta_a = \infty$ and $\tau_u = -\{w + c(x) - \lambda\}$.*

Proof. When the regulator uses both taxes simultaneously, the firm's objective functional is

$$J_F = \int_0^\infty e^{-rt}\{\tau_a P(q)q - wq - \tau_u q - c(x)q\}dt. \qquad (20)$$

The first-order necessary conditions include $\tau_u = \tau_a\{P'(q)q + P(q)\}$ $- w - c(x) + \lambda$. Substituting this into the regulator's objective functional, I get

$$J_R = \int_0^\infty e^{-rt}[B(q) + P(q)q + \tau_a P'(q)q^2$$

$$- wq - c(x)q - D(x) + \lambda(t)q]dt. \qquad (21)$$

Now let $\tau_a \geq 0$. Since the regulator's current value Hamiltonian is linear and decreasing in τ_a, it is optimal to set $\tau_a = 0$. This in turn implies that $\zeta_a = \infty$ and that $\tau_u = -\{w + c(x) - \lambda\}$.   □

Proposition 2 tells us that when the regulator chooses to use both taxes simultaneously, it is optimal for him to levy an infinite *ad valorem* tax and impose a unit subsidy equal to $-\{w + c(x) - \lambda\}$, where λ solves (7) with $\lambda^* = 0$. Using $\tau_a = 0$ in (21) and comparing the resulting equation with the corresponding equation in Batabyal (1996), I find that when the regulator uses unit and *ad valorem* taxes simultaneously, he is able to force the monopolistic firm to behave competitively. This is because the simultaneous use of unit and *ad valorem* taxes allows the regulator to shift and rotate the inverse demand function. As a result, he is able to confront the monopolistic firm with an infinitely elastic non-stationary function. Note that unlike the competitive industry studied in Batabyal (1996), the simultaneous use of two taxes does not make one tax redundant.

4. Dynamically Consistent Taxes

The problem with inconsistent policies, i.e., open loop policies is that such policies are not credible. The forward looking firm will recognize that at $t = 0$, the regulator will set a tax trajectory from which he will want to deviate. Thus, such a tax trajectory will not be believed by the firm and hence the original policy will fail to achieve its objectives. This lack of credibility of open loop policies provides a rationale for the study of dynamically consistent policies.

I shall obtain consistent controls by using a method employed in Buiter (1983) and in Karp (1984). While other methods — see Karp (1991) — for obtaining consistent controls exist, there are two advantages to using the Buiter/Karp method. First, this method makes the logic of the solution transparent. Second, the method facilitates the comparison of results obtained in Section 3 with the results to be derived in this section. The basic idea is as follows. In a Stackelberg game, it must be possible to use the follower's first-order condition to eliminate the leader's control from his objective functional. When this has been done and the leader's problem has the form

$$J_R = \max_{q(t)} \int_0^\infty [e^{-rt}\{g(q,x) + hq(t)\lambda(t)\}]dt, \quad h \in \mathbb{R}, \quad (22)$$

$$\dot{x} = q(t), \ x(0) = x_0 > 0, \quad (23)$$

$$\dot{\lambda} = r\lambda + c'(x)q(t), \ \lambda(t) \le 0, \quad (24)$$

where $g(q,x)$ in my case is a linear combination of the derivatives of the benefit, damage, inverse demand, and the stock dependent cost functions, one can obtain consistent controls by using Theorem 1.

Theorem 1. *When the leader's problem has the form* (22)–(24), *consistent controls can be found by solving*

$$\hat{J}_R = \max_{q(t)} \int_0^\infty e^{-rt}g(q,x)dt, \quad (25)$$

subject to (23). Theorem 1 can be proved as in Karp (1984, pp. 94–96). Note that while the proof requires that the function multiplying the follower's costate variable be linear in the leader's control, the proof does not depend on h or the follower's costate variable being non-negative.

Put differently, in the class of problems that can be stated as (22)–(24), the leader obtains consistent controls by disregarding the effect that the follower's marginal value of the state has on his own payoff. The logical basis of this method is as follows. One way to eliminate the inconsistency of the open loop solutions of Section 3 lies in removing the term which makes the solution dependent on x_0. This can be done in two ways. The first approach is to posit that the stock dependent cost function is constant. Then $c'(x) = 0$ and the inconsistency disappears. However, this is a strong and, *a priori*, unrealistic restriction. The second approach lies in making $(x_0 - x)$ vanish. This is exactly what the above described method for obtaining consistent controls does "... by treating the [regulator's] problem as [a] sequence of short open loop problems, which in the limit becomes an infinite sequence of static optimization problems" (Karp, 1982, p. 117). Intuitively, one can think of a regulator who revises his tax policy whenever air quality declines by some set amount. The idea is to let this set amount and hence the time interval between successive revisions approach zero. When the regulator does not set a specific tax trajectory at the beginning of the game but continuously revises his control, x_0 in $(x_0 - x)$ must be replaced by $x(t)$. When this is done, $(x_0 - x)$ vanishes and the resulting solution is dynamically consistent. The only disadvantage of the above method lies in the requirement that the function multiplying $\lambda(t)$ be linear in the leader's control. This means that this approach cannot be used to find consistent controls for the general case in which the regulator uses an *ad valorem* tax. However, even in this case, for specific functional forms, the method can be used.

Consistent controls always result in a lower payoff to the regulator than do open loop controls except when the two kinds of controls coincide. This stems from the fact that forcing the controls to satisfy the principle of optimality completely eliminates any gain accruing to the regulator from setting policy at the beginning of the game. Alternatively, when the regulator uses consistent controls, his "period of commitment [shrinks] to zero" (Buiter, 1989, p. 244). In a manner analogous to Karp (1984, p. 88) the claim in this paragraph can be verified formally by observing that

$$\max_{q(t)} \left[\int_0^\infty \{e^{-rt} g(q,x) + \lambda q\} dt \right]$$

$$\geq \left\{ \max_{q(t)} \left[\int_0^\infty e^{-rt} g(q,x) dt \right] \right\} + \int_0^\infty \hat{q} \hat{\lambda} dt, \quad (26)$$

where $\hat{q}$ and $\hat{\lambda}$ are the optimized values of the output rate and the follower's marginal value of the state which arises from the solution to the maximization problem on the RHS of (26). The constraints for both problems are the same and are given by (23) and (24). Equality in (26) holds if and only if $\hat{\lambda} = 0$, a condition which holds when the pollution dependent cost function is constant. When this last condition holds, the open loop and the consistent controls coincide.

I now obtain dynamically consistent controls, in turn, when the regulator uses a unit tax, and then when the regulator uses an *ad valorem* tax.

4.1. *The dynamically consistent unit tax*

When the regulator uses a unit tax, the first-order conditions to his problem are

$$B'(q) + q^2 P''(q) + 3qP'(q) + P(q) - w - c(x) + \sigma = 0, \quad (27)$$

and

$$\dot{\sigma} = r\sigma + c'(x)q + D'(x), \quad (28)$$

where σ is the costate variable associated with (5). The steady state level of pollution, x^*, solves

$$B'(0) + P(0) - w - c(x^*) - D'(x^*)/r = 0. \quad (29)$$

4.2. *The dynamically consistent ad valorem tax*

When the regulator uses an *ad valorem* tax, the method proposed in Theorem 1 cannot be used to solve for the consistent tax in the general case owing to the nonlinearity of $\Psi(q)$. However, for some functional forms, $\Psi(q)$ is linear. In what follows, I shall analyze the impact of an *ad valorem* tax when $P(q) = q^{-\alpha}$, $\alpha \in (0, 1)$. In this case, $\Psi(q) = q/(1 - \alpha)$ and Theorem 1 can be used to conduct the analysis. When the regulator uses an *ad valorem* tax to control pollution, the first-order conditions to his problem are

$$B'(q) + (1 - \alpha)q^{-\alpha} - \{w/(1 - \alpha)\} - \{c(x)/(1 - \alpha)\} + \sigma = 0,$$

$$(30)$$

and

$$\dot{\sigma} = r\sigma + c'(x)q/(1 - \alpha) + D'(x), \qquad (31)$$

where σ is the costate variable associated with (5). I close this subsection by deriving an equation satisfied by x^*. Using (30), this equation is

$$B'(0) - \{w/(1 - \alpha)\} - \{c(x^*)/(1 - \alpha)\} - D'(x^*)/r = 0. \quad (32)$$

4.3. *Analysis*

I now compare the steady state output and pollution effects of the two policy instruments. Recall that $q^* = 0$ in every case analyzed in this chapter. I first compare the open loop policies with the dynamically consistent policies.

The results of this paragraph are summarized in Table 1. The two equations which I shall use to compare the pollution levels with the open loop unit tax and with the dynamically consistent unit tax are (18) and (29). The subsequent analysis concentrates on special functional forms. If the relevant functions in (18) and (29) are arbitrary but $c'(x) = 0$, then a comparison of (18) and (29) tells us that the open loop unit tax and the consistent unit tax both give rise to the same level of pollution. Using $B(q) = \gamma q - (1/2)q^2$, $D(x) = (1/2)\delta x^2$, $P(q) = a - bq$, $c(x) = \alpha_1 x$ in (18) and (29) and assuming that $\gamma > w$, I find that the open loop unit tax leads to a lower (higher) level of pollution as compared to the consistent

Table 1. Steady state pollution effects of the open loop unit tax versus the dynamically consistent unit tax.

Functional forms	Restrictions on parameters	Open loop unit tax
$B(q) = \gamma q - (1/2)q^2$ $D(x) = (1/2)\delta x^2$ $P(q) = a - bq$ $c(x) = \alpha_1 x$	$\gamma > w$ and $\alpha_1 x_0/\{2\alpha_1 + \delta/r\} <$ $[[\{\gamma + a - w\}/\{\alpha_1 + (\delta/r)\}] -$ $[\{\gamma + a - w\}/\{2\alpha_1 + (\delta/r)\}]]$	Lower pollution
$B(q) = \gamma q - (1/2)q^2$ $D(x) = \delta x$ $P(q) = a - bq$ $c(x) = \alpha_1 x$	$\gamma + a > \{w + (\delta/r)\}$ and $\alpha_1 x_0/2\alpha_1 <$ $[[\{\gamma + a - w - (\delta/r)\}/\alpha_1] -$ $[\{\gamma + a - w - (\delta/r)\}/2\alpha_1]]$	Lower pollution
$B(q) = \gamma q - (1/2)q^2$ $D(x) = \delta x$ $P(q) = q^{-\alpha}, \alpha \in (0,1)$ $c(x) = \alpha_1 x$	$\gamma > \{w + (\delta/r)\}$ and $\alpha_1 x_0/2\alpha_1 <$ $[[\{\gamma - w - (\delta/r)\}/\alpha_1] -$ $[\{\gamma - w - (\delta/r)\}/2\alpha_1]]$	Lower pollution

unit tax as $\alpha_1 x_0/\{2\alpha_1 + \delta/r\} < (>)[[\{\gamma + a - w\}/\{\alpha_1 + (\delta/r)\}] - [\{\gamma + a - w\}/\{2\alpha_1 + (\delta/r)\}]]$. Now consider $B(q) = \gamma q - (1/2)q^2$, $D(x) = \delta x$, $P(q) = a - bq$, $c(x) = \alpha_1 x$. If $(\gamma + a) > \{w + (\delta/r)\}$, then as compared to the consistent unit tax, the open loop unit tax leads to a lower (higher) level of pollution as $\alpha_1 x_0/2\alpha_1 < (>)$ $[[\{\gamma + a - w - (\delta/r)\}/\alpha_1] - [\{\gamma + a - w - (\delta/r)\}/2\alpha_1]]$. Finally, consider $B(q) = \gamma q - (1/2)q^2$, $D(x) = \delta x$, $P(q) = q^{-\alpha}$, $\alpha \in (0,1)$, $c(x) = \alpha_1 x$ and let $\gamma > \{w + (\delta/r)\}$. Then as opposed to the consistent unit tax, the open loop unit tax leads to a lower (higher) level of pollution as $\alpha_1 x_0/2\alpha_1 < (>) [[\{\gamma - w - (\delta/r)\}/\alpha_1] - [\gamma - w - (\delta/r)/2\alpha_1]]$. Inspection of (18) and (29) tells us that the effects of these two taxes essentially depend on the properties of the pollution dependent cost function. The other functions affect both the equations in a similar manner.

Now consider the steady state pollution effects of the open loop and the dynamically consistent *ad valorem* taxes, with $P(q) = q^{-\alpha}$, $\alpha \in (0,1)$. The relevant equations are (19) and (32). Table 2 summarizes the results contained in this paragraph. Let $B(q) = \gamma q - (1/2)q^2$, $D(x) = (1/2)\delta x^2$, $c(x) = \alpha_1 x$ and let $(1 - \alpha)\gamma > w$.

Table 2. Steady state pollution effects of the open loop *ad valorem* tax versus the dynamically consistent *ad valorem* tax.

Functional forms	Restrictions on parameters	Open loop *ad valorem* tax
$B(q) = \gamma q - (1/2)q^2$ $D(x) = (1/2)\delta x^2$ $P(q) = q^{-\alpha}, \alpha \in (0,1)$ $c(x) = \alpha_1 x$	$(1-\alpha)\gamma > w$ and $[\alpha_1 x_0/\{2\alpha_1 + (1-\alpha)\delta/r\}] <$ $[[\{(1-\alpha)\gamma - w\}/$ $\{\alpha_1 + (1-\alpha)\delta/r\}] -$ $[\{(1-\alpha)\gamma - w\}/$ $\{2\alpha_1 + (1-\alpha)\delta/r\}]]$	Lower pollution
$B(q) = \gamma q - (1/2)q^2$ $D(x) = \delta x$ $P(q) = q^{-\alpha}, \alpha \in (0,1)$ $c(x) = \alpha_1 x$	$(1-\alpha)\{\gamma - (\delta/r)\} > w$ and $\alpha_1 x_0/2\alpha_1 <$ $[[\{(1-\alpha)\gamma - w -$ $(1-\alpha)\delta/r\}/\alpha_1] -$ $[\{(1-\alpha)\gamma - w -$ $(1-\alpha)\delta/r\}/2\alpha_1]]$	Lower pollution

Then the open loop *ad valorem* tax gives rise to a lower (higher) level of pollution than does the consistent *ad valorem* tax as $\alpha_1 x_0/\{2\alpha_1 + (1-\alpha)\delta/r\} < (>) [[\{(1-\alpha)\gamma - w\}/\{\alpha_1 + (1-\alpha)\delta/r\}] - [\{(1-\alpha)\gamma - w\}/\{2\alpha_1 + (1-\alpha)\delta/r\}]]$. Next, consider the case where $B(q) = \gamma q - (1/2)q^2$, $D(x) = \delta x$, $c(x) = \alpha_1 x$ and where $(1-\alpha)\{(\gamma - \delta/r)\} > w$. Now as compared to the consistent *ad valorem* tax, the open loop *ad valorem* tax leads to a lower (higher) level of pollution as $\alpha_1 x_0/2\alpha_1 < (>) [[\{(1-\alpha)\gamma - w - (1-\alpha)\delta/r\}/\alpha_1] - [\{(1-\alpha)\gamma - w - (1-\alpha)\delta/r\}/2\alpha_1]]$.

I note that these results depend crucially on the properties of the stock dependent cost function. Depending on the magnitudes of the various parameters, there are a number of situations in which the use of consistent taxes leads to a higher level of pollution. However, it is important to recognize that the use of consistent taxes does *not* always lead to a higher level of pollution.[12] Note that because $q^* = 0$ in every case and because $D'(x) > 0$, in my model, higher steady

---

12. By specifying parameter values, this claim can be easily verified. See Batabyal (1996) for the details of such an exercise.

Table 3. Steady state pollution effects of the consistent unit tax versus the consistent *ad valorem* tax.

Functional forms	Restrictions on parameters	Unit tax
$B(q) = \gamma q - (1/2)q^2$ $D(x) = \delta x$ $P(q) = q^{-\alpha}, \alpha \in (0, 1)$ $c(x) = \alpha_1 x$	$(1 - \alpha)\{\gamma - (\delta/r)\} > w$ and $[\alpha\{(\delta/r) - \gamma\}/\alpha_1] < 0$	Higher pollution
$B(q) = \gamma q - (1/2)q^2$ $D(x) = (1/2)\delta x^2$ $P(q) = q^{-\alpha}, \alpha \in (0, 1)$ $c(x) = \alpha_1 x$	$(1 - \alpha)\gamma > w$ and $\alpha\gamma/\{\alpha_1 + (1 - \alpha)\delta/r\} <$ $[[(\gamma - w)/\{\alpha_1 + (1 - \alpha)\delta/r\}] -$ $[(\gamma - w)/\{\alpha_1 + (\delta/r)\}]]$	Lower pollution

state pollution implies lower social welfare — as embodied in the regulator's objective functional — in the steady state [13] This means that although consistent taxes can lead to higher steady state levels of pollution, the use of such taxes is more plausible because open loop tax policies are not credible.

I now compare the steady state pollution and output levels that result from the use of dynamically consistent taxes. Table 3 summarizes the results. In the rest of this paragraph, I shall use $P(q) = q^{-\alpha}$, $\alpha \in (0, 1)$. Substitute $B(q) = \gamma q - (1/2)q^2$, $D(x) = \delta x$, $c(x) = \alpha_1 x$ in (29) and (32) and suppose that $(1 - \alpha)\{\gamma - (\delta/r)\} > w$. I find that the level of pollution with a consistent unit tax is more (less) than the level of pollution with a consistent *ad valorem* tax as $[\alpha\{(\delta/r) - \gamma\}/\alpha_1] < (>)0$. Next substitute $B(q) = \gamma q - (1/2)q^2$, $D(x) = (1/2)\delta x^2$, $c(x) = \alpha_1 x$ in (29) and (32) and suppose that $(1 - \alpha)\gamma > w$. Then the level of pollution with a consistent unit tax is less (more) than the level of pollution with a consistent *ad valorem* tax as $\alpha\gamma/\{\alpha_1 + (1 - \alpha)\delta/r\} < (>) [[(\gamma - w)/\{\alpha_1 + (1 - \alpha)\delta/r\}] - [(\gamma - w)/\{\alpha_1 + \delta/r\}]]$.

My next task is to rank the steady state pollution levels with the four taxes. Table 4 summarizes the results of this paragraph. In the

---

13. This result does not hold in models with state equations more complicated than (5).

Table 4. Steady state pollution rankings of the alternate policy instruments.

Industry structure	Functional forms	Restrictions on parameters	Ranking of instruments
Monopoly	$B(q) = \gamma q - (1/2)q^2$ $D(x) = \delta x$ $P(q) = q^{-\alpha}, \alpha \in (0,1)$ $c(x) = \alpha_1 x$	$\Theta > w$ and $\Delta > \{\gamma - (\delta/r) - w\}$	$\tau_u^{OL} > \tau_a^{OL} > \tau_u^{DC} > \tau_a^{DC}$
Monopoly	$B(q) = \gamma q$ $D(x) = \delta x$ $P(q) = q^{-\alpha}, \alpha \in (0,1)$ $c(x) = \alpha_1 x$	$\Theta > w$ and $\Delta > \{\gamma - (\delta/r) - w\}$	$\tau_u^{OL} > \tau_a^{OL} > \tau_u^{DC} > \tau_a^{DC}$

rest of this paragraph, $a > b$ means that a leads to a greater level of pollution than b and $a \Leftrightarrow b$ means that a and b both give rise to the same level of pollution. Denote the open loop unit tax, the open loop *ad valorem* tax, the dynamically consistent unit tax, and the dynamically consistent *ad valorem* tax by τ_u^{OL}, τ_a^{OL}, τ_u^{DC}, and τ_a^{DC} respectively. I shall use Equations (18), (19), (29), and (32) for comparative purposes. When $B(q) = \gamma q - (1/2)q^2$, $D(x) = \delta x$, $c(x) = \alpha_1 x$, $P(q) = q^{-\alpha}$, $\alpha \in (0,1)$, I conclude that $\tau_u^{OL} > \tau_a^{OL} > \tau_u^{DC} > \tau_a^{DC}$ as long as $[(1 - \alpha)\{\gamma - (\delta/r)\}] \equiv \Theta > w$, and $[\alpha_1 x_0 + \alpha\{(\delta/r) - \gamma\}] \equiv \Delta > \{\gamma - (\delta/r) - w\}$. This ranking also holds — with the same restrictions on the parameters — when $B(q) = \gamma q$ and the other functions are as above. This analysis once again brings out the sensitivity of the qualitative results to the choice of functional forms and in particular to the properties of the stock dependent cost function.

I close this section by asking at what level the two taxes should be set when the regulator chooses to use both dynamically consistent taxes simultaneously. The answer is contained in Proposition 3.

Proposition 3.   *When the regulator uses both taxes simultaneously, it is optimal for him to set* $\tau_u^{DC} = -\{w + c(x) - \lambda\}$ *and* $\zeta_a^{DC} = \infty$.

Proof.   (Outline): The procedure for demonstrating this result is very similar to that employed in the proof of Proposition 2. Hence, I omit a formal proof.   □

The reader will note that while continuous revision of the tax by the regulator alters the solution to his optimization problem, it does not alter his optimal course of action when he chooses to use both taxes simultaneously.

5. Conclusions

In this chapter, I analyzed the interaction between a monopolistic, polluting firm and a regulator as a Stackelberg differential game in which the regulator leads. I studied the effects of open loop and consistent unit and *ad valorem* taxes. I demonstrated the dynamic inconsistency of open loop policies and I discussed the equivalence of the open loop and the consistent policies when production costs are unrelated to the stock of pollution. The non equivalence of the unit tax and the *ad valorem* tax was demonstrated.

By way of numerous steady state examples, I showed how to interpret the general results and then I ranked the four taxes in terms of their ability to control pollution. These examples demonstrate the sensitivity of the qualitative results to (a) the choice of functional forms for inverse demand and stock dependent cost and (b) the nature of the taxes.

Five policy conclusions flow from the analysis in this chapter. First, owing to the sensitivity of the results to the choice of functional forms, in any given regulatory scenario, empirical research will be needed to estimate the parameters of the relevant functions and hence serve as a guide to regulatory action. Second, as I have shown here and in Batabyal (1996), while a unit tax and an *ad valorem* tax are equivalent in a competitive industry, this equivalence breaks down in a monopolistic industry. Third, if the regulator's control set is sufficiently large, then he can force the monopolistic firm to behave competitively. Fourth, as far as policy credibility is concerned, the efficiency of regulatory action depends on the properties of the stock dependent cost function. If production costs are unrelated to the stock of pollution, then it makes no difference whether the regulator announces a policy trajectory at the beginning of the game or whether he continuously revises his policy. Finally, there is a basic tradeoff between policy payoff and policy credibility. Open loop policies yield a higher payoff to the regulator than do consistent policies. This is a possible explanation as to why many regulators are loath to use dynamically consistent policies.

Despite Samuel Johnson's pronouncement that "he is no wise man that will quit a certainty for an uncertainty," I believe that the most promising extension of this research lies in analyzing the issues that I have addressed in a stochastic framework. Such an analysis will substantially increase the model's realism and hence its policy conclusions.

References

Batabyal, A.A. (1995). Leading Issues in Domestic Environmental Regulation: A Review Essay. *Ecological Economics* 12:23–39.

Batabyal, A.A. (1996). Consistency and Optimality in a Dynamic Game of Pollution Control I: Competition. *Environmental and Resource Economics* 8:205–220.

Bator, F.M. (1958). The Anatomy of Market Failure. *Quarterly Journal of Economics* 72:351–379.

Baumol, W.J. and Oates, W.E. (1988). *The Theory of Environmental Policy*, 2nd edn. Cambridge, UK: Cambridge University Press.

Buiter, W.H. (1983). Optimal and Time-consistent Policies in Continuous Time Rational Expectations Models. *NBER Technical Working Paper*, NBER, Cambridge, Massachusetts.

Buiter, W.H. (1989). Policy Evaluation and Design for Continuous Time Linear Rational Expectations Models: Some Recent Developments. *In* W.H. Buiter (ed.), *Macroeconomic Theory and Stabilization Policy*. Ann Arbor, Michigan: University of Michigan Press.

Chen, C.I. and Cruz, J.B. (1972). Stackelberg Solutions for Two Person Games with Biased Information Patterns. *IEEE Transactions on Automatic Control* AC-17:791–798.

Cropper, M. and Oates, W.E. (1992). Environmental Economics: A Survey. *Journal of Economic Literature* 30:675–740.

Karp, L.S. (1982). *Dynamic Games in International Trade*. Unpublished Ph.D. dissertation, University of California, Davis.

Karp, L.S. (1984). Optimality and Consistency in a Differential Game with Non-renewable Resources. *Journal of Economic Dynamics and Control* 8:73–97.

Karp, L.S. (1991). Monopsony Power and the Period of Commitment in Nonrenewable Resource Markets. *In* L. Phlips (ed.), *Commodity, Futures, and Financial Markets.* Dordrecht, The Netherlands: Kluwer Academic Publishers.

Karp, L.S. and Newbery, D.M. (1993). Intertemporal Consistency Issues in Depletable Resources. *In* A.V. Kneese and J.L. Sweeney (eds.), *Handbook of Natural Resource and Energy Economics*, Vol. III. Amsterdam, The Netherlands: Elsevier.

Simaan, M. and Cruz, J.B. (1973a). On the Stackelberg Strategy in Nonzero Sum Games. *Journal of Optimization Theory and Applications* 11:533–555.

Simaan, M. and Cruz, J.B. (1973b). Additional Aspects of the Stackelberg Strategy in Nonzero Sum Games. *Journal of Optimization Theory and Applications* 11:613–626.

Van der Ploeg, F. and de Zeeuw, A. (1992). International Aspects of Pollution Control. *Environmental and Resource Economics* 2:117–139.

Weitzman, M.L. (1974). Prices vs. Quantities. *Review of Economic Studies* 41:477–491.

Chapter 16

A STOCHASTIC MODEL OF WASTE MANAGEMENT WITH ON AND OFF SITE STORAGE[1]

with L. P. Freitas

When the regulatory threshold which specifies the maximum amount of waste that can be stored on site is exceeded, a waste generating firm must move waste to an off site location. Given that off site storage is costlier than on site storage, how much waste ought a firm — operating in a probabilistic environment — to produce in the time period of interest? This salient question has received insufficient theoretical attention in the extant literature. Therefore, we analyze a stochastic model with on and off site storage that is relevant to the management of a broad class of wastes. We first derive a representative waste generating firm's long run expected cost function. Next, we conduct comparative statics exercises to demonstrate the impact of key parameter changes on the firm's long run expected cost. Finally, we show that the optimal waste production level we seek is the solution to a specific cost minimization problem.

1. Introduction

Firms engaged in the production of economically desirable "goods" typically also produce economically undesirable "bads" in the form of wastes. Because all modern production processes generate some level of waste, federal and state regulatory agencies in most nations

1. This chapter is the outcome of an independent study project conducted by L.P. Freitas under the supervision of A.A. Batabyal. We thank Cutler J. Cleveland and two anonymous referees for their helpful comments on a previous version of this chapter. In addition, Batabyal acknowledges financial support from the Gosnell endowment at RIT. The usual disclaimer applies.

have produced a voluminous body of regulatory requirements with which waste generators must comply. In the United States, the Environmental Protection Agency (EPA) and, to a lesser extent, the Department of Energy (DOE) have detailed regulatory requirements that govern the conditions of waste generation, transportation, and storage. In addition, individual states in the United States often have their own rules and regulations concerning the ways in which waste can, and on occasion must, be managed.

There are many ways in which one can categorize waste. For instance, waste can be nuclear or non-nuclear, it can be hazardous or non-hazardous, and it can be solid or liquid. In this chapter, we shall be concerned with the activities of goods producing firms that also generate waste. The goods production aspect is clearly an important part of the existence of these firms. Even so, because our chapter is about waste management, in what follows, we shall abstract away from the goods production activities and the profit maximization problems of these firms and focus exclusively on their waste generation. Further, given that these firms generate waste, we shall pay particular attention to their *on* site *versus off* site waste storage decision.

Now, quite apart from the specific classification scheme — such as hazardous or non-hazardous — one uses to categorize the waste under consideration, in the United States, a decision faced by most waste generators is the on site *versus* off site storage decision. From the standpoint of a cost minimizing waste generator that is subject to exogenous regulatory requirements concerning the maximum amount of waste that can be stored on site, this decision involves determining the *optimal* waste production level in the time period of interest. Because off site waste storage is generally costlier than on site storage, this optimal waste production level will have a direct bearing on a firm's long run expected cost of waste management. The reader should note that the two related issues of the optimal waste production level and the on site versus off site storage decision together comprise the centerpiece of the analysis that we undertake in this chapter.

Researchers have now studied the subject of waste management from various perspectives. Chapman (1990) has analyzed the connection between the evolution of the nuclear power industry and the costs of centralized and on site storage of spent fuel. Focusing on solid wastes, Keeler and Renkow (1999) have studied the welfare effects of public versus private waste disposal with and without flow controls. Conrad (1999) has shown that the theory of the firm can be expanded to incorporate the trinity of waste reduction, waste recycling, and waste disposal. In a study of the Netherlands, Dijkgraaf and Gradus (2003) have determined the extent of the cost savings that arise when refuse collection is contracted out. A similar question in the context of Spain has been analyzed by Bel and Miralles (2003). The Swedish paper industry has been analyzed by Samakovlis (2003). She shows that contrary to previous life cycle studies, waste paper and fossil fuels are substitutes and that waste paper and electricity are complements. In a study of Yucatan state in Mexico, Drucker and Latacz-Lohmann (2003) have pointed to the advantages of cost minimizing economic instruments over command and control approaches in the treatment and disposal of pig slurry. Finally, Mickwitz (2003) has shown that permits specifying waste discharge limits can be quite effective in regulating the waste water emissions of Finnish industry.

The papers that we have just discussed in the previous paragraph have certainly advanced our understanding of various aspects of waste management. Further, very recently, Batabyal and Nijkamp (2009) have analyzed aspects of waste management from the viewpoints of a waste generator and a recipient. Even so, our basic contention that the extant literature has paid insufficient theoretical attention to the determination of the optimal waste production level in a stochastic environment with on and off site storage remains true. Given this state of affairs, we complement the recent analysis of Batabyal and Nijkamp (2009) and study a probabilistic model with on and off site storage that is pertinent to the management of a broad class of wastes. Specifically, we first derive a representative waste generating firm's long run average or expected cost of waste management. Next, we conduct comparative statics exercises to show the effect that key parameter changes have on the above long run expected cost function. Finally, we demonstrate that the optimal waste production level we seek is the solution to a specific cost minimization problem.

The rest of this chapter is organized as follows. Section 2.1 briefly delineates renewal-reward processes and the renewal-reward theorem that will form an important part of our subsequent analysis. Next, Section 2.2 computes the long run expected cost for our representative waste generating firm's management strategy involving both on and off site waste storage. Then, Section 2.3 qualitatively discusses the effect that changes in the central parameters of our problem have on our waste generating firm's long run average cost. Section 2.4 endogenously determines the optimal waste production level for our firm. Finally, Section 3 concludes and discusses avenues for further research on the subject of this chapter.

2.   The Theoretical Framework

2.1.   *Preliminaries*

As Ross (2003, pp. 416–425) has pointed out, a stochastic process $\{Z(t) : t \geq 0\}$ is said to be a counting process if $Z(t)$ denotes the total number of counts that have taken place by time t. Clearly, since $Z(t - 1)$, $Z(t)$, $Z(t + 1)$, etc. are random, the time between any two counts $Z(t)$ and $Z(t - 1)$ is also random. This time between any two counts is called the interarrival time. A counting process in which the interarrival times have a general cumulative distribution function is said to be a renewal process. A special kind of a renewal process is the Poisson process. For a Poisson process, the interarrival times are exponentially distributed.

Consider a renewal process $\{Z(t) : t \geq 0\}$ with interarrival times X_z, $z \geq 1$, which have a cumulative distribution function denoted by $H(\cdot)$. In addition, suppose that a monetary reward R_z is earned when the zth renewal is completed. Let $R(t)$, the total reward earned by time t, be given by $\Sigma_{z=1}^{Z(t)} R_z$, and let $E[R_z] = E[R]$, and

$E[X_z] = E[X]$. The renewal-reward theorem — see Ross (2003, p. 417) or Tijms (2003, p. 41) — tells us that if $E[R]$ and $E[X]$ are finite, then with probability one,

$$\lim_{t \to \infty} \frac{E[R(t)]}{t} = \frac{E[R]}{E[X]}. \tag{1}$$

In words, if we think of a cycle being completed every time a renewal occurs, then the long run expected or average reward — the left hand side (LHS) of Equation (1) — is simply the expected reward in a cycle or $E[R] = E[$reward per cycle$]$ divided by the expected amount of time it takes to complete that cycle or $E[X] = E[$length of cycle$]$. The reader should note that the renewal-reward theorem holds for positive rewards such as profit and for negative rewards such as costs. With this background, we are now in a position to compute the long run expected cost per unit time for our representative waste generating firm's management strategy involving both on and off site waste storage.

2.2. Long run expected cost

Consider a representative waste generating firm in a particular geographic region of a country such as the United States. This firm's goods production process yields waste that is initially stored on site. We suppose that the amounts of waste that are produced by this firm in successive *months*, the time period of interest, are independent and identically distributed random variables with finite first two moments μ_1 and μ_2. The first moment is also known as the mean and the second moment can be thought of as the variance about the origin. Opportunities to remove the waste that is currently stored on site by our firm occur at the end of each month. Consistent with the regulatory requirements for a broad class of wastes including universal and hazardous wastes,[2] our firm uses the following control

---

2. Go to http://dep.state.ct.us/wst/mercury/uwrule.htm for an example of Connecticut's regulatory requirements concerning the management of "universal waste." See United States Department of Energy (1999) for more on hazardous waste generator requirements.

rule to manage the waste it produces. If, at the end of a month, the total amount of waste on site is larger than the maximum legally permissible level or threshold W, then all waste presently stored on site is moved to a location off site.[3] Otherwise, the on site waste is not moved. Our representative waste generating firm incurs a fixed cost F when it moves the accumulated waste stored on site to the off site location. In addition, this firm also incurs a variable cost of v for each unit of waste in excess of the threshold W that it moves to the off site location.

The outstanding task before us now is to compute our waste generating firm's long run expected cost per unit time. Specifically, we want to use the renewal-reward theorem (Equation (1)) to compute this expected cost function. Let us first compute E[length of cycle]. In this regard, note that the process delineating the amount of waste present at the end of each month is a regenerative or renewal process. Further, the regeneration or renewal epochs are the months in which our firm moves waste to the off site location. Now, let the random variable X denote the amount of waste that is produced by our firm in any month and let $G(x) = \text{Prob}\{X \leq x\}$ denote the cumulative probability distribution function of this random variable X. In addition, let $M(x)$ be the renewal function[4] associated with the cumulative probability distribution function $G(x)$. Now, the renewal function $M(x)$ and some thought together tell us that

$$E[\text{length of cycle}] = 1 + M(W). \tag{2}$$

The computation of the E[cost per cycle] is a little more involved. Let us begin our computation of this expectation by first letting

---

3. For instance, in the state of Connecticut, the W for universal waste equals 5000 (10,000) kilograms for small (large) quantity handlers. See the sources cited in the previous footnote for additional discussion of these and other similar numbers.

4. The renewal function tells us the expected number of renewals that have occurred by a certain time. It is of interest to us in our analysis because a renewal function uniquely determines an underlying renewal process. See Ross (2003, pp. 403–404) or Tijms (2003, pp. 35–37) for more on the renewal function.

$\gamma(W)$ denote the amount of waste in *excess*[5] of the threshold W when a removal of waste to the off site location occurs. Some thought will convince the reader that $E[\text{cost per cycle}] = F + \nu E[\gamma(W)]$. Given this finding, let us compute the expectation of $\gamma(W)$ or $E[\gamma(W)]$. Equation (7.9) in Ross (2003, p. 414) and Lemma 2.1.2 in Tijms (2003, p. 37) tell us that $E[\gamma(W)] = \mu_1\{1 + M(W)\} - W$. Using this last result we reason that

$$E[\text{cost per cycle}] = F + \nu\mu_1\{1 + M(W)\} - \nu W. \qquad (3)$$

Now, applying the renewal-reward theorem and simplifying the right hand sides (RHSs) of Equations (2) and (3), we get an expression for our representative waste generating firm's long run expected cost per unit time (LREC) and that expression is

$$\text{LREC} = \frac{E[\text{cost per cylce}]}{E[\text{length of cycle}]} = \frac{F + \nu\mu_1\{1 + M(W)\} - \nu W}{1 + M(W)} \qquad (4)$$

with probability one.

Generally speaking, the computation of the renewal function $M(W)$ is not straightforward. Therefore, to proceed further with our analysis, we shall assume that the regulatory threshold W is sufficiently large relative to the first moment μ_1. Having made this assumption, we can now use an asymptotic expansion for the renewal function $M(W)$ given in Equation (2.1.6) in Tijms (2003, p. 37) to simplify the ratio on the RHS of Equation (4).[6] This asymptotic expansion tells us that $M(W) = (W/\mu_1) + (\mu_2/2\mu_1^2) - 1$.

---

5. The excess random variable is the time elapsed from renewal epoch t until the next renewal after epoch t. See Ross (2003, pp. 414–415) or Tijms (2003, pp. 37–38) for more on the properties of this excess random variable.

6. As noted in Tijms (2003, p. 37), this asymptotic expansion can only be used if the pertinent interarrival times have a positive density on some interval. We assume that this condition is satisfied for the scenario that we are analyzing in this chapter.

Using this expression for $M(W)$, we can rewrite the long run expected cost per unit time function in Equation (4). We get

$$\text{LREC} = \frac{E[\text{cost per cycle}]}{E[\text{length of cycle}]} = \frac{2\mu_1^2 F + \mu_1\mu_2 v}{2\mu_1 W + \mu_2}. \qquad (5)$$

This completes the derivation of our representative waste generating firm's long run expected cost function. Our task now is to conduct comparative statics exercises and thereby demonstrate the impact that changes in the key parameters of our model have on the long run expected cost in the RHS of Equation (5).

2.3. *Comparative statics*

We shall sequentially study the impact of changes in the fixed cost parameter (F), the variable cost parameter (v), and the exogenous waste threshold (W), on the LREC in Equation (5). Now, differentiating the LREC expression with respect to each of the three parameters F, v, and W, we get

$$\frac{\partial(\text{LREC})}{\partial F} = \frac{2\mu_1^2}{2\mu_1 W + \mu_2} > 0,$$

$$\frac{\partial(\text{LREC})}{\partial v} = \frac{\mu_1\mu_2}{2\mu_1 W + \mu_2} > 0,$$

$$\frac{\partial(\text{LREC})}{\partial W} = -\frac{(4\mu_1^3 F + 2\mu_1^2\mu_2 v)}{(2\mu_1 W + \mu_2)^2} < 0. \qquad (6)$$

Mathematically, the signs of the first two derivatives in (6) are positive because the fixed and the variable cost parameters F and v appear only in the numerator of the ratio describing our firm's LREC. Put differently, our waste generating firm's long run expected cost is clearly a positive function of the fixed and the variable costs it encounters when moving waste to the off site location. Therefore, *ceteris paribus*, if either F or v go up then we expect the LREC to go up and this is indeed what happens.

In contrast, the regulatory waste threshold W appears only in the denominator of the expression for the LREC and this is why an increase in its magnitude lowers our firm's long run expected cost. From an economic perspective, as W increases, our firm is able to store more waste on site and hence avoid the costs of off site storage. This is why the relationship between W and our firm's LREC is negative and this is indeed what the sign of the third derivative in (6) also shows. In other words, all three results in (6) conform well with our intuition about the direction of the changes we expect. We now proceed to our third and final task in this chapter. This task involves the endogenous determination of the optimal waste production level by our firm.

2.4. *The optimization problem*

For the optimal waste production level determination problem to be meaningful, it must be possible for our firm to control some aspect of the underlying problem in a way so as to directly affect its long run expected cost function given in Equation (5). Now, recall from the Section 2.2 discussion that the amounts of waste that are produced by our waste generating firm in successive months are independent and identically distributed random variables with finite first two moments μ_1 and μ_2. Given this specification, in the rest of this section, we suppose that our firm can control the first moment μ_1 or the mean of the distribution delineating the random waste generation process. Inspection of our waste generating firm's LREC in Equation (5) reveals that the nature of the impact of changes in the first moment μ_1 on the firm's LREC is ambiguous because μ_1 appears in the numerator and in the denominator of the ratio describing the firm's LRAC.

With the choice of control variable resolved, we can now state our waste generating firm's cost minimization problem. Formally, this firm solves

$$\min_{\{\mu_1\}} \left[\frac{2\mu_1^2 F + \mu_1 \mu_2 v}{2\mu_1 W + \mu_2} \right]. \tag{7}$$

The first-order necessary condition for an optimum to this problem is[7]

$$4FW\mu_1^2 + 4F\mu_2\mu_1 + \mu_2^2 v = 0. \tag{8}$$

Equation (8) is a quadratic equation in μ_1. Therefore, using the standard method, the two possible roots of this quadratic equation are given by $\{-4F\mu_2 \pm \sqrt{16F^2\mu_2^2 - 16FWv\mu_2^2}\}/8FW$. Now, to ensure that the two roots are real, we must have $16F^2\mu_2^2 > 16FWv\mu_2^2$ and hence we suppose that this inequality holds. In addition, one of these roots — and therefore the mean waste production by our firm — is clearly negative and hence we discard this root. This leaves us with the remaining root. Accordingly, we conclude that without imposing further constraints on our cost minimization problem, the most reasonable solution to this problem is given by

$$\mu_1^* = \frac{\sqrt{F^2\mu_2^2 - FWv\mu_2^2} - F\mu_2}{2FW}. \tag{9}$$

Given that off site storage is costlier than on site storage, how much waste ought a firm operating in a probabilistic environment to produce in — a month — the time period of interest? We posed this question in the introductory section of this chapter. The analysis thus far provides us with an answer to the above question. Specifically, this analysis tells us that the optimal mean waste production in a month by our firm ought to equal the quantity given by the RHS of Equation (9).

3. Conclusions

In this chapter, we analyzed a probabilistic model with on and off site storage that is pertinent to the management of a broad class

---

7. The second-order sufficiency condition $8FW\mu_1 + 4F\mu_2 > 0$ is satisfied. Further, the minimand in (7) is strictly convex in the control variable μ_1 and hence this cost minimization problem is well posed.

of wastes. Specifically, we first derived a representative waste generating firm's long run expected cost function. Next, we conducted comparative statics exercises to show the effect that key parameter changes have on the above long run expected cost. Finally, given that our firm is subject to regulation concerning the maximum amount of waste that can be stored on site, we showed that the optimal mean waste production level is the solution to a particular long run expected cost minimization problem.

The analysis in this chapter can be extended in a number of directions. In what follows, we suggest two possible extensions. First, independent of the regulatory threshold W, space constraints may limit the amount of waste that our firm is able to store on site. Therefore, it would be interesting to incorporate this feature of the problem into the analysis explicitly and then study a waste generating firm's management strategy involving both on and off site storage.

Second, in our chapter, the regulatory threshold W is exogenous to the waste generating firm. Therefore, it would be useful to construct and analyze a game model in which a waste regulator and a waste generator interact among themselves and the optimal value of the regulatory threshold W emerges endogenously from this interaction. A study of these aspects of the problem will permit richer analyses of the connections between on and off site regulatory requirements and the waste management decisions of polluting firms.

References

Batabyal, A.A. and Nijkamp, P. (2009). Two Aspects of Waste Management from the Viewpoints of a Waste Generator and a Recipient. *Applied Economics Letters* 16:337–341.

Bel, G. and Miralles, A. (2003). Factors Influencing the Privatisation of Urban Solid Waste Collection in Spain. *Urban Studies* 40:1323–1334.

Chapman, D. (1990). The Eternity Problem: Nuclear Power Waste Storage. *Contemporary Policy Issues* 8:80–93.

Conrad, K. (1999). Resource and Waste Taxation in the Theory of the Firm with Recycling Activities. *Environmental and Resource Economics* 14:217–242.

Dijkgraaf, E. and Gradus, R.H.J.M. (2003). Cost Savings of Contracting Out Refuse Collection. *Empirica* 30:149–161.

Drucker, A.G. and Latacz-Lohmann, U. (2003). Getting Incentives Right? A Comparative Analysis of Policy Instruments for Livestock Waste Pollution Abatement in Yucatan. *Environment and Development Economics* 8:261–284.

Keeler, A.G. and Renkow, M. (1999). Public vs. Private Garbage Disposal: The Economics of Solid Waste Controls. *Growth and Change* 30:430–444.

Mickwitz, P. (2003). Is It As Bad As It Sounds Or As Good As It Looks? Experiences of Finnish Water Discharge Limits. *Ecological Economics* 45:237–254.

Ross, S.M. (2003). *Introduction to Probability Models*, 8th edn. Amsterdam, The Netherlands: Academic Press.

Samakovlis, E. (2003). The Relationship Between Waste Paper and Other Inputs in the Swedish Paper Industry. *Environmental and Resource Economics* 25:191–212.

Tijms, H.C. (2003). *A First Course in Stochastic Models*. Chichester, England: Wiley.

United States Department of Energy (1999). *RCRA Information Brief Hazardous Waste Generator Requirements*. Washington, District of Columbia: Office of Environmental Policy and Assistance.

Chapter 17

THE IMPACT OF INNOVATION ON A POLLUTING FIRM'S REGULATION DRIVEN DECISION TO UPGRADE ITS CAPITAL STOCK[1]

with P. Nijkamp

The extant literature has paid scant *theoretical* attention to the tripartite inter-action between increasing environmental regulations, the resulting decision by a polluting firm to upgrade its capital stock, and the impact of innovation on this capital stock improvement decision. Hence, we theoretically analyze this tripartite interaction when the polluting firm faces adjustment costs to upgrade its capital stock. First, we construct a dynamic model of regulation driven investment by a polluting firm. Second, we specify the conditions characterizing efficient investment. Third, we study the impact of an *unantici-pated* increase in innovation on the polluting firm's steady state capital stock. Fourth, we analyze the impact of an *anticipated* increase in innovation on the polluting firm's steady state capital stock. Finally, we discuss the relationship between the polluting firm's internal shadow price of capital and the stock market value of a unit of this firm's capital.

1. We thank the Editor Sergio J. Rey, two anonymous referees, and workshop participants in Free University, Amsterdam, for their helpful comments on a previous version of this chapter. In addition, Batabyal thanks Cassandra Shellman for drawing the figures in this chapter and he acknowledges financial support from the Gosnell endowment at RIT. The usual disclaimer applies.

1. Introduction

The passage of the Clean Air Act in 1970[2] in the United States (US) has given rise to a substantial literature on the impact of stringent environmental regulations on economic activity. One key question analyzed by researchers in this literature concerns the impact that environmental regulations have on the productivity of firms. In an early study, Barbera and McConnell (1986) showed that pollution abatement capital expenditures had a significant negative impact on both labor and capital productivity in chemical, primary metal, and stone, clay, and glass industries in the US. Gray (1987) showed that environmental regulations were responsible for 12% to 19% of the slowdown in economic activity in the US manufacturing sector in the 1970s. Focusing on plant level productivity in the paper, oil, and steel industries, Gray and Shadbegian (1995) found a negative relationship between a plant's abatement costs and productivity levels.[3] Frondel *et al.* (2007) have used a data set derived from a OECD survey and have shown that cleaner production technologies are used a lot more frequently by polluting firms than are end-of-pipe technologies.

Despite the negative findings obtained by three of the above cited studies, it is not obvious that the effects of increased environmental regulations will always be negative. This is because there is a direct and an indirect effect of environmental regulations. The direct effect — documented by the three studies cited in the previous paragraph — is typically negative because environmental regulations

---

2. This Act was subsequently revised in 1977 and again in 1990.

3. In a related line of inquiry, Montero (2002) and Fischer *et al.* (2003) have studied the implications of using alternate regulatory instruments in the presence of technological innovation. Montero (2002) shows that relative to tradeable permits, emission standards can offer greater incentives for environmental research and development (R&D). However, when markets are competitive, he shows that tradeable and auctioned permits provide equal incentives for environmental R&D. Comparing three different pollution control instruments, Fischer *et al.* (2003) show that the relative welfare ranking of these three instruments depends on the costs of technological innovation, the extent to which innovations can be imitated, the slope and the level of the marginal environmental benefit function, and the number of polluting firms.

raise total input costs for the same level of output. This may in particular be true for short-term technological changes where it is useful to make a distinction between technology substitution and succession in the context of path dependency, technological trajectories, and technology architectures (see Abernathy and Utterback (1975), Nelson and Winter (1977), and Henderson and Clark (1990)).

In contrast, Hamamoto (2006) has noted that the indirect effect is likely to be positive. This is because environmental regulations may change the amount or the combination of conventional inputs and encourage firms to upgrade their capital stock and this decision can lead to productivity improvements. Therefore, in principle, it is possible that the net effect of environmental regulations might be *positive*. This is, in fact, one way of stating the now prominent "Porter hypothesis" initially advanced by Porter (1991).[4]

Several researchers have explored the validity of the Porter hypothesis. Jaffe and Palmer (1997) have shown that stringent environmental regulations do have a positive impact on R&D expenditures in US manufacturing industries. Xepapadeas and de Zeeuw (1999) point out that tough environmental regulations can increase the average productivity of the capital stock. Brunnermeier and Cohen (2003) show that environmental innovations do respond to increases in pollution abatement expenditures and that such innovations are more likely to occur in internationally competitive industries. Finally, Greaker (2003) has noted that under certain conditions, stringent environmental regulations can increase the competitiveness of domestic industries. In contrast to these four studies, Palmer *et al.* (1995), Simpson and Bradford (1996), and Ulph and Ulph (1996) have all credibly claimed that the Porter hypothesis is

---

4. The Porter hypothesis says that strict environmental regulations lead to the discovery and the introduction of cleaner technologies and environmental improvements thereby making production processes more efficient. The cost savings from this "innovation effect" can compensate for both the compliance costs of environmental regulations and the costs of innovation. See Porter (1991) and Porter and van der Linde (1995) for more on this hypothesis.

unlikely to be valid in general. Therefore, a fair conclusion about the Porter hypothesis is that the evidence concerning its validity is *mixed*.

Our discussion thus far demonstrates that the connections between stringent environmental regulations and economic activity have been analyzed quite thoroughly in the existing literature. Even so, this literature has paid scant *theoretical* attention to the *tripartite* interaction between increasing environmental regulations, the ensuing decision by a polluting firm to upgrade its capital stock, and the impact of innovation on this capital stock improvement decision.

In a prominent paper, Tobin (1969) formulated an economic theory of investment in which a variable known as q plays a central role. This q represents the ratio of the market value of a firm's existing shares (share capital) to the replacement cost of this firm's physical assets, i.e., the replacement cost of the share capital. Specifically, Tobin's investment theory states that the normal value of q is unity. However, if the value of q exceeds unity ($q > 1$) then additional investment in a firm would make sense because the profits generated by this investment would exceed the cost of this firm's assets. On the other hand, if the value of q is less than unity ($q < 1$) then the firm would be better off selling its assets instead of trying to put them to use. This q-theoretic investment framework is well suited to an analysis of the tripartite interaction mentioned in the previous paragraph.[5] Even so, not only has this framework not been used previously to analyze this tripartite interaction but, to the best of our knowledge, only one paper in the environmental economics and regional science literatures has used Tobin's (1969) framework to conduct its analysis. Therefore, we now comment on the contents of this one paper.

---

5. For a textbook treatment of Tobin's q model, see Obstfeld and Rogoff (1996, pp. 105–113).

Garofalo and Malhotra (1995) have utilized this q-theoretic framework to conduct an *empirical* analysis of the effect of environmental regulations on regional capital formation in the manufacturing sector in the US. This paper does a good job of demonstrating that environmental regulations have a modest impact on net capital formation and that such regulations influence different regions differently. This notwithstanding, several unstudied questions concerning the tripartite interaction mentioned above remain. Therefore, the purpose of this chapter is to shed light on three of these unexamined questions. We now briefly discuss these three questions.

As noted by Kort (1994) and Rubio and Fisher (1994), polluting firms frequently respond to stringent environmental regulations by upgrading their capital stock. Now, in principle, this upgrading response can occur over time, over space, or over both time and space. The temporal dimension of the upgrading response is rather obvious and hence this does not require any further comment on our part. However, the spatial and/or the temporal and spatial dimensions do require some additional commentary. This is because a polluting firm may respond over space by either relocating to an alternate location or, if it is a multi-plant firm, by altering the production mix in its various plants. In this regard, the reader should note that an extreme upgrading response would be one in which a polluting firm decides to exit the industry under consideration.

Koetse *et al.* (2008) have shown that in the context of energy and environmental policy, one is often confronted with a technology-efficiency paradox in which the high transition and transaction costs of new technologies act as a deterrent to the prompt adoption and implementation of clean technologies.[6] Thus, the adoption of clean technologies calls for a careful analysis of various benefit and cost components and it is therefore important to comprehend that firms

---

6. See Dosi (1982) and Unruh (2000) for more on this issue.

cannot upgrade their capital stock costlessly. To model this, we theoretically analyze the abovementioned tripartite interaction for a representative polluting firm in a regional economy which faces adjustment costs to upgrade its capital stock. In Section 2, we first construct a q-theoretic dynamic[7] model of regulation driven investment by our polluting firm. We then specify the conditions characterizing efficient investment by this polluting firm. In Section 3, we study the first of this chapter's three questions. This involves determining the impact of an *unanticipated* increase in innovation on our polluting firm's steady state capital stock. In Section 4, we address this chapter's second question. This involves ascertaining the impact of an *anticipated* increase in innovation on our polluting firm's steady state capital stock. In Section 5, we take up this chapter's third and last question and this involves discussing the relationship between our polluting firm's internal shadow price of capital and the stock market value of a unit of this firm's capital. Finally, in Section 6 we conclude and then we discuss ways of extending the research described in this chapter.

2.   Theoretical Framework

2.1.   *Preliminaries*

Our representative polluting firm's objective is to maximize the present value of current and future profits. This polluting firm faces the market interest rate $1 + r$. Time in our model is discrete and in time period t, our polluting firm uses capital K_t and labor L_t to

---

7. Our model is dynamic but not explicitly stochastic. Section 2.2 discussion shows that even in this dynamic model, it is not possible to obtain unambiguous analytical results. This is why we resort to a qualitative analysis of the model using phase diagrams. We are *not* suggesting that issues of expectations and decision making under regulatory and technological uncertainty are unimportant. However, given that we cannot obtain unambiguous analytical results with our dynamic model, the addition of these stochastic considerations will complicate the basic model even more and hence make qualitative analysis more difficult. This and our ongoing work — in which we are attempting to incorporate stochastic considerations into the model — jointly explain why we have not accounted for probabilistic considerations in the model of this chapter.

produce output Υ_t. The price of output Υ_t is normalized to unity. We assume a positive relationship between output Υ_t and the pollution generated by our polluting firm. The reader will note that the focus of this chapter is on our polluting firm's *capital stock*. In addition, in what follows, we shall use phase diagrams to qualitatively describe the solution to our firm's profit maximization problem. Therefore, to keep the focus on the firm's capital stock, we assume that the wage continually adjusts in the background so that our firm wishes to employ exactly L workers in every time period.

Given the above assumption, we can write our polluting firm's production function as $\Upsilon_t = A_t F(K_t)$, where A_t is the firm's innovation parameter. This parameter A_t captures the outcome of in-house R&D undertaken by our firm. A positive outcome of in-house R&D will be reflected in an increase in the magnitude of the innovation parameter A_t and, *ceteris paribus*, this increase will have a positive impact on our polluting firm's output.

Increasing environmental regulations force our polluting firm to take steps to internalize the negative effects of its polluting activities. We do not model these regulations directly. However, following Kort (1994), Rubio and Fisher (1994), and others, we suppose that our polluting firm responds to these environmental regulations by investing and thereby upgrading its capital stock. The key thing to note now is that capital cannot be installed or dismantled by our polluting firm without incurring *adjustment costs*. Further, the quicker the speed with which this polluting firm attempts to upgrade its capital stock the higher are the adjustment costs that it must bear. To model these features of the problem, we suppose that our polluting firm must pay $\chi I^2/2$ in adjustment costs in any time period in which it invests at rate I.[8] In the above quadratic adjustment cost function, $\chi > 0$ is a parameter.

---

8. In the model of this chapter, the adjustment costs are internal to our polluting firm. Alternately, one can also model and study adjustment costs at the level of, say, a regional economy.

2.2. *Profit maximization problem*

We are now in a position to state our polluting firm's profit maximization problem. Specifically, this firm solves

$$\max_{\{I,K\}} \sum_{s=t}^{\infty} \left(\frac{1}{1+r}\right)^{(s-t)} \left[A_s F(K_s) - I_s - \frac{\chi I^2}{2} \right], \tag{1}$$

subject to the capital stock improvement equation[9]

$$K_{t+1} - K_t = I_t. \tag{2}$$

As a prelude to solving the above maximization problem, let us denote the Lagrange multiplier for the capital stock improvement equation in time period t by q_t. Our polluting firm's profit maximization problem can now be written as

$$\max_{\{I,K\}} \sum_{s=t}^{\infty} \left(\frac{1}{1+r}\right)^{(s-t)}$$

$$\times \left[A_s F(K_s) - I_s - \frac{\chi I_s^2}{2} - q_s(K_{s+1} - K_s - I_s) \right]. \tag{3}$$

Differentiating the expression in (3) with respect to I_s and K_s, we get the two first-order necessary conditions to our polluting firm's optimization problem. These conditions are

$$q_s = 1 + \chi I_s \tag{4}$$

and

$$q_s = \frac{1}{1+r}[A_{s+1} F'(K_{s+1}) + q_{s+1}]. \tag{5}$$

Equations (4) and (5) characterize efficient investment for our polluting firm. Now, recall that q_s is the shadow price of capital in place

---

9. We are modeling innovation — also see the penultimate paragraph of Section 2.1 — and the capital stock improvement decision in a particular way. For the purpose of mathematical tractability, we are not explicitly accounting for the fact that in practical settings, investment by a firm in a context such as ours will tend to be affected by the relative speed of innovation and by the possible lumpiness of the capital stock.

at the end of time period s. Therefore, Equation (4) tells us that the shadow price of capital (the LHS) equals the marginal cost of investment including adjustment costs (the RHS). The reader will note that Equation (4) can also be written as

$$I_s = \frac{q_s - 1}{\chi}. \tag{6}$$

Equation (6) tells us that our polluting firm's investment in capital stock improvement is positive only when the shadow price of upgraded capital exceeds unity.

Equation (5), the second optimality condition, can be thought of as an investment Euler equation. Specifically, this equation tells us that at the firm's optimum, the time period s shadow price of capital (the LHS) equals the discounted sum of capital's marginal product in the next time period and the shadow price of capital in the next date (the RHS).

To continue the analysis, we want to specify a two equation dynamic system in K and q. To do this, let us combine Equations (2) and (6). This gives us the first of our two equations and this equation is

$$K_{t+1} - K_t = \frac{q_t - 1}{\chi}. \tag{7}$$

Combining Equations (4) and (5) we get the second of our two equations and this equation is

$$q_{t+1} - q_t = rq_t - A_{t+1}F'\left(K_t + \frac{q_t - 1}{\chi}\right). \tag{8}$$

2.3. *Phase diagram*

To gain more insight into the investment dynamics represented by Equations (7) and (8), we now draw and analyze a phase diagram[10] for the implied behavior of the two variables of interest, namely, q

---

10. Textbook discussions of phase diagrams can be found in Chiang (1984, pp. 628–638) and in Simon and Blume (1994, pp. 689–703).

and K. Further, we temporarily assume that the innovation parameter is constant at level A. Our model's steady state is defined by the levels q^* and K^* of the endogenous variables which, once they are concurrently reached, remain constant over time. Setting $K_{t+1} - K_t = \Delta K = 0$ in Equation (7) gives us $q^* = 1$. This tells us that capital is constant in the steady state. In addition, setting $q_{t+1} - q_t = \Delta q = 0$ in Equation (8) we see that K^* satisfies $AF'(K^*) = r$. This last expression says that only in the steady state is the marginal product of capital equal to r. Put differently, the steady state in our model is *independent* of adjustment costs even though these costs do determine the speed of transition to the steady state.

Figure 1 represents the dynamics of the system given by Equations (7) and (8). The schedule labeled $\Delta K = 0$ shows points in the (K, q) plane at which our polluting firm's capital stock is stationary. The discussion in the previous paragraph tells us that this schedule is horizontal at $q = q^* = 1$. For $q > 1$ our firm's capital stock is rising and this is indicated by the rightward pointing arrows parallel to the K axis and above the $\Delta K = 0$ schedule. Conversely, for $q < 1$ the

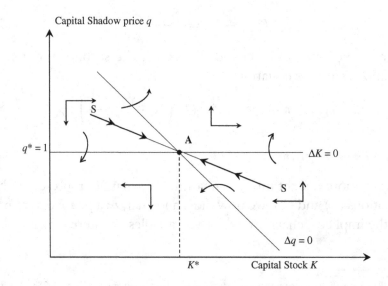

Fig. 1. Steady state behavior of K and q.

capital stock is falling and this is depicted by the leftward pointing arrows parallel to the K axis and below the $\Delta K = 0$ schedule.

The schedule labeled $\Delta q = 0$ shows points at which the shadow price of capital q is stationary. The slope of this $\Delta q = 0$ schedule is

$$\left.\frac{dq}{dK}\right|_{\Delta q = 0} = \frac{AF''\left(K + \frac{q-1}{\chi}\right)}{r - (1/\chi)AF''\left(K + \frac{q-1}{\chi}\right)} < 0, \tag{9}$$

where $F''(\cdot) < 0$, and the negative sign in Equation (9) explains why the $\Delta q = 0$ schedule is drawn as a negatively sloping line in Fig. 1. For q above (below) the $\Delta q = 0$ schedule, q is rising (falling) and this is indicated by the upward (downward) pointing arrows parallel to the q axis and to the right (left) of the $\Delta q = 0$ schedule.

The dynamic system depicted in Fig. 1 is saddle point stable. This means that this system has a unique path — marked SS in Fig. 1 — that converges to the steady state marked A. In particular, for any initial capital stock K_t, there is a single value of q_t that places our polluting firm on the stable adjustment path SS. The unstable paths in Fig. 1 — shown by divergent arrows — are suboptimal. To see this, first consider paths that arise in the north-east quadrant of Fig. 1. These paths call for both K and q to rise forever at accelerating rates. This clearly cannot be optimal because the marginal product of capital is declining over time. Next, consider the paths that arise in the south-west quadrant of Fig. 1. Here, both K and q are declining rapidly and this simultaneous decline will cause both these variables to turn negative in finite time if they are to continue to satisfy Equations (7) and (8). This is clearly an economic impossibility. This discussion tells us that none of these unstable paths maximizes our polluting firm's discounted profits.

In contrast to the suboptimality of the unstable paths discussed in the previous paragraph, the dynamics delineated by the saddle path SS make sense. To see this clearly, consider, for example, the situation in which our polluting firm begins with a capital stock below the steady state level of capital K^*. In this scenario, the marginal product of the firm's capital exceeds the interest rate. Therefore, the firm will want to raise — and thereby upgrade — its capital stock to K^*. However, our firm cannot do so in an instant because such a course of action would result in prohibitively high adjustment costs. Consequently, our firm gradually raises — and upgrades — its capital stock to K^*. However, the high — relative to r — marginal product of installed capital will result in a high — relative to 1 — value of q and an expectation that q will fall in the future as the capital stock is improved. Consistent with this line of reasoning, as q falls toward 1 along the stable path SS, the initially high investment falls to zero.

3. Unanticipated Increase in Innovation

We are now ready to shed light on the first of this chapter's three questions. Recall from the discussion in Section 1 that this involves determining the impact of an *unanticipated* increase in innovation on our polluting firm's steady state capital stock. We model this unanticipated increase by letting the innovation parameter A rise permanently from A to A'. We can now use Fig. 2 to study the

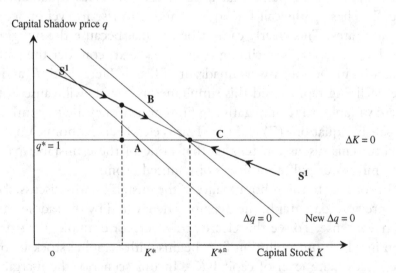

Fig. 2. Impact of an unanticipated increase in innovation.

impact of this permanent rise in the innovation parameter on our polluting firm's steady state capital stock.

The innovation parameter A enters only into the $\Delta q = 0$ schedule. Therefore, as shown in Fig. 2, a rise in A shifts this $\Delta q = 0$ schedule immediately and permanently to the right. As a result, the steady state capital stock rises from K^* to K^{*n}. As shown in Fig. 2, the unique convergent saddle path SS also shifts to the right, becoming $S^1 S^1$. Now, because the initial capital stock K^* is less than the new capital stock K^{*n}, q rises in the short run, investment by our polluting firm surges, and the initial equilibrium shifts from point A to point B on the new saddle path. However, over time, q falls back to 1, investment by our firm decreases, and the long run equilibrium shifts from point B to point C in Fig. 2. At point C, the new capital stock is K^{*n}.

We now have an answer to the basic question of this section. Specifically, the discussion in the previous two paragraphs tells us that an unanticipated increase in innovation that, *ceteris paribus*, expands our polluting firm's output Y also increases this firm's steady state capital stock. Therefore, an increase in innovation improves our polluting firm's steady state capital stock and this allows our firm to better respond to the environmental regulations it confronts as a result of its production related pollution generation.

4. Anticipated Increase in Innovation

We now address the second of this chapter's three questions. Recall from the discussion in Section 1 that this involves ascertaining the impact of an *anticipated* increase in innovation on our polluting firm's steady state capital stock. We model this anticipated increase as follows. Assume that the dynamic system given by Equations (7) and (8) is initially in the steady state marked A in Fig. 1. The reader will note that in this steady state, the innovation parameter is at level A. Now, our polluting firm learns (by surprise) on date t that this innovation parameter A will rise permanently from A to A' at some future date T. We now use Fig. 3 to analyze the impact of

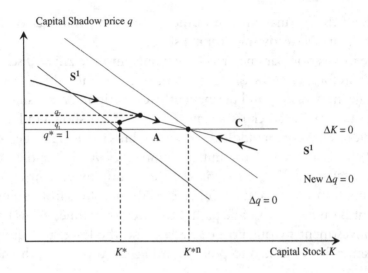

Fig. 3. Impact of an anticipated increase in innovation.

this permanent rise in the innovation parameter on the firm's steady state capital stock.[11]

We can find the new equilibrium by working backward from date T. In this regard, it is important to understand that because no further change in the innovation parameter is expected to occur after date T, our firm must be on the new saddle path $S^1 S^1$ by that date. In addition, in order to smooth its investment costs, our polluting firm will actually move away from the initial equilibrium at point A in Fig. 3 *before* date T. In particular, between dates t and T, K and q will follow the original equations of motion, i.e., Equations (7) and (8) with the innovation parameter A and not A'.

Thus, the initial response of our firm to the news of a future increase in the value of the innovation parameter is to raise capital's shadow price to q_t in Fig. 3. After this, q continues to gradually rise until it just equals q_T on the new saddle path $S^1 S^1$. This shadow price

---

11. To comprehend the chain of events that we have just described, suppose that our polluting firm learns at date t that it will be able to use a new and innovative technique that enhances production but not until the patent has expired at time T.

is reached precisely when the jump in the innovation parameter to A' occurs.[12] Thereafter and as shown in Fig. 3, q steadily falls to its steady state value of 1 at point C and capital K reaches its new steady state value K^{*n}.

We now have an answer to the second question of this chapter. Specifically, the discussion thus far in this section tells us that an anticipated increase in innovation increases our polluting firm's steady state capital stock. Further, comparing the results of this section with those in the previous Section 3 we see that, qualitatively, unanticipated and anticipated increases in innovation both lead to an increase in our polluting firm's steady state capital stock. However, inspection of Figs. 2 and 3 clearly tell us that the transitional dynamics or the way in which our polluting firm gets to the new steady state equilibrium — point C in Figs. 2 and 3 — from the initial equilibrium — point A in Figs. 2 and 3 — is very different. As in Section 3, once again we see that an increase in innovation improves our polluting firm's steady state capital stock and this permits our firm to better respond to the environmental regulations it is faced with as a result of its production related pollution generation.

5. Relationship Between q and the Stock Market Value of a Unit of Our Firm's Capital

We now address the third and final question of this chapter: What is the relationship between our polluting firm's internal shadow price of capital and the stock market value of a unit of this firm's capital? We already know that our polluting firm's internal shadow price of capital is q. Let V denote the stock market value of our polluting firm. Then, the stock market value of a unit of our firm's capital

---

12. In this chapter, we are not interested in analyzing the impacts of an anticipated *decrease* in innovation. Even so, the reader should note that an anticipated *decline* in the value of the innovation parameter A would result in an initial fall in q followed by a subsequent decline until the new and lower q_T is reached precisely when A falls to, say, $\bar{A}$. After this, q would rise to 1 as K gradually approached its new and *lower* steady state level.

is V/K. Our task now is to determine the relationship between q and V/K.

Obstfeld and Rogoff (1996, pp. 111–113) have noted that when there are no adjustment costs, we can expect the relationship $q = V/K$ to hold. In addition, Hayashi (1982) has shown that even in the presence of adjustment costs, when a firm is a price taker, this firm's production function is linear homogenous in capital (K) and labor (L), and the adjustment cost function itself is linear homogeneous in capital (K) and investment (I), then the relationship $q = V/K$ will hold. This last equality is often referred to as the equality between "marginal" q and "average" q.

In the model that we have been analyzing in this chapter, the adjustment cost function $\chi I^2/2$ is *not* linear homogeneous in capital (K) and investment (I). Therefore, marginal q is unequal to average q in this model. Put differently, our polluting firm's internal shadow price of capital is not equal to the stock market value of a unit of this firm's capital. The reader can verify that if we normalize adjustment costs by capital (K), i.e., if we replace the adjustment cost function of this chapter $(\chi I^2/2)$ with the alternate function $(\chi I^2/2K)$ then marginal q would equal average q. As one might expect, this is because this last adjustment cost function is linearly homogeneous in both capital (K) and investment (I).

6. Conclusions

In this chapter, we analyzed a q-theoretic dynamic model of regulation driven investment by a polluting firm. We first specified the conditions characterizing efficient investment by this firm. Then, we studied the first of this chapter's three questions. This involved determining the impact of an *unanticipated* increase in innovation on our polluting firm's steady state capital stock. Next, we addressed this chapter's second question. This involved ascertaining the impact of an *anticipated* increase in innovation on our polluting firm's steady state capital stock. Lastly, we focused on this chapter's third question and this entailed discussing the relationship between our polluting firm's internal shadow price of capital and the stock market value of a unit of this firm's capital.

The analysis conducted in this chapter can be extended in a number of directions. In what follows, we offer four suggestions for extending the research described in this chapter. First, it would be interesting to include pollution directly in the model. In this case, a more conclusive result concerning the validity of the Porter hypothesis might be found because when pollution is directly in the model, the stringency of environmental policy might be related to anticipated environmental costs (see Hemmelskamp *et al.* (2000) and Cole *et al.* (2005)). In this case, in accordance with the Porter hypothesis, strict environmental policy might generate either absolute cost advantages or a competitive advantage due to the introduction of better products. Second, it would be useful to analyze a scenario in which the adjustment costs incurred by our polluting firm depend negatively on the amount of capital that is already in place. Such an analysis will involve working with an adjustment cost function of the sort discussed in the last paragraph of Section 5. Third, it would also be helpful to model pollution regulations as one or more constraints that directly impact the firm's profit maximization problem. Finally, it might be useful to consider the endogenization of the innovation parameter A_t. Studies of the regulation driven behavior of polluting firms in a regional economy that incorporate these aspects of the problem into the analysis will provide additional insights into the tripartite interaction between increasing environmental regulations, the resulting decision by a polluting firm to upgrade its capital stock, and the impact of innovation on this capital stock improvement decision.

References

Abernathy, W. and Utterback, J.M. (1975). A Dynamic Model of Product and Process Innovation. *Omega* 3:639–656.

Barbera, A.J. and McConnell, V.D. (1986). Effects of Pollution Control on Industrial Productivity: A Factor Demand Approach. *Journal of Industrial Economics* 35:161–172.

Brunnermeier, S.B. and Cohen, M.A. (2003). Determinants of Environmental Innovation in US Manufacturing Industries. *Journal of Environmental Economics and Management* 45:278–293.

Chiang, A.C. (1984). *Fundamental Methods of Mathematical Economics*, 3rd edn. New York: McGraw Hill, Inc.

Cole, M.A., Elliot, R. and Shimamoto, K. (2005). Industrial Characteristics, Environmental Regulations, and Air Pollution. *Journal of Environmental Economics and Management* 50:121–143.

Dosi, G. (1982). Technological Paradigms and Technological Trajectories. *Research Policy* 11:147–162.

Fischer, C., Parry, I.W.H. and Pizer, W.A. (2003). Instrument Choice for Environmental Protection When Technological Innovation is Endogenous. *Journal of Environmental Economics and Management* 45:523–545.

Frondel, M., Horbach, J. and Rennings, K. (2007). End-of-pipe or Cleaner Production? An Empirical Comparison of Environmental Innovation Decisions Across OECD Countries. *In* N. Johnstone (ed.), *Environmental Policy and Corporate Behaviour*. Cheltenham, UK: Edward Elgar.

Garofalo, G.A. and Malhotra, D.M. (1995). Effect of Environmental Regulations on State-level Manufacturing Capital Formation. *Journal of Regional Science* 35:201–216.

Gray, W.B. (1987). The Cost of Regulation: OSHA, EPA, and the Productivity Slowdown. *American Economic Review* 77:998–1006.

Gray, W.B. and Shadbegian, R.J. (1995). Pollution Abatement Costs, Regulation, and Plant-level Productivity. NBER *Working Paper 4994*, Cambridge, Massachusetts.

Greaker, M. (2003). Strategic Environmental Policy: Eco-dumping or a Green Strategy? *Journal of Environmental Economics and Management* 45:692–707.

Hamamoto, M. (2006). Environmental Regulation and the Productivity of Japanese Manufacturing Industries. *Resource and Energy Economics* 28:299–312.

Hayashi, F. (1982). Tobin's Marginal q and Average q: A Neoclassical Interpretation. *Econometrica* 50:213–224.

Henderson, R. and Clark, K. (1990). Architectural Innovation. *Administrative Science Quarterly* 35:9–30.

Hemmelskamp, J., Rennings, K. and Leone, F. (eds.) (2000). *Innovation Oriented Environmental Regulation*. Heidelberg, Germany: Physica-Verlag.

Jaffe, A.B. and Palmer, K. (1997). Environmental Regulation and Innovation: A Panel Data Study. *Review of Economics and Statistics* 79:610–619.

Koetse, M., de Groot, H. and Nijkamp, P. (2008). Barriers in Investments in Energy Saving Technologies in Small Firms: The Energy-efficiency Paradox Revisited. *Studies in Regional Science* 38:1–15.

Kort, P.M. (1994). The Effects of Marketable Pollution Permits on the Firm's Optimal Investment Policies. *Central European Journal for Operations Research and Economics* 3:139–155.

Montero, J.P. (2002). Permits, Standards, and Technology Innovation. *Journal of Environmental Economics and Management* 44:23–44.

Nelson, R.R. and Winter, S.G. (1977). In Search of a Useful Theory of Innovation. *Research Policy* 6:36–76.

Obstfeld, M. and Rogoff, K. (1996). *Foundations of International Macroeconomics*. Cambridge, Massachusetts: MIT Press.

Palmer, K., Oates, W.E. and Portney, P.R. (1995). Tightening Environmental Standards: The Benefit-cost or the No-cost Paradigm? *Journal of Economic Perspectives* 9:119–132.

Porter, M.E. (1991). America's Green Strategy. *Scientific American* 264(4):168.

Porter, M.E. and van der Linde, C. (1995). Toward a New Conception of the Environment-competitiveness Relationship. *Journal of Economic Perspectives* 9:97–118.

Rubio, S.J. and Fisher, A.C. (1994). Optimal Capital Accumulation and Stock Pollution: The Greenhouse Effect. *Revista Espanola de Economia* Special Issue:119–140.

Simon, C.P. and Blume, L. (1994). *Mathematics for Economists*. New York: W.W. Norton and Company.

Simpson, R.D. and Bradford, R.L. (1996). Taxing Variable Cost: Environmental Regulation as Industrial Policy. *Journal of Environmental Economics and Management* 30:282–300.

Tobin, J. (1969). A General Equilibrium Approach to Monetary Theory. *Journal of Money, Credit, and Banking* 1:15–29.

Ulph, A. and Ulph, D. (1996). Trade, Strategic Innovation, and Strategic Environmental Policy: A General Analysis. *In* C. Carraro, Y. Katsoulacos and A. Xepapadeas (eds.), *Environmental Policy and Market Structure*. Dordrecht, The Netherlands: Kluwer Academic Publishers.

Unruh, G.C. (2000). Understanding Carbon Lock-in. *Energy Policy* 28: 817–830.

Xepapadeas, A. and de Zeeuw, A. (1999). Environmental Policy and Competitiveness: The Porter Hypothesis and the Composition of Capital. *Journal of Environmental Economics and Management* 37:165–182.

INDEX

ad valorem tariff, 236
ad valorem tax, 273, 278, 279, 281,
 285, 287
adjustment costs, 37, 313, 315, 316,
 323
alien species, 223, 224, 232, 252
antibiotics, 12, 91

ballast water, 27, 224, 234, 258
biodiversity, 113, 114, 123, 124, 141,
 142
biodiversity prospecting, 143
biological diversity, 5
biological invasion, 225, 257, 260, 262
Brownian motion, 12, 98, 199, 203

capital stock, 36, 307, 313, 314
capital theory, 45
comparative statics, 302
complex adaptive system, 201
conservation, 113, 123, 141
conservation decisions, 53
conservation policy, 125, 134
consistent ad valorem tax, 288, 289
consistent controls, 284
consistent tax, 33
consistent unit tax, 289
containers, 27, 212, 224, 233, 257,
 258
continuous time Markov chains, 257,
 261
conversion process, 113, 117, 128, 134

cost minimization, 295, 297, 298,
 303–305
Cournot competition, 30, 223, 228,
 246, 249, 250

decision rule, 11, 82
discrete-time Markov chain, 200, 201
drug susceptibility, 97
dynamic inconsistency, 271, 272, 291
dynamic programming, 169
dynamically consistent, 284
dynamically consistent policies, 283
dynamically inconsistent, 33, 273, 276,
 278

ecological economics, 5
ecological functions, 165
ecological resilience, 114
ecological strategy, 95
ecological-economic systems, 4, 161,
 162, 178, 199, 200
economic cost minimization, 257
economic cost reduction, 260
ecosystem resilience, 124, 142
ecosystem services, 25, 202
environmental regulation, 4, 271, 272,
 307, 308, 311
exhaustible resources, 4
exotic species, 144
expected damage, 29, 235, 238, 251
expected profit, 78, 81
expected utility, 18, 144, 145, 152,
 155

exponential, 165
exponential distribution, 26, 165, 232, 233
exponentially distributed, 265, 298

fines, 211, 218, 260
flexibility premium, 18, 78, 85, 141
forest management, 45, 54
functional forms, 34, 275, 286, 290, 291

generalist species, 164, 167, 172
generating function, 230
genetic information, 142
grazing cycle, 8, 67
grazing period, 185

habitat conversion, 14, 123, 136, 137, 148, 151
history, 280
homeopathic, 99

import tariffs, 251
indivisible, 10, 76
infinitesimal look ahead stopping rule (ILASR), 115
information, 146
innovation, 36, 307, 312, 314, 319, 323
inspection, 5, 171, 211, 214, 259, 265
inspection stringency, 257
intensity function, 52, 116
international trade, 29, 226, 252
interventionist strategy, 95
invasive species, 4, 211, 224, 226, 233, 257
invasive species management, 5
inverse demand function, 279, 280–282
investment, 307, 310, 322
investment under uncertainty, 136, 155
irreversibility, 202, 203
irreversible, 10, 76, 80
isoelastic, 280

jointly determined, 178
jump state constraint, 276

keystone species, 200

land, 10
land development, 11, 75, 77
learning, 137
likelihood function, 99, 104
limiting distribution, 205
limiting probabilities, 216
linear homogeneous, 38, 322
linearly homogeneous, 322
long run, 9
long run average net cost, 187
long run average or expected cost, 297
long run expected cost, 100, 295, 296, 300, 302, 303
long run expected net cost, 181, 183, 213

management, 162
manager, 167
market structures, 223
Markov chain, 7, 47, 216
Markov decision process, 113, 127
memoryless, 26, 205
monetary damage, 229, 231, 232
monopolist, 223, 242, 272
monopolistic firm, 34, 291
monopolistic polluter, 274
multiple use, 192

Nash equilibrium, 201
natural habitat, 113, 135, 141, 154
natural resource management, 5
natural resources, 70
negative binomial distribution, 230
non-interventionist strategies, 106

off site location, 295
off site storage, 295, 304
off site waste storage, 296
on site storage, 295, 296, 304
open loop, 33
open loop ad valorem tax, 288
open loop policies, 282, 291
optimal control, 95

optimal management, 178, 201
optimal stopping, 6, 113, 120, 126, 145
optimal stopping rule, 114
optimal tariff, 239, 241, 250
option value, 10, 76
Ornstein–Uhlenbeck stochastic process, 201

paddock, 181
perfect competition, 30, 223, 238
persistence, 20, 161–163, 172
pesticides, 91
phase diagram, 37, 312, 313, 315
Poisson process, 7, 48, 63, 79, 116, 147, 149, 151, 229, 234, 261, 266, 298
policy credibility, 292
policy payoff, 292
polluter, 272
polluting firm, 307, 308, 312, 320, 322
pollution dependent cost function, 276, 285
porter hypothesis, 309
post-invasion, 259
pre-invasion, 259
price control, 33
principle of optimality, 284
profit function, 79, 243
profit maximization, 313, 323
protected area, 130, 134

q-theoretic investment, 310
quasi-option value, 76
queuing theory, 7

range management, 8, 58, 182, 192
range manager, 177, 183
rangelands, 22, 58, 177, 180
rational expectations constraint, 278
regional economy, 37
renewable resources, 4
renewal function, 300
renewal process, 63, 186, 189, 195, 219, 220, 298, 300
renewal theoretic, 182

renewal theory, 62, 100, 183, 186
renewal-reward process, 23, 64, 298
renewal-reward theorem, 64, 101, 186, 298, 299, 301
renewal-theoretic, 62, 71
research and development (R&D), 116, 313
resilience, 14, 200
resistance, 12, 91, 162
risk, 31
risk loving, 257, 265

saddle point stable, 317
safe minimum standard, 5, 199, 202, 206
seaport, 214, 219, 225, 257
season length (time) restrictions, 71
shadow price of capital, 307, 314, 321, 323
short duration grazing, 22, 180, 188
social planner, 16, 123, 126, 128, 132, 135, 141, 143, 145
social welfare, 223, 227, 236, 245, 249, 289
specialized grazing systems, 180
species, 47
specific import tariff, 236
specific tariff, 238
stability, 20, 162, 200, 258
stability domain, 200
Stackelberg differential game, 33, 271, 272, 291
Stackelberg game, 283
stationary probabilities, 7, 49
steady state, 7, 51, 316
steady state capital stock, 319, 321, 322
steady state output, 275, 286
steady state pollution, 275, 279, 287
stochastic differential equations, 173
stochastic process, 7, 52, 115, 129, 136, 151, 186, 298
stock dependent cost function, 276, 288, 290, 291
stock externality, 271
stocking rate, 8, 58

stopping rule, 14, 77
strong sustainability, 201
submerged aquatic vegetation, 172

tariff, 30, 213, 223, 227, 252, 260
tax, 33
temporal flexibility, 87
terms of trade, 243
time dependent decision rule, 86–88
time independent decision rules, 87
time reversibility, 50
trade policy, 5, 226, 229, 252
transitional dynamics, 37, 321

treatment cost, 104
tropical forests, 126

unanticipated increase in innovation,
    318, 322
uncertainty, 6, 61
unit tax, 273, 281, 285

value function, 170
variability, 162

waste, 295, 299, 305
waste management, 35, 305

Printed in the United States
By Bookmasters